Good Anger

John Giles Milhaven

Sheed & Ward

Sheed & Ward™ is a service of National Catholic Reporter Publishing
Company, Inc.

Library of Congress Catalog Card Number: 89-61217

ISBN: 1-55612-264-0

Published by: Sheed & Ward
             115 E. Armour Blvd. P.O. Box 419492
             Kansas City, MO 64141-6492

To order, call: (800) 333-7373

Contents

Introduction v

I. For Example

1. Blaming for Blaming's Sake 3
2. One Moment of Love 24
3. The Critic 37

II. The Question

4. The State of the Question? 59
5. Anger of Aristotle? Anger of Christ? 77
6. Practical Point to the Question? 91
7. The Right Attitude Towards Anger? 109

III. An Answer

8. Take Me Seriously! 123
9. To Feel Pain Can Be Good. 137
10. To Cause Pain Can Be Good In Itself? 158
11. Feel My Power! Feel My Pain! 168
12. Vindictive Anger, Activists and Feminists 184
13. Contemplation in Action 194
14. Saint Angela 209

For Shelly, for reasons that are nobody's business

Introduction

The mind is a houn'dog. It does not know where it is going. It follows a scent. These days my mind keeps following the same scent. It keeps asking: What good, if any, is there in human anger? By "anger" I mean, not its nobler species, but the vulgar passion of wanting to get back at, to get even with, to get revenge on, to punish simply for the sake of punishing, to get someone for wrong they did to me or mine, etc. It is usually labelled "vindictive anger."

I write this book in pursuit of my question. I put in print what I am discussing with fellow ethicists and other scholars, with other professionals such as psychologists, psychotherapists and counselors, with students, graduate and undergraduate, and with generally educated persons, such as Brown University alumni and church groups. I discuss it with Christians, Jews, Muslims, Hindus, Buddhists, and with nonreligious persons. If you fall into any of these categories, I invite you to read the book and join the discussion.

I cannot remember anyone who at the end of discussion has said, "You are right!" "You've convinced me!" I hear over and over: "You've got me thinking." This is my aim for fellow discussants and myself. This is what I aim at for readers of this book. To get you thinking. Perhaps some day I or someone else will bring out a book proving that the answer reached tentatively in the present book is true. Or is not.

My discussion partners in their turn get me thinking. Most of the pages of this book have been rewritten at least once as a result of discussion. When I re-read them now, I hear often the voice of a discussion partner uttering words which I make blithely my own. The chapters represent where I and others are now in discussion. We are in mid-pursuit of the question. Some of us think we have gained some clarity. We think on in a strenuous, disturbing, promising way.

The only evidence we appeal to in support of our answer is experience. We get ideas from Aristotle and Thomas Aquinas, from Jesus and Paul, from modern psychology and social science, and from contemporary black and feminist thinkers. But our argument is solely phenomenological. We appeal only to experience.

We do not appeal to experience as detached observers or as scientists reporting objectively on questionnaires and other statistics. We appeal to our own experience. We appeal to what we directly experience and what we experience through empathy or identification with others: with a battling husband and wife or with a victim of rape or other abuse or with people oppressed for gender or race. We exert ourselves only to expand this experience of ours and to open ourselves more to it. We want to experience more. We want to see more clearly what we experience. Our concentration on our own experience is one reason why any answer we come to is incomplete and tentative as well as invaluable and promising.

The book has three parts. In the first, we gather by anecdote and story experiences that are commonplace and usually ignored. They are experiences of vindictive anger that seems to be more good than evil. It seems even to be love. This raises our question, "What good, if any, is there in this anger?" In the second part of the book, we work at getting clearer what we ask and why we ask it. In the third part, we offer a tentative beginning of an answer. We argue for it by invoking experience not only of anger but of other human passions. The thrust of our whole inquiry is not only to clarify what is good in anger. It is also through that clarification to suggest something of what is good generally in the nonrational, passionate, embodied dimension of our personal life.

As I say, I invite you along. Each chapter is intended to provoke you, as it provokes us. The most powerful passion, Voltaire noted, is the passion for truth. One needs to add that it is the hardest to arouse. I set down these chapters to arouse your passion for a suspicious line of questioning. Halloo!

I
For Example

1

Blaming for Blaming's Sake

A commonplace phenomenon of current Western society is the blaming of adults by other adults. Blaming overlays, like a fungus, large areas of most individuals' lives. One can easily condemn much of this without noting how puzzling it is. It does not seem to make sense. One can also fail to note that if one blames the blamers, one joins the phenomenon.

In the following pages, I do not blame blamers in genus or species. Nor do I justify them. I attempt no moral judgments. I attempt no causal explanation as, for example, a psychologist or sociologist could do. I fix my gaze on the phenomenon itself, the blaming. It is puzzle enough! What is it? For answer, I look closer at it.

I invite you, hardy reader, to examine with me some of what goes on more or less consciously when one blames someone else. Perhaps what transpires in the dim reaches of our consciousness can illuminate from below the opaque enigma of the surface. This fixed gaze on the everyday experience itself may, for you and me, turn into a slow revelation. What shall we find?

First of all, what is the puzzle? The simple fact that one person blames another person is not puzzling. There can be a good reason for blaming someone.

Imagine someone in our society who acts regularly in a racist or sexist way. He continues to do so until someone publicly blames him for it. He then desists. Perhaps the blame by others made him realize that he himself "deep down" disapproved what he was doing. Perhaps the

3

blame made him afraid of the disfavor of important people of his social life. In any case, the blame made him cease at least some of his racism and sexism. One can imagine circumstances under which advocates of social equality knew no better way to stop his public bigotry. Blaming makes sense here. It has a real basis: the objectively wrong actions of the sexist or racist. Its aim is realistic: that the offender cease his actions.

How much of the blaming we observe is realistic and reasonable? Western literature, great and small, celebrates the human penchant to angrily and sincerely blame someone on little or no evidence that the person did what one blames him for. Witness Othello or Don Quixote or Oedipus, many a detective story or TV comedy or soap opera.

This notorious human failing is not merely comic or tragic. It is mysterious. *Why* didn't I look in my desk to see whether I had ever mailed the letter? *Why* didn't I check whether my boss had said what was reported to me on hearsay? *Why* didn't I first ask my husband why he didn't meet me at the station? In each case, the thought crossed the back of my raging mind that perhaps the other person had not done what I was blaming him or her for. A vague memory flickered of having been mistaken before in this kind of thing. I did not care. Gridley was ready. Fire away! What *did* I care about? What was I up to?

It is not enough for the other's action to be wrong or harmful for it to merit blame. We recognize "inculpable ignorance." We do not *blame* honest error. Blaming implies that the persons blamed do the wrong knowingly. They have enough knowledge for us to hold them responsible for what they do. Otherwise we could only criticize their action and urge them to do otherwise in the future. We could not blame them.

Even blame that is neither moral nor juridical implies knowledge aforethought on the part of the person blamed. When, face red and heart pounding, I blame my bridge partner for leading a heart, I am not just telling her she made a mistake. I am not just correcting her or expressing my vigorous disapproval. If I blame her, I declare, among other things, "You know better!"

How rarely do blamers verify that their targets know better! Those who oppose abortion blame those who would permit it for murdering human beings. Those who would permit abortion blame those who would prohibit it for dictating what a woman should do with her body. The tone of blame implies here that the other group knows the heinous thing they do. Words like "murder" or "dictate" include in their meaning that one knowingly does the act or gives the command.

But in fact pro-choice people do not believe that the fetus is a human being. If they are killing human beings, they do not know they are doing it. Pro-life people do not believe that the fetus is part of the woman's body. They hold that it is a distinct person. If they are dictating to the woman what she should do with her body, they do not know they are doing so.

Pro-choicers and pro-lifers have stated repeatedly what they believe and do not believe. Each side knows the position of the other. Pro-life people know that pro-choice people do not believe that the fetus is a human being. Pro-choice people know that pro-life people do not believe the fetus is part of the woman's body. There is no basis for charging that either pro-choicers or pro-lifers are insincere in the position they hold and that they really know better. And sincere error does not call for blame. But the debate rings with the rhetoric and tone of blame. Blame makes no sense here. What is going on?

Other public debates are similarly baffling. Those who would increase defense spending and those who would decrease it blame each other. Those who would increase governmental social services and those who would decrease them blame each other. Those who would protect homosexuals against discrimination and those who would discriminate blame each other. Blame is not as omnipresent in these public debates as in the abortion debate, but it is common. And it is commonly as unrealistic as in the abortion debate. Blame implies that the opponents are not simply in error. Blame implies that they, at least in their heart of hearts, know better. But no effort is made to verify this implication. Why?

Since blame presupposes that the accused know the evil they do, blamers often fill out the picture with appropriate motives and corresponding character traits. Why indeed do those politicians knowingly bring the world closer to destruction by escalating the arms race? Surely love of combat or money or power drives them on. They are the kind of persons who do this sort of thing.

6 Good Anger

Common in public debates like these are insinuations or outright charges of despicable motives and attitudes. Those who disagree with us are warmongers, trigger-happy, power-hungry, timid, irresolute, calloused, lazy, sex-obsessed, libertine, dictatorial, etc. Which motives and characteristic attitudes one alleges in each case depends on the particular policy being criticized, but we make no effort to prove that the proponents of the policy have these motives and attitudes. Another mystery! Not that the proof is inadequate. But that no proof is attempted. Why?

The unreality of public, accusatory rhetoric is so commonplace that one takes it for granted. One rarely notes how mystifying it is. How do sincere, intelligent speakers, often well educated, critical intellectuals, supported by a chorus of peers, come to affirm knowledge, motive and attitude of others without even looking for evidence for the affirmations? This is blame with no concern for a real basis. It is irrational. It makes no sense.

There is at times method in the madness. The blamer may wield the lash of blame because she judges it more effective than mere criticism or disapproval to discourage a given activity. In this situation the unreality and irrationality of blame does not diminish its social force. The senator may not in fact look down on women. But to accuse him publicly of this may be the only effective way to move him to withdraw support of a certain discriminatory bill.

But what of the more common instances where blame is not likely to discourage the objectionable conduct? Usually, in connection with public issues such as those cited above, the blamed will never hear the speech or conversation. The speakers do not seem to care. Speakers and listeners may be realistically practical in their determination to vote against or picket the activity they object to. But what practical purpose does it serve to fire volleys of blame into the air? Blame does not logically support the action of voting or picketing, since the reasons for or against abortion, nuclear armament, governmental social services, homosexuality, etc., are independent of the bad intentions or unworthy motives which those holding the other view may have. Why then the ardent accusation, explicit or implicit, of bad intentions or unworthy motives?

The puzzle thickens in conversations where speakers and listeners show they have no interest in any good coming from the condemnation. Listen to two or three gathered together in blame of Ronald Reagan, Howard Cosell, Margaret Thatcher, or Andrew Greeley. The tone of the laughter betrays that it is blame, and not mere criticism, going on. The humor hinges on the implication that the individual really knows better and/or has unworthy motives. Dumb as Reagan is said to be, he is also said to be heartless. "Heartless" implies he knows what will result from his actions and is indifferent.

Almost ritual is the rhythmic participation of the conversation partners as the innards of the victim's personality are drawn and quartered. Soon, usually abruptly, the speakers move on to other subjects, having evidently accomplished what they wanted. No one shows inclination to follow up the blame with proposals to do anything. All appear grimly satisfied with their words.

I led university alumni recently in a discussion of "Religion in America Today." Talk fixed at one moment on the mercenary motives of certain purveyors of popular religion on TV. No one suggested anything to do about it. Obviously, nothing could be done by any of us. But the conversation absorbed our group as several underscored how reprehensible this exploitation of religion was. The eagerness in the room was palpable.

This kind of occurence was so familiar that only afterwards did I realize its opacity. To what end was our chorus of blaming? If we could do nothing about the object of blame, why blame? And why prolong an exercise of impotence? With such avidity? Most mysterious of all, why the evident satisfaction—nodding of heads, pursing of lips, settling back in the chair—as we left the subject? Incidentally, no one criticized the popular religion being purveyed.

The blamer's lack of interest in halting the activity for which he blames someone is more striking and bewildering when the person blamed is present. I refer to the innumerable instances where the blame works against the blamer's practical purpose in blaming and the blamer had good reason to expect that it would. At a departmental meeting, a colleague proposes additional requirements for our Political Science major. I oppose it. Long experience as departmental undergraduate advisor and informal discussion with others of the pro's and con's have convinced me that we have enough requirements for a meaningful major. Additional ones will work against the department's educational goals, agreed upon by all of us. But I do not bring these arguments forward in my opposition to the new proposal. I choose rather to denounce it—in oblique, diplomatic language, of course—as characteristic of the proposing colleague's tendency to value legalistic regulation for its own sake.

I not only attribute to my colleague attitude and motivation that I do not know him to have. I sabotage my own purposes, for, as I do know, my other colleagues tend to react unfavorably to the kind of *ad hominem* arguments I choose now to advance. They suspect them, and are influenced rather by the kind of practical, empirical reasons which I have but elect not to present. Why do I not present them? Why do I choose blame to achieve my purpose when I know blame will defeat it?

Intimacy teems with this blatantly unproductive or counterproductive blaming, though the tactic and camouflage can be intricate and subtle. I generally go to the movies only when my wife suggests it. I do so inwardly resisting. I succeed often in making my wife feel guilty afterwards, e.g. by observing how boring the film was. She in turn may make me feel guilty of intellectual snobbery by cooing, "Oh, you see so much more in the picture than I do!" In this three-cushion blaming, we do not keep score.

My wife halted it once when she ceased suggesting our going to the movies. I soon felt frustrated and resentful. Life was emptier. I missed the movies. I experienced a start of joy one evening months later when my wife suggested movies. Why then did I once more go about making her guilty? "Well, you know the reviews were mixed. I'll go, but next Saturday we spend the evening home together." What was my object? My gain?

Peeling back the skin of our society, we see blame flowing back and forth everywhere. People blame people for making love, for making it poorly, for not making it at all, for raising taxes, for not offering public services, for lowering educational standards, for not admitting their child to the school, for not earning more money, for being materialistic, for not getting in touch, for staying too long, for imposing on them, for drinking too much, for disapproving of drinking, for letting their dog run around, for doing a poor term paper, for being pedantic, for not listening more carefully, for not working harder, for not having friends, for trying hard to be popular, etc. You can make your additions to the list.

My illustrative cases of the preceding pages are oversimple and partly fictional. But I submit that real cases of blaming, randomly selected, often turn out under examination to be unreasonable because unrealistic, in at least one of the four ways indicated above. The blamer shows little concern whether the action for which he blames someone was done by that person. The blamer shows little concern whether the person blamed knew what he did was wrong. The blamer shows little concern whether the other has the motives and attitudes for which he blames him. The blamer shows little concern whether his blame will help halt the objectionable action. In brief, the blamer shows little concern whether his blaming has a basis in reality and whether it really serves the purpose he believes he has in blaming.

By blaming, the blamer claims, at least implicitly, that he has this quadruple concern. He may be sincere. He may even feel some such concern. But, as I have illustrated above, the rest of what he says and does, or fails to say and do, belies his claim. His effort in full stride of blaming reflects so little of this concern, that any concern he has must be negligible.

The blamer usually shows that he is indeed deeply concerned about something. Blame is taken seriously in our society. When one begins to blame, one's voice gathers force and urgency. Looking back at one's day, one may often find that the most strongly felt incident or the moment in which one felt most personally engaged came when one was blaming. But what can one be concerned about, if it be not the apparent basis and purpose of one's blaming? We have a passion to blame. We blame with passion. What passion is it?

The moment may seem ripe to bring value judgments crashing down on unrealistic blaming. Or to solve the puzzle by identifying causes of a psychological, sociological and/or religious nature. I stay with the phenomenon. It itself, I submit, makes sense. The uncovering in the experience of that immanent sense should precede any evaluation or causal explanation. *Zurück zu den Sachen*! Back to the things! Let the reader judge whether his or her experience confirms or belies the following description of what one is often dimly conscious of in the very act of blaming.

*   *   *   *   *

We looked mostly at instances of blaming where the blamed person is absent. It is easier here to catch how the blamer often lacks the concern that blaming seems to imply. We now turn our scrutiny more to experiences of blaming someone who is present. It is easier here to uncover what is really going on.

Let us ponder another everyday sample of unrealistic blame. "You still haven't made the appointment for Rose. That's two weeks now. How can you be so indifferent? Do I have to do everything myself?" In fact, my wife is not indifferent to my daughter's pains. She has just forgotten, absorbed as she is in the myriad things she does for the family as well as in her professional work. I do not care that I accuse her falsely. Nor can I be blaming in order to assure that the appointment be made. Knowing my wife, I know that a simple reminder would be just as effective to that end. Why do I choose to blame? What is my object?

I obviously have an object. In my blaming I am concerned about something. As I start to blame, I exert myself consciously. I strain internally, which I would not do if I were simply reminding my wife of the appointment to make. I struggle to launch my blame and land it on target. Desire mounts in me, as well as anxiety that I may fail. This whole troubled, tense thrust of my person is not to get the appointment made, for, as we saw, I could do that by a quiet reminder. What is my object? I struggle and strain towards something. What can it be?

I put the conundrum to friends and colleagues. They had no trouble recalling experiences of this sort. They suggested purposes that were extrinsic to the immediate experience. "To divert attention from recent mistakes of yours." "To maintain superiority in your relationship with your wife." "To project your own guilt feelings on another."

I probably had purposes of this sort in blaming my wife for not making the appointment. But I look for something else. What is my *immediate* purpose, making possible the further goals suggested by friends and colleagues? What do I strive to effect here and now in the very act of blaming? *What* will draw attention from my own recent mistakes? *What* will shore up my position of superiority? *What* is the bridge over which I will pass my guilt feelings to her? We must probe the blaming phenomenon further, without looking to consequences.

What then do I strive to immediately bring about in unrealistic blaming? Many things, undoubtedly, for our "phenomenon" is in fact many different phenomena. Moreover, any single case of human action is usually determined by a multiplicity of motives. But in unrealistic blaming one fact emerges most of the time. The blamer feels satisfaction in the act of blaming the other. His desire comes to rest in the climax of his denunciation, delivered in reality or fantasy to the other. Blaming may be for him a means to further goals, but he experiences it also as an end in itself. He blames, at least in part, for blaming's sake.

This satisfaction is clue in our investigation. The blamer is at least dimly conscious of seeking and getting his satisfaction. The attentive observer can pick it up. Take a conversation disposing of Edward Meese or Jerry Falwell or Phyllis Schlafly. Note the eagerness in entering the subject. The half-suppressed smiles as the work goes on. The occasionally surfacing undertone of relish. The peace that settles on the group when all is done.

I catch, several levels down in myself, the same sense of satisfaction as I belabor my wife for not making the appointment. As I allege and excoriate my colleague's legalism. Something in the act of blaming gives me definitive satisfaction. I can go back then to being kind to my wife and cordial with my colleague. I blamed simply for blaming's sake. Now I have other things to do.

The puzzle of unrealistic blaming becomes the puzzle of blaming for the sake of blaming. One can uncover also in many instances of realistic blaming a generous dollop of this satisfaction in the blaming itself. What kind of satisfaction is it? What satisfies? How can blaming anyone, just by itself, satisfy? What in that act sates my passion? What passion?

Listening to true stories told by Jewish friends, I sicken with anger at atrocities done to Jews by Nazis in concentration camps. I speak out my outraged condemnation. Looking back later at the conversation, I recall, like silt at the bottom of my consciousness, the satisfaction that I felt at my words. In the back of my imagination, Nazi guards stood helplessly caught, pale, panic-stricken, cringing beneath my strokes. I took grim pleasure in the agony and despair I caused them.

What yielded the pleasure? Justice done? That the Nazis get their just deserts in the fantasy of my mind? Yes, but I must ask how their agony and despair constitute justice for me. We will return to this issue later in the book. In any case, my pleasure seems more personal than devotion to my ideal of justice would warrant. Justice seems the cover, not the cause, as my anger swells and I radiate contempt on the men I imagine.

Justice gives me title to say, "You creeps!" Justice may dictate objectively that they should suffer this way. But my savage pleasure in making them suffer at my words has none of the objectivity I associate with justice. It is my pleasure in their knowing that now I've got them. It is a bleak pleasure that I share with my Jewish friends. It brings us closer.

Listen once more to a conversation in which a group begins to indict an absent person or persons. The target may be—to vary our examples—a former mayor of Providence, the Roman Catholic bishops of the United States, American physicians in general or the president of the University. Excitement rises as the group goes to work. Righteous indignation clouds all, but can one miss the whiffs of relish at "getting them"? For this happy, though serious, moment, we have them at our mercy. They writhe under our blows. Eventually satisfied, we let them go. What did we do to them that sated our roused appetites?

Sometimes, the feeling is easier to verify, for it is the only strong one. The insignificance of the event brings into relief the intense satisfaction I experience in blaming. I overhear my husband telling a visitor that he is a friend of a certain eminent person. He barely knows the person. No harm is likely to result from the fib. But in the following hours I return often to the prospect of telling him I heard him lie. I rehearse the scene. When I start to actually do it, my heart pounds. As I do it, I cannot meet his eyes lest he see my glee. I got him!

"You said, 'Turn left.'" "I did not." "You did too. Ask Shelly." At stake is nothing practical, for we have now found the right route. At stake and crucially important to me is to blame my friend solidly. Part of it is perhaps to avoid being blamed by her for this minor delay in our trip. But strongest is that irresistible slope of inclination to get the soursweet position of "having her." What does the experience of having her consist in?

It is not enough that my friend recognize and admit she was wrong. If she did that on her own, it would spoil my pleasure. What intensely satisfies, though I would not admit it at the moment, is that I force my statement upon her in triumph. In my eyes, her pain comes much less from recognizing her mistake than from my statement penetrating her in our mutual awareness. From this inflicting of pain comes my satisfaction.

The thicket of the phenomenon thickens as we push into it. The inflicting of sharp pain, the secure sense of having the other person, cannot come from simply catching my husband in a harmless fib or my friend in giving false, soon corrected, directions. As we noted, the most dramatic, exciting event I experience on some days is a moment of blaming for blaming's sake. Frequently, the matter of blame was trivial. I was then most aroused, and afterwards most content, though shaken. What do I say that gives me such pleasure and mastery as it forces such helpless pain on the other? Let us listen attentively to more sample scenes.

As our psychic ears have become attuned, the voice of blame has already turned out to be a jumble of voices. It first sounded single: "You did this bad thing." We soon recognized a polyphony: "And you did it knowingly. You did it out of bad motives." "You're the kind of person who does this kind of thing." Finally, in the hiss of rage, the sigh of satisfaction, we caught a third message: "I've got you! Take that!"

But what is "that"? How have I got him? The blamer must be saying something more, something of rocking impact; for in the blamer's mind, and often in the blamed one's too, the blamer skewers the blamed person with pain. In the film, *The Conversation*, the protagonist, an expert in the use of electronic hearing devices, has the task to record secretly the sounds of a crowd in a plaza and find out what a particular young couple say. Replaying his tape repeatedly, he manipulates the dials of his machine to let all other sounds recede and the conversation of the couple come out. He succeeds in isolating portions of their conversation, finding out that they are arranging a rendezvous. But he cannot get the rest of their words. Only towards the end of the film, after much replaying and exquisite adjusting of dials, can he bring out the whole conversation. It is not what was expected. They plan a rendezvous, not for love, but for murder.

Let us replay experiences of someone blaming someone just for the sake of blaming him or her. Let us listen over and over to the "Now I've got you! Take that!" We have already concluded that the blamer must be saying to the other person something more concrete and specific than this vague statement. We hear him say things like, "See how foolish a person you are!" Or: "How phony or contemptible or cruel or childish you are!" "You always . . ." "Are you again . . ." "Why do you have to. . ." But we already noted that the unrealistic blamer has little concern whether these denunciations of motive or characteristic attitude are true. How then do they convey the blow that pins the blamed person down?

When the blame reaches the blamed persons, they often know that the accusations are false. They may know that the blamer deliberately exaggerates or fabricates. They may contest the point: "I don't *always*. . ." "How can you say I'm indifferent to her needs when I . . ." But this scarcely lessens their pain and panic at the blame. What then pains and panics so effectively?

If we keep reliving some of the experiences, listening intently, we can pick up at least one message that by itself penetrates with power. It can be put in words, though the blamer usually does not. It travels into the blamed person rather as a tone of voice, a quality of the expelled air that forms the farcical accusation. This message is not farcical. We hear at last something that is absolutely true. Both blamer and blamed know that it is. We hear how the blamer feels at this moment about the blamed.

The feelings are rarely put into words, but they could be. "I don't like you!" "I despise you!" "You bore me!" "You make me laugh!" Brutal feelings like these explode into final, primitive force, the hook at the end of the lash: "I can't stand you!" "I want to get rid of you!" "Why do I have to put up with you!" More succinctly: "Get lost!" "Get out!" "Go!"

Blamed persons have no defense against this missile because they cannot deny it. The blamer tells how she feels. She is the authority on the subject. Moreover, in the mutual awareness that climaxes successful blaming, the blamed person experiences somehow these feelings of the blamer. She feels the contemptuous dismissing hiss of the blamer's heart. She does not have to take her word for it. She knows.

Blame crushes all the more irresistibly when, as usually happens, the "I" echoes with "We." "We don't like you !" "We despise you!" "You bore us!" "You make us laugh!" "We wish you'd go away!" When I blame someone, I generally take a certain tone as speaking in a chorus of voices, all yea-saying my disgust and dismissal.

This is why I denounce my opponents as murderers or warmongers or voluptuaries. My society differs in what it feels about abortion or escalating armament or homosexual behavior. It is of one mind in what it feels about murderers, warmongers and voluptuaries. To call you a murderer swells my voice with the rage (itself murderous?) of "everybody" against murderers.

That in fact you are not a murderer is inconsequential because my real message is how we feel about you. Ultimately we feel: "We can't stand you! Get lost!" Cloaking myself with the primal fury of my society, I feel irresistible, at the head of a host, sure of getting on top and giving you the triumphant blow. If you sense my confident merging with our society, it multiplies the force of my blame in your consciousness. It reaches, like the nerve of a tooth, your fear, unrealistic, too, but deep, of your society's dismissing you forever.

In the trivia of intimacy, with you standing before me, it is similar. "We" can't stand people who tell lies for no good reason. If you sense my confident merging with our society, it multiplies in your consciousness the force of my blame on the occasion of your fibbing about having a friend or denying that you gave wrong directions. Yet only you and I are here. I deftly draw in the social consensus about lies only to add weight to what *I* really feel and mean: "*I* can't stand you." "*I* wish I were rid of you."

"I want to be rid of you!" Beneath this is there not another utterance, dimmer, almost lost? "I wish you were dead." "Drop dead!" "I want to kill you!" A desire, ineffective surely, but real? Our inquiry will not follow up this line of questioning. Or look for other utterances which we may snarl in whisper when we blame for blaming's sake.

Can this be true? Do I want to get rid of you, my spouse? Or child or parent or close friend or fellow worker? In the paroxysm of blame: Yes!

That is what I feel now. And I want you to feel this desire of mine. Yet my desire has little impetus toward real fulfillment. I want to get rid of you, but I do not want to take steps towards getting rid of you. My desire is a desire in fantasy. I desire in fantasy, for instance, when I desire to unclothe someone, perhaps to one way or another communicate my desire to the person, but have little inclination to actually do it.

The desire of fantasy can fill my consciousness and overwhelm me. But it does not move me to carry it out. In fantasy, the very desire gives me sweet pleasure. More pleasure floods me if I imagine that my desire of unclothing or getting rid of the other penetrates the awareness of that person. Exquisite is the pleasure if I experience my desire actually penetrating the awareness of that person standing here and now in front of me. That the person knows I have no intention to actually fulfill my desire does not dull my pleasure.

"Fantasy" can mean different things. I mean by it no more than what I have said. I want terribly to do something but have little or no inclination to do it. Fantasy is flesh and bone of real life as we can discover if we continue to unfold familiar experiences of blaming for the sake of blaming.

I want to be rid of you, though I have no inclination to bring it about. I communicate this desire to you. You share my fantasy. I am satisfied. I feel no urge now to continue to desire or to share the desire with you. My interest passes to other things. My fantasy is finished.

I was sick and tired of you, and wanted you to know it. I wanted you to be stricken by my wish to be free of you. In my ecstacy of blaming, everything resounded, openly or in disguise, with this cried desire. Everything except perhaps that at that climax, dimmer still, I wanted you to stay with me. In fantasy, even shared fantasy, contradictions are unimportant.

Fantasy is not make-believe, not pretense. Fantasy is an experience of the mind, lived for itself, with no movement towards realization. To cover the fantasy, I make believe that my wife knowingly failed to make my daughter's appointment. I make believe that she is indifferent to my daughter's health. I make believe that blaming her is the only way to get her to be less forgetful in the future. All this is false and part of me knows it. But that beneath the play-acting of blame, I desire frantically to be free of my wife is true, however much I may deny or ignore it. My desire is real. This is real life, mine and my wife's.

I call my desire "fantasy" because it does not impel me to get what I desire. It gets its satisfaction in my feeling it and my wife's feeling it. If need arose, I believe I would instantly and without questioning fight, even at risk of death, to prevent fulfillment of my desire to be rid of my wife. I desire it in fantasy because I desire much more strongly to be with her.

Yet this desire to dismiss the blamed person is real. Recall once more: perhaps at no other moment of the day do I desire so completely and satisfy myself so richly as when, exposing the nonexistent sins of Reagan or my husband or fellow-worker, I want to be rid of them forever. The desire engages me from the ground up. I give myself to it without restraint (even if also giving myself to the contradicting desire). The earth moves beneath me. I am here to an extent I rarely am.

*   *   *   *   *

We have an initial solution to the puzzle with which we started. With a closer look, the phenomenon of blaming that bewildered us makes sense. It is blaming for blaming's sake. It has a real basis: my real desire to be rid of the blamed person. It has a realistic goal, which I aim at in the act of blaming: to communicate this desire to the person I want to be rid of.

What kind of reality is this? How does this reality of our conscious life compare with other kinds of reality we may believe in? With "external" reality that the individual ascertains by reason or brings about by choice? With the conscious reality of our reasoning and our choosing? With the really real, which if Augustine be right, we yearn restlessly for under all other desires? With the reality of that yearning? With the reality of a loving God and of the individual's faith in Him?

To compare these realities lies beyond the scope of this book. I suggest only that desire and its satisfaction are the movement of all human conscious life. Reason, choice and faith are forms of this desire and satisfaction, this vital flow and ebb. So, too, are the strong desires of fantasy, which we are examining. So, too, are the strong desires which, unlike fantasy, move us to carry them out. All these *are* elemental human life. They are not fabricated by our civilization however much they be affected by it. We study in this chapter only one form of elemental human life: one desire in fantasy that runs beneath the mechanisms of much apparently senseless blaming.

But this desire in fantasy presents its own puzzles. For the purpose of this book's inquiry, we sidestep some of the puzzles. We sidestep the puzzle why our desire in fantasy passes sometimes out of fantasy and into action and we start unclothing this person or taking steps to get that person out of our life once and for all. We bypass, too, the puzzle why we sometimes make no effort to communicate our desire to its object, but stay completely in solitary fantasy, excited there, gripped and finally satisfied. Neither Reagan nor the concentration camp guards nor our employee need ever know. It is enough that in our imagination they cringe and cower under our desire to dismiss them. Desire and satisfaction here are perhaps of a masturbatory sort, but not less real for that. We come alive, though alone. Not totally alone, for like much masturbation, this intense condemnation of absentees is a way of being with them.

It is not puzzling that we feel a desire to be rid of someone. We usually can find reasons in real life for that. The desire is understandable even when we feel more often and much more strongly the contrary desire, to remain with this person. In real life there are usually advantages and disadvantages, gains and losses, pains and pleasures, in living together with someone and so we have, at different times, sometimes at the same time, feelings for and against being with the person.

But why do we want to communicate the desire to the other person when we have little interest in carrying it out? Even if alone in fantasy with absent, probably now dead, Nazi guards I imagine myself communicating my feelings to them and it is the communicating that pleases and satisfies me. It is the look in their face, as my message penetrates them, that excites me and gives me a fierce satisfaction. In most of these fantasies, I do not go on to imagine the guards executed or sentenced to life in prison. If I do, what is essential to my fantasy is that as they are executed or sentenced they thereby know how I or "we" feel about them.

This is the puzzle we fasten on. Why, in blaming for blaming's sake, do we desire so fiercely and are satisfied so sweetly to communicate our desire to be rid of these guilty parties, when we have relatively little intent to actually get rid of them? What do we want and get from doing this? The puzzle is both more acute and more easily soluble if we recall instances when not in mere imagination but in actual fact we communicate our desire to others. Here we do not stay in solitary fantasy. We blame openly the blamed persons. Our blaming expresses, in patent disguise, our real desire. We say: You should be concerned about so-and-so. We mean: You should go away. We don't say so, but they know. We say: Shape up. We mean: Get lost. They understand.

What do we get by disguising this desire as we express it? I can offer no answer within the limits of the present chapter and book. I suggest that it has something to do with the fact that our current civilization, despite fanfare to the contrary, taboos human passion.

Our question is: What do we get by expressing this desire when we intend to leave it ineffective? One answer is often verified in the kind of incident exemplified earlier in this chapter where blame is openly expressed but the blamed person is not present. Other blamers are. By blaming together, the blamers come closer to each other. Such closeness can be highly worthwhile for itself. It can also generate a confident vitality carrying over to the rest of their lives. As a black ethicist remarked, commenting on this chapter in an earlier form, oppressed people reap often this harvest from meetings where accusations are made against people who are not there and are not likely ever to hear the charges.

We, however, in this book shape the question more narrowly. We ask it of the kind of incident, exemplified more in the later part of this chapter, where blame is expressed to the blamed person. What do we want and get, when we blame the person to the person's face in order to convey to them our ineffective desire to be rid of them? What gives us keen satisfaction? Let me start an answer, trailing off as I close the chapter. I invite you then to stop reading for a while and pursue the question for yourself. Take as a working hypothesis this beginning answer.

Reflect again on instances where I blame persons to their face. Beneath the farce of blame, I convey to you my disgust with you and my need never to see you again. In fear and trembling and joy, I bare to you my passion to send you away. My joy comes when I see my passion reflected in your eyes or the tightening of your lips. I sense what you feel. I've been on the receiving end and know what it's like.

A colleague wrote me a surly note upbraiding me for not attending a lecture which he had organized and to which he had invited me. He announced he would never invite me to another. There was no reason to be upset. I had had to be out of town and had communicated my regrets to the lecturer. Moreover, my colleague is notoriously volatile. The next scene would undoubtedly be renewed friendship and cooperation.

But in reading the note, my stomach knotted. My throat tightened. Words of rebuttal raced through my head. Beneath my flood of rage shot a pang of terror. Panic circled frantically. Laughing at myself and my colleague, I chose to ignore the note. As expected, peace and harmony returned the next day.

But why the pang of terror? In this instance, the terror was dim, weak, safely under control. But what terrified me? Psychologists might identify a reaction carried over from childhood, but what triggers the reaction, panics the child in me now? I had nothing terrible to fear from my colleague. When in reflective recall I isolate that clutch of terror, that scurry of panic, it becomes clear that I feared something monstrous.

What emerges from the mist as I keep watching? Is it not someone faceless smiling grimly over me? And then walking away forever? Sitting in my office at my cluttered desk, seeing outside my window students going to the Library, holding the note in my hand, I feel primitive agony at being abandoned.

In blaming for blaming's sake I strive to effect a union with the person blamed. Having experienced my own, I now experience your agony at my disgust and dismissal. You are terrified at my possibly walking away from you for good. This satisfies me and you feel that, too. Resisting it with all your force, you still have to accept my satisfaction at your terror. That acceptance satisfies me, too, and you know it. It is not an infinite regress, but a shared globe of mutual awareness, however odious.

This violent, incandescent union seems, at least in some instances, to be not completely odious. Waspish, I address my son, home on vacation from college. "How come you're so late? What've you been up to?" Dread crosses his face and is gone, but a note of it remains in his casual explanation. Why is he alarmed? After twenty years, he knows he can count on me. He does so regularly. There's no longer question of punishments for lateness or for anything else. I treat him as an adult now. Besides I can tell he hasn't done anything worrisome tonight.

The fear in his eyes was of the look in mine. He turned his gaze away immediately. He dreaded what I was doing to him with my gaze and tone of voice. He stood exposed to the searing fall of what my voice and looks conveyed. While he mastered his fright immediately and replied with calm factualness, I knew I had inflicted on him something monstrous, something we never talked about, but which I had done to him many times before.

Weary of worrying endlessly about him and what he was becoming, I wished suddenly and savagely that he were not in my life, that he was not at all. I told him this by the timbre of my voice and fixed glare. I wanted him to hear me. He heard me. For a second, we both knew how we both felt. He felt agony. I felt satisfaction at his agony and at causing it.

We each might have reacted to that collision in a variety of ways. We went into the kitchen, drank warm milk, and talked of the Red Sox. Would it have been better if we had talked about our violent flare of emotion over nothing at all? It felt good as it was, at the kitchen table. For all its ugliness, our flare-up had been a touching, strangely satisfying.

Was it somehow an act of love? Did he sense that I wearied so violently of him because he was entwined in my guts? As I wearied at times of myself? In receiving my primal dismissal of him, did he sense its determined impotence? Did he sense how dwarfed it was by my other twenty-year-old primal, inescapable desire from which it grew: that I be with him forever? I think so.

Such vicious, loving embrace has all sorts of outcome. In the iron confines of intimacy, the desire behind blaming for blaming's sake may pass from expressed fantasy into execution. Repeated daily in the guise of blame, the desire to be rid of the other may grow harder, speak louder, and eventually move one of us to leave the other.

It can work other ways. Some lovers' mutual blaming for blaming's sake has enough humor in it to be love's fool. Their love delights and battens on it. Other lovers are dead serious, as they beat each other wildly to collapse fondly on each other afterwards, year after year.

Such a fight of rage and love, this one serious and then humorous, is illustrated by the climax of the film, *The Turning Point*.

Some lovers have passion for each other only when they fight. Only when they blame each other for blaming's sake, do they feel strongly, and feel each other's feelings. They feel their own and the other's panicked pain and mordant joy as the battle rages back and forth. They press into each other with their longing to be rid of each other.

Years of practice assure that the blades go deep. Locked in combat, they have neither intention nor power to break apart. Their vicious, impotent dismissal of each other makes a real embrace. Only with their bared longing to be rid of each other, do they bare their desire to be with each other. With angry words, they grip each other desperately, rocking on the porch.

Blaming for blaming's sake is often like an erotic dance of two dancers who are also lovers. In the dance they act their real desire to make love, without making love. For the moment they satisfy their desire by disclosing it to each other in movement and gesture. They share their satisfaction by similarly disclosing it. If an observer watching the dance knows that the two are real lovers, he thrills not only at their art but also at their acted desire and satisfaction. Their desire and satisfaction are erotic and real though different from what they would be in actually making love. By their dance they reveal in patent disguise to each other their real desire and satisfaction. This is the actual sense of this duo's dance.

All this, of course, is to suggest that a moment or life of mutual blaming for blaming's sake can be a blaming for love's sake. How marvelously humans love by hating! How ingenious, by moral accusation, to share secret passion! How close, in the barrage of rage, is the union of lover and loved one in fantasy! How real the life lived in play-acting! It makes sense. It makes sense that is not sense to our civilized thinking.

It makes sense, but is it truly love? Ever? Or if it be "love" in some sense of the word, is it good? Humanly good? Morally good? In this book, we ask this not about what we see that blamers *do*, but what we see that they *feel*. We ask this about such anger whether or not blaming be the act it surges towards. We ask about this vindictive fury at the other: Can it be love? Can it be good?

I answer "Yes!" We will hear this "Yes!" supported by the great Greek philosopher, Aristotle, by Jesus and Paul in the New Testament, and by the great Christian theologian, Thomas Aquinas. We will hear certain contemporary writers, particularly black and feminist, support the answer, "Yes!" But my argument for "Yes!" will be simply appeal to the reader's experience.

The nub of our question is: How? How can it be loving or good to want to cause, in mutual awareness, another person's pain? Before undertaking, in Chapter 4 on, to get clearer ideas both of our question and our foolhardy answer, let us stay a while longer staring at experience. In the next chapters I offer two bits of fiction to stimulate further the reader's imagination and memory. In both stories the climax comes when the hero recognizes his passion to cause another person pain and is glad he feels the passion!

I hope that in these stories, as in this first chapter, a further thing will grow evident. The rational categories that we automatically apply do not apply. The usual concepts with which we tend to represent good and evil do not fit the good and evil of passion in these experiences. Our stubborn pursuit of our question takes us into a strange world. It is a familiar dimension of our experience, yet the more we look squarely at it, the more it bewilders us.

2

One Moment of Love

The road from Lawton twists and turns to get over the hills and down into Burrisville. Around eleven one Monday night, descending into a turn of the road, Paul Muelder drove onto a sheet of ice which he did not see and the sander had missed. His steering had no effect. The car shot ahead off the road and rolled down a fifty foot embankment, bouncing off rocks and small trees as it plummeted. Near the end Paul flew out of the car and bounced the rest of the way by himself, like a straw doll.

He came to on his back under a huge tree that disappeared up into fine, falling snow. His head was propped up on a root. A shining transparent figure stood before him looking at him with penetrating gaze and evident perplexity. "Extraordinary," murmured the figure. "Balanced exactly between life and death. Not in either. Won't move forward or backward. Never saw anything like it before." The figure paused, then shrugged its shoulders. "Well, let's count him dead."

"No!" cried Paul. The figure raised its eyebrows. "I don't want to die!"

"You've got nothing to worry about, Paul. You made it. Some purgatorial fire first, but you'll get to heaven eventually."

"How much purgatory?"

The figure pondered, moving lips in rapid calculating.

"Eleven years, give or take one or two."

"Eleven years! That can't be. It's a mistake. I'm an active, church-going Christian. I teach Sunday school. I publish articles in religious publications. Besides, I'm a family man, an assistant principal, a liberal Democrat, a . . .," Paul realized he was getting incoherent.

24

"You can appeal," conceded the figure. "I've never been overturned but it's bound to happen some day. Purgatorial time does go slow. A minute feels like a year."

Desperation galvanized Paul's ingenuity. The spirit apparently exercised a certain autonomy of judgment. Could he be reasoned with? Persuaded?

"Look, maybe I have no right to ask. But what have I done to merit eleven years of pain? I haven't done *anything* real bad."

"Pain is not the point, though purgatory *is* horribly painful." The spirit shuddered. "It's a burning of purification. It's purifying you into pure love, so you can enter the kingdom of love.

"Merit is not the point either. The point is that you need eleven years of purgatory. You've loved so little in your earthly life that there's not much love in you. All your dross has to be burned away so your fire of love can grow and fill you. Inasmuch as a human being doesn't transform himself into a fully loving person in his earthly life, we do it by fire after death. Somebody's got to do it."

"Loved so little? Not much love in me? Me? Love is my single ideal. It's my whole philosophy of life. I've written on the subject and it's been greatly appreciated. I'm known as a guy who's always available for people, always ready to speak up for others, always ready to help.

"I'm not perfect. I have faults. I'm not always loving. But every day I do a lot of it."

"Wanna bet?" said the figure. "I'll make a deal with you. Your present situation is so unprecedented in my experience that I have to come up with an unprecedented solution in any case."

"What's the bet?" asked Paul cautiously.

"The stakes are life or death. We bet whether you had one moment of love in the last twenty-four hours, one moment when you were mainly loving someone."

"Just one moment?"

"Right. If you can find it, I'll push you gently back into life. If you can't, I'll push gently into death. And into your eleven-year term."

"That's a walk in!" exclaimed Paul. "It's a bet! Wait a minute. What do you mean by 'loving'?"

"What do *you* mean by 'loving'?"

Though still stretched out under the tree, Paul instinctively folded his hands on his stomach and revolved his thumbs. He always did this when speaking on his favorite subject, love, whether to teenagers in his Sunday school class or those in his Guidance class in the high school or his friends over afterdinner drinks. Paul did have a Ph.D. in philosophy and his dissertation had been on concepts of love.

"Love is caring. To love is to care about another person. It may entail caring *for* the person, too, if they need it. But you also care *about* them if you love them. You take the person as the unique, important individual he or she is. You. . . ."

"All right, all right!" interrupted the spirit, biting its lip in a vain attempt to hide its amusement. "That'll do. It's a bet."

The figure added ruminatively, "It would have been more interesting if you had defined loving to include loving yourself. We would have had an argument or two, I suspect. Humans, particularly Christians, think that loving yourself is so common and easy. But ultimately, you'd have realized you haven't loved yourself any more than anyone else in the last day."

"I said: love is caring about other persons," Paul said pugnaciously. "How do we settle the bet?"

"Easy," said the spirit. "You can replay any scene of the last twenty-four hours that you want. If you turn up one moment of love, a moment when your main attitude was one of love, you win the bet. You live. If you can't find any, I'll take you away."

"Well," cried Paul exultantly, "how about that talk with Rita Santos?"

The woods were gone and he was in his office at school watching himself at the desk. He *was* getting old. Rita sat by the side of the desk facing him. She held her head in her hands and shook with sobs. The oldest child of a family of nine, she had to get all the other children off to school. This morning had been chaos and violence and agony because, among other difficulties, the only heat was from the stove, the only thing to eat was corn flakes with water, and one child had no dry shoes.

Paul heard his warm tones, sympathetic and yet encouraging. At the same time, he heard in the background, like a second interfering station on the radio, the bass whisper of his unspoken feelings. "Who else in this school would give the poor kid the time? Nobody would really feel for her but me. That's why she just burst in here. I'm a warm, sensitive person. I feel for people, no fooling around. I really love them. . . ."

"Do you think that would work, Mr. Muelder?" asked Rita softly.

"It may work, Rita. But it might do harm. Go very carefully. Things have to get better. The winter's nearly over." The bass whisper went on: "Didn't catch her idea. I get so caught up in the sorrows of others I don't hear their words. My compassion comforts her. Lucky kid she came in to me."

Paul shook his head in embarrassment and was back in the woods. "Well," he muttered to the figure. "I did have some feeling of compassion for Rita."

"You did. But the bet's about your main attitude. That's what the basso profundo expresses. You were chiefly thinking and feeling about yourself. Not about your real self, incidentally, but one you imagine."

"How many scenes can I review?"

"As many as you like, as long as they are from the last twenty-four hours. But I can save you time. I've been with you every minute of these hours and I don't remember a single minute when you loved anyone. I'll be honest, my memory is not as good as it used to be. That's been pointed out to me recently. I may be forgetting something you did. But I doubt it. Come on. Let's forget the bet. The sooner you start your eleven years, the sooner you'll be finished."

"No!" Paul was determined. "I want to live some more. I'd much rather purify myself in loving before I die than afterwards."

"Don't blame you," replied the figure, and was gone.

As Paul called up one scene after another, the sick sensation spread in his stomach. How could he have been feeling this way! And yet he could not deny the accuracy of the basso profundo. He remembered. How was it that he had not noticed his actual feelings then and now could recall how strong they had been?

Scorn was what he felt for the principal, Al Hutchings, as he enthusiastically supported Al's latest project. He knew it would go no further than any other of the flimsy dreams with which Al justified his position. "How can he kid himself this way?" muttered the basso profundo.

At the school board this evening, he pleaded eloquently the plight of the talented youngster, bored by classes aimed at average students. But what he eagerly sought was the board's admiration for him as dedicated educator. He did not embarrass the board by any concrete proposals, for they would cost money and he knew the board would refuse them. Besides, there were no talented kids in the school.

In the afternoon, he lectured the honors class on James Joyce without hope that they would get anything out of it. Small-town kids, farm kids, how could they have the slightest inkling of "the spell of arms and voices: the white arms of roads . . . and the black arms of tall ships . . . ."? But the spell intoxicated Paul for the millionth time and his voice rang in the classroom like the meditation of a shaman alone on the hilltop.

After class, one student stopped to sneer that Joyce was just overemotional. Paul viewed with satisfaction the tense five minutes when step by step, through Socratic questioning, he brought Jonathan Rhinestein, him of the straight A's, to acknowledge that he did not understand why Stephen Daedalus left Dublin. Masterful midwivery in bringing Jonathan to the wisdom of recognizing his ignorance! But the basso profundo bellowed hoarsely, "Now I got you, you son of a bitch!" Paul recognized that was exactly how he had felt in the back of his chest.

Because of the school board meeting in the evening, Paul did not go home for supper. From 5 to 8, with a brief break at the diner for a ham sandwich and soup, he brought up to date student records and files with the meticulous thoroughness for which he was noted. Did he not care? But the basso profundo simpered the whole time, "What a good boy am I!"

Paul did not bother replaying his attentive listening to Eva Mallia, the young art teacher. He needed no replay to remember that, while she poured out to him as usual the latest exciting thing to happen to her, he had been occupied in undressing her mentally and dizzily fantasizing further. His basso profundo would probably be doing heavy breathing. Paul could not remember what she had told him about today.

In desperation, Paul turned to the morning rush at home. As he watched, he defended himself as not awake enough to love. And how could he love his wife while she talked a blue streak about one thing after another with no pause for him to respond? He nodded interestedly and thought of other things. Wait!

Stopping his daughter at the door, he reminded her in even, kind accents that he was worried about her grades. He could not permit her to sign up for Driver's Ed till she began to pass the science tests. Surely he showed loving concern here. His tense stance showed it took effort of will. But the basso profundo only snarled angrily, "I always passed my courses. Pass yours! What must they think of me?"

Paul stared at his still, slumped body now white with snow. He had set the bet up wrong. No wonder the angel smiled. If he had only defined love as doing good to another. . . . In the last twenty-four hours, he had gone about doing good. The replays had not shown a single incident when he had failed to work more good than harm. Even the school board showed, by their faces, that Paul had given them something to think about, though they would do nothing. Jonathan Rhinestein profited perhaps the most. His eyes lit up with new ideas and his "See you" rang with respect for Paul.

Perhaps Paul's mistake had not been to take love as caring. His mistake was to evalutate his past twenty-four hours with the presupposition that caring was principally a matter of feelings. Paul recognized each time with sinking dismay how accurately the basso profundo voiced the dominant feelings he had at the particular moment. But perhaps love, caring, was principally a matter of the will.

Flat on his back, closed in by falling snow, Paul had no illusions. If he took love as essentially an act of the will, he was espousing a definition he had repeatedly and heatedly denounced as "disembodied," "inhuman," "unreal." The kind of love he always championed was something one felt deeply because it was an "experience." Still the present moment was not one for theoretical argument.

However emotionally disinterested he had been in those he had dealt with today, he had surely willed their good. Most of them anyway. He would remind the angel—that is what the figure must be—that the great scholar and Christian, C. H. Dodd, rendered the Biblical definition of love as "to will good." An angel of the Lord should respect the Word of God and not insist on a false definition, even if initially agreed on by angel and Christian.

"Did you will the good of anybody in the last twenty-four hours?" The figure was back, apparently as amused by Paul's new claims as he had been by his former ones. "I won't quibble. Take 'love' or 'caring' as willing the good of the other. Let's forget about your feelings and talk about your intention or purpose." The figure laughed. "You're right. You helped everybody you dealt with in the scenes you replayed. You did good to them. But you didn't mean to. You didn't care what happened to them. You did good despite yourself." The figure shook his head chuckling. "If you find one time today when you intended the good of someone, you win the bet."

Paul stared at the figure mistrustfully. He was certain this was false. He could win the bet now. But he had been certain before, and wrong. This was his last chance. He licked his lips, said nothing and thought hard.

"Did you, for example," the figure began jovially, "intend to help Al realize his crazy project? You did intend to help him think he was a great principal. But you know he's not and you don't believe it's good for him to keep kidding himself that he is. Remember that talk you gave students on self-deception, dishonesty with self?

"You didn't intend to help talented students by your plea to the board since you knew the board would do nothing. You did make the board members think a little but you couldn't have cared less about that. You always dismiss them as 'idiots.' You just wanted them to appreciate you and you achieved that.

"You didn't expect any student to get anything out of your Joyce lecture. And that work on student records and files. You know that 80% of your ordering and recording will never be of use to anyone. You just like to have—just have to have?—neat, complete files. And be a good boy.

"You made Eva less lonely but that's not what absorbed your interest. If you had cared about easing someone's loneliness, you wouldn't have broken away from Edith, the librarian, a few minutes earlier when she wanted to tell you about her weekend. Edith is an old friend, but she's too old and thin to give your fantasy what you wanted."

"Is this the Last Judgment?" murmured Paul.

"No. We're settling a bet. Was it really your daughter's good you intended as you threatened her about her science grades? Is that private school and its fast pace turning out to be too much for her? Giving her harmful, unnecessary stress and tension as she's trying to grow up? Why haven't you asked yourself that? Do you care?"

The angel was cheating. It ticked each incident off on its fingers, as if it were reviewing all the scenes Paul had called up. "You skipped one!" Paul was grimly arch.

"I skipped three," the figure replied. "Shall we take another look at the exchange with Jonathan?"

"That's not what I refer to." Paul did not want to examine why his complete victory over Jonathan had left him disappointed. But now as he turned his mind away, he knew why. The dawning light in Jonathan's eyes and his eager respect was not what Paul wanted. He wanted a glare of cringing defeat or grudging surrender. He wanted Jonathan conquered, not co-victorious with himself.

"No. I meant Rita. I willed her good. I did care about her in that sense, even if I was enraptured mainly by my own compassion. I did want to help her."

They were back in his office again, with Rita crying at the side of his desk. It was the end of their conversation. "Look!" said the figure sharply. "No, not at you. At her. What do you see?"

After a moment, Paul replied with surprise, "There's something wrong. She's shaking all over. Even her lips. Is she sick?"

"She has pneumonia. Fortunately the teacher of her first class caught it and sent her home. Her father, back from the night shift, brought her to the hospital. I can't foresee the future, but I think she'll pull through."

"I was so concerned with her crushed spirit I didn't notice her body."

The figure raised a finger and the scene halted. They had now a still shot. "Look at her again. The face!" Above the hands, behind the tears, the eyes flashed with fury. The action continued and Rita whispered softly, "Do you think that would work, Mr. Muelder?"

Now Paul saw the savage flicker of her lips and heard the murderous hiss. "Whom is she mad at? What is she proposing to do?"

"Good questions, Paul. Now you do care about her. You didn't then. You weren't trying to help the person sitting before you. You didn't notice her. You weren't willing the good of the real Rita. You didn't know she was there."

The figure sighed. "This is unpleasant. I've never had to conduct someone over the border before. Let's get it over with."

Paul smiled for the first time, ruefully. "It was a bad day to go off the road." He was silent. "It wasn't one of my better days, was it?"

The figure weighed its answer. "On some days you would have won the bet," it said gently.

"Come along now. Much of purgatory is just like reliving the days of your life over and over. Like you've just done. You've got eleven years to see what your other days were like. You'll find out, too, what else . . . happened today. Let's go. The sooner you start, the sooner you finish."

The figure's voice broke slightly, almost imperceptibly, after "what else." It picked up immediately but not quite as sonorously as before. The figure had abruptly lost its assurance only to regain composure quickly, but not completely. Had it suddenly recalled an event of Paul's day that it had forgotten? An event that could throw the wager in Paul's favor?

"Not yet. Let me think a few more minutes."

"You have to come. Time's up."

"We put no time limits on the bet."

"The whole matter has to be settled today. It's midnight."

Paul looked at his watch. "I have ten minutes left. Leave me alone." The spirit, annoyed, disappeared.

Paul strained his memory desperately, racing through all hours of the day. Nothing promising. There was that crazy happening with Luce on the cellar stairs. It was surely neither loving nor caring. Neither reason nor will played a part in it. It was in good part violent, even vicious. Still it was also strange . . . .

He was in the cellar once more. Vanessa had left for school. Paul had been searching for his overcoat in the hall closet when the thin, strident voice of his wife summoned him down. Now she was pointing out to him the flooding at the foot of the stairs, the flooding in his basement den, the flooding in the linen closet, the flooding over by the windows, the flooding across the entry. The first time *this* had happened. As usual she had put the old blankets against the walls. Last night and early this morning she had put each blanket in the automatic dryer and got the water out. But what was he going to do about it? He had said he'd take care of it last year. Last summer. Last month. Yesterday morning. He had done nothing about it. Was he going to continue to do nothing about it?

Paul, in basso profundo, roared, "Bitch! Doesn't she ever stop? How can I get out of here quick?" Paul, watching, winced at his irresponsible callousness and childish urge to flee. He was no more loving here than in any other event of the day.

"Sorry, Luce," he mumbled, "but I'll be late for my appointment with Al if I don't head off. I'll do something about it."

Paul moved towards the stairs to go up. Since they were narrow, he expected her to step back and let him pass or to go up ahead of him. She did neither. She stood there, hands at her side, glaring with speechless rage. Paul halted in mid-stride waiting for her to move. She did not budge and her stone face leaned forward in fury.

Paul's basso whispered, "Help! Help!" Then tensely, "I'm going through." Paul thrust into the inches between his wife and the wall of the staircase. Though Paul's wife was taller, younger and in better shape than he, his abrupt charge banged her up against the opposite wall. Paul just about squeezed into the space, hoping to get between them, when Luce counter-attacked. She had big, bony hips with crushing force.

They fought their way up the stairs. No breath for words. Grunts and gasps. Paul couldn't manage to pull ahead of her and free himself. Luce couldn't get ahead to block him or send him reeling down with a massive hip swivel. Paul was hampered by the railing on his side, Luce by the ledge with cans on hers. Before they reached the top, cans were bumping loudly down.

The walls pressed Paul and Luce so close together that their vicious thrusts of shoulder, elbow, hip or knee, delivered with utmost effort, traveled only three or four inches and never gained enough force to cause great pain or harm. Indeed the two of them were so squeezed together in arm and leg that the heaving of the one to get a step ahead actually helped the other along.

Paul's basso profundo was scarcely more verbal than his lips or Luce's. The basso, too, mainly grunted and gasped though it gave out an occasional "Bitch!" "Take that!" "Damn you!" which Paul did not say aloud. Luce did once snarl aloud "Bastard!" as she ground in a good elbow jab.

Paul, watching now, heard the pants and snorts change tone as Luce and he wormed slowly, convulsively upward. By the time they finally reached the top—it took a good three minutes, he figured—they were clearly laughing. They were struggling not to; they were trying to hide it; they were laughing. At the top, Paul finally managed to use a two-inch lead to forge clearly ahead. But that freed Luce's hips so she could give finally a weighty blow from behind that sent him sprawling on the landing. Her momentum sent her on her back along side of him. He, on hands and knees, looked down at her on her back, looking up. They laughed helplessly. They could not move for laughter.

"May you live forever!" boomed Paul's basso profundo. "Let's do it again!" gasped Luce still on her back. "Tomorrow!" promised Paul through the tears of his mirth. Reaching for the wall, he worked himself weakly to his feet.

"I'm late. You know I'm never late." He blew her a kiss, lying there, rushed for his overcoat and was out the door.

The scene was gone. Paul found that he had turned onto his hands and knees in the snow, reached for the trunk and worked himself up weakly to his feet. He was now stepping forward gingerly and his legs held up. He started shakily climbing back up the embankment. It was steep, almost vertical in places, but he pulled himself up by snow-covered branches and shrubs. The snow was moist and heavy, not slippery underfoot. He did not hurry, but he did not halt. An enormous, wordless determination inside him propelled him steadily up.

He stood on the road awhile, getting his breath. It was only a half mile downhill into Burrisville. He wondered what the insurance company would give him. His head was a little misty and swirling like the snow coming down, but he could see clear enough. He probably had a slight concussion. That would explain his delirium about an angel. Paul smiled incredulously at the memory and began limping down the road.

He would loan Jonathan his old, college-days copy of *Ulysses*. He mused how Jonathan would react to his faded jottings in the margin. And what Al might think about his giving a student a book once banned as pornographic. Paul smiled again, as he took the turn-off. He'd be home in five minutes. The key was already in his hand.

*   *   *   *   *   *

I invite you, reader, to ponder this careless story. I ponder it, too, for it came spontaneously, unplanned, out of me. I have questions about it to which I do not know the answers. Fellow discussants and I recognize the story as somehow familiar. It expresses some truth. We grope together in it, end up with something, but know we have only part of its truth. We see it dimly, as in a dark glass.

Can we get it a little clearer? How is the fight on the stairs a moment of love? What makes Paul want Luce to live forever? Why does Luce want to do it again? Why is the key so soon in Paul's hand? Is the violent anger of Paul and Luce at each other a kind of love? What kind? A willing of good for the other? What good? How can their battering of each other carry out their love?

Could it be that passion for violence in family, whether the violence be physical or verbal, is commonly so destructive and evil, not because the violence is pure evil, but because it is a kind of loving that is basically good but hideously corrupted? Could it be that Paul and Luce on the stairs model the less common instance when the violent anger of two who love each other is a loving that is more good than evil? That in such instances the couple should afterwards, like Luce and Paul, be glad they got angry? If so, what does this suggest about the possibility and nature of *good* anger?

3

The Critic

I

There once was a man named Martin who was known for his elegant, pointed reviews. He wrote book reviews, review essays, and recent literature bulletins on a given question. Specialists in his field, that of seventeenth century Western thought, read his reviews religiously. No one else marked out as surely where a new book or article repeated work already done and where it advanced new claims. No one else sliced as deftly under the claims to expose what basis or lack of basis they had in historical evidence. And—it was generally recognized—no one was more fair and objective in his stringent criticism. If some murmured that Martin might some day write something maintaining a position of his own so that others could review *him*, the murmur was, in a sense, irrelevant. In any case, it never reached Martin's ears.

One December morning, as the snow pattered on his office window, Martin, a tall, thin man with a receding shock of red hair, pounded at his old typewriter. He abruptly stopped typing. He stopped for two years. That morning, he suddenly did not want to write another publishable word. He felt infinitely weary. He was completely dissatisfied with all he had written and was likely to write. He tried to lift his hands back to the keyboard. He could not.

From his first days of school, in a way, from birth on, Martin had always been a critic. It was his personality, his bent. His greatest ambition in life had been to do learned criticism. He had never ambitioned anything else. He did it now with eminent success. Why was it then so wearying,

37

flat, stale and unprofitable? It had been so, he realized, for some years. Always? Why?

Was he that morning just sensing the vanity of all human endeavor? Or the non-being the existentialists talked about, which he had never understood? Or was his heart asserting its restlessness for God in the midst of worldly success? Or was it the onset of the mid-life crisis? Martin doubted any of these. But sitting there he knew two things. One: he could not write another word. Two: the fact that he could not was due to another fact, namely, that if he had finished the paragraph he had been typing, he would have ripped the paper out of the machine and stuffed it into the overflowing wastepaper basket. And started a better paragraph. And another. And another.

Of course, he would have ended up with an excellent review. Whoever read Martin's reviews admired their figure-skating grace of style and the firm, smooth progression of the criticism. No reader guessed that the reviews emerged out of violent torment, out of a jagged process of whipsaw mental conflict and countless castings and recastings of word.

By my magic wand I have Martin now enter into two years of extraordinarily successful psychotherapy. But already, at the moment of collapse that winter morning, he has the loose thread in hand. He knows what's wrong. There are thirty pounds of lead in his gut and he no longer has the stomach for the bloody battle that writing a review was for him. That's what's wrong. The inevitable victory is no longer worth the struggle, if it ever was.

The struggle Martin went through each time was, as he saw it, a moral one. There were two stages—one could say, two successive drafts—in producing the review. In the first, he wrote by hand, the hand trembling and lashing at the paper, the mouth in silent spasms. He was invariably enraged that the author presumed to say some of the things he or she had said. Martin's first draft swam with accusations of ignorance, naivete and incompetence, with condemnatory innuendo and outright blame, with sarcasm and even invective.

Finally limp, intellectually and emotionally, Martin swivelled over to the typing table. He knew he could not publish the review in its present state. Now began the laborious purging of all that was vicious, unfair, untrue or simply unproven. The paper basket filled up as he carried out the purification and welded the remnants into the unity of sheer objectivity he was known for.

Though Martin tried, on occasion, to do it otherwise, he could write satisfactory reviews only by this brutal two-stage process. He derived some consolation from the fact. If he was excessive in moral indignation, he was morally scrupulous in pruning the excesses. In his moral conflict, he remained moral master of himself and what he did. In the final stage he could and did pound away at his own words so that all that appeared in print was justified criticism, responsible, fair and often kind. He just didn't feel like doing it any more.

So I send Martin into therapy and in two years he comes out completely cured. If this were real life, therapy might not be the best thing or even a good thing for the individual in Martin's shoes. And if it were a good thing, a complete cure in two years is improbable. But a completely successful therapy helps the purpose of this story to show anger at work. So off Martin goes into therapy. I describe it as he experienced it. His therapist would surely tell another, though perhaps not contradicting, story.

Martin's first discovery in therapy is that he mistook the nature of his turmoil in writing. He conceived it in moral terms. Overrun by excessive moral indignation in writing his first draft, in his second he obstinately regained the ground, foxhole by foxhole, for truthfulness and justice and, on occasion, kindness. He sees now that this was not what went on. His struggle was not a moral one at all.

He comes to see what the struggle was in part because he comes to recognize the same struggle holding sway, in various guises and disguises, in other sectors of his life, from childhood on. But in a brief chapter, I can focus only on the struggle that possessed him in writing reviews.

That struggle was not moral. True, the flaws of scholarship which he exposed in the literature he reviewed were failures in the professional responsibility of the authors reviewed. They were, therefore, moral faults, however unintentional. The qualities he made sure dominated every piece he published were moral traits: truthfulness and justice as well as general professional responsibility. Therapy does not weaken Martin's conviction that the flaws in scholarship he exposed are reprehensible and that justice and truthfulness are essential to scholarly writing. Therapy takes none of these moral principles away.

Therapy will only give him some new ones, as we'll see. But therapy first forces on Martin, not a new moral principle, but a correction of his error of fact. That unremitting struggle of which he finally became so weary that he could not write another word was not a moral struggle. It was not a moral struggle because the conflict and the motives that compelled the conflict were not on the moral level.

What *were* the motives that drove Martin first one way in moral indignation, and then the other way to assure truthfulness and justice? They were not what held the forefront of his consciousness as he wrote. They were not his conviction of the professional irresponsibility of the author reviewed, and they were not any concern he had for justice, truthfulness or kindness. Reenacting in therapy the exhausting conflict within himself in which he wrote, Martin becomes aware of the iron impulses that create the struggle. They are brutal desires that strike Martin as neither moral nor immoral. They have not reached the moral level, because in their obscurity they have been subject to no judgment of reason and to no deliberate choice by him.

At first, Martin can't make out what these conflicting desires of his really desire. He scrutinizes first that regular final frenzy of his to be honest and just and kind in his printed piece. His need to end up with a morally impeccable review came—in waves that Martin thinks must be like birth labor—from a panicky desire not to be condemned, not rejected, not disapproved, not dismissed, not taken lightly. But surely he desired to have these things NOT happen to him because he desired something else, something positive. What did he really want?

It could not be the esteem and respectful use which his reviews did receive, for he felt little satisfaction at this reception. Acknowledgments in the scholarly literature of his critical contributions provoked in him a curious melange of emotions: a small, passing pleasure, a dull, opaque frustration that seemed familiar, and a lot of numbness. The question broadens. Why with so little satisfaction did he unhesitatingly go back and start anew the excruciating process of writing another review? What was he trying to get out of it?

The mystery did not open up for Martin by his understanding this pseudo-moral surgery with which he gave final shape to the review. His first glimmer of truth illumined, rather, the anger that preceded. On the surface, this anger of his, this frantic fury flailing at the author beneath his pen, was so monstrously unintelligible that even at the time he wrote, carried away with wrath, a part of him felt bewildered and ashamed. In his righteous indignation, he put down things he did not know were true. At times he put down things he knew were not true. He let himself do this, of course, because he knew he would go on, in his second stage of operation, to check all his statements and excise all that were false or dubious. But what made him write them in the first place? With such fervor and conviction, even when in the back of his mind he knew they were false?

What flood roared up from his guts to pour groundless denunciations onto the page? Was he insane? He was certainly ludicrous. A grown man sitting alone at his desk ranting away at an absent person for something he had as yet no reason to think the person did!

At the steady nudges of the therapist, Martin makes himself look closer at his memories of these rages. Did not fantasies flicker in his mind as he slashed away with his pen? Yes, he seemed indeliberately, almost unwittingly, to spasmodically imagine what he hoped his acid words would do. The author kneeled before him, his face crumpled in the agony of being exposed as a scholar far inferior to what he claimed to be and infinitely inferior to the scholar who was masterfully exposing him. In Martin's dim fantasy, other scholars knelt, too, all around Martin. Their faces were crushed with humiliation at not having appreciated Martin's greatness and at sharing thus in the author's exposure. This is just one of his fantasies of vindictive punishment that Martin forces with horror into the glare of his full consciousness. Other fantasies are more horrifying. I spare you the details.

The memories embarrass Martin and revolt him. When he first recalls one, it takes several sessions before he can describe it to the therapist, though she shows no sign of being revolted. Some ethicists might stop Martin right here. They would say, "Martin boy, let fantasies be fantasies. You didn't choose to have them. You couldn't help it. You don't act on them. No trace appears in your reviews. Don't give them a further thought."

Martin gives them further thought. Not, strangely enough, because he wants to get rid of them. He is eventually able to laugh at them. But the fantasies hint at a different Martin from the one he thought he knew. In the back of Martin's mind, a hound begins to bay. Martin will later look back at this as the first time in his life he begins to seek truth for its own sake.

What is the truth about Martin and his rages? What was he trying to do in his futile fury? The fantasies expressed a desire he truly felt. The desire was grotesque, unrealistic, silly, childish, disgusting, humiliating. It was desire to punish, to take revenge on his colleagues. But after he accepts his desire as part of himself, and as in memory he goes back and forth reliving his experience of this desire in its various fantasized forms, he begins to remember other fantasies, fantasies of a different kind.

The image fades of his colleagues kneeling around in awe and dismay. His colleagues now dance a jig around him. They each wave in hand a copy of his latest review. They shout words he cannot catch, but which are obviously exclamations of delight and enthusiasm about him and what he has written. Bounding highest and crying most loudly is the author reviewed. He is overcome with gratitude by what he has learned about his subject from Martin's writing. Another time, when Martin lets himself go in fantasy without knowing what to expect, his colleagues sweep him up on their shoulders and carry him around cheering, as *he* waves his latest pages. These seem to be fantasies of Martin's younger days. They persist, though weaker than the later, punitive ones.

One day Martin stares at the floor in front of his therapist as he feels,— not concludes, but feels—what he really wants with his writing. It is not far from the last two fantasies mentioned. In his gut, he wants his peers, after they read his review, to do something like race to the phone and to shout hoarsely to him their marvelling joy at it. He wants them to tell others excitedly about it. No wonder the sober respect he got from his reviews tasted flat, stale and unprofitable. Few writers in Martin's field were respected as much as he. But respect was not the glad celebration he wanted. And couldn't help wanting.

Now that Martin feels finally in full awareness his desire for raves about his writing, he feels also the despair that riddles it. He feels like a boy again, a boy dreaming a boy's dreams, but man enough to dream them as they are, that is, impossible. He desires with his whole being what in his very desiring he knows cannot be. He feels so sad. Sitting there, he is ashamed of the self-pity washing over him. But he can do nothing about it. He knows what he wants, and has no hope. Sometime in his scholarly life—when and for what reason, good or bad, he is ignorant—he abandoned hope in his desires.

This is why he came to write only in rage. This is why the fantasies changed from colleagues making a jig to colleagues kneeling in abasement. It was the impotent, vindictive rage of the defeated. Martin called his author names because he had no sticks and stones. The *pain* of his colleagues would make them take him as seriously as he wanted them to, since he could not give them enough *pleasure* to have the same effect. All in fantasy, of course. In reality, his rage, put in print, would have made his readers take him much less seriously than they did. It would have made more impossible his dream of being celebrated for his reviews. So after frantically raging, he frantically corrected. His two-stage writing with its elegant, pointed product was simply the exercise of the same desire in *despair*. Spare!

Can Martin spare himself this despair? Within the singeing of the strong sun? The therapist asks, "Is your fantasy really impossible? Is it impossible to make your colleague dance—equivalently—over your writing?"

"I certainly can't do it with reviews." The therapist says nothing. Silence follows. "You know," says Martin, "I might as well admit to myself that I *have* a unique understanding of seventeent-century thought. I see *certain ways* the whole time moves together. No one else has seen them. At least, no one else ever put it in print."

"Where have you put it in print?" asks the therapist.

"I haven't. But it's behind all my reviews. It's the hidden power that makes my critical judgment so effective. I've never laid it out." Martin grins, "I always fired from cover." Silence follows. "Could I convince anybody? They'd laugh at me. Dismiss it. They'd call it naive, pretentious, boring. Never take me seriously again. I guess that is what always set me in a rage. I have worked out over the years a unique understanding that would enrich the approach to my field and no one appreciates me for it."

The therapist says only, "Do you want to tell them about it?"

Before concluding my story, let me suggest that Martin going home from one of his last therapy sessions and turning over incredulously in his mind this new crazy project of writing what *he* thinks, also turns over implicitly a constellation of new moral questions. I list three moral questions which Martin stirs vaguely and which illustrate the kind of questions that awareness of one's dominant passions can force on one's morality and ideals.

First: Is it right, good, worthwhile, to devote one's energies to gain the excited admiration, acclamation, celebration, enthusiastic gratitude of others for one's achievement? Can this, for example, be part of a good Christian life? Good Jewish life? The good secular humanistic life generally praised in our time?

The *second* moral question concerns Martin's anger. Now that he yearns uninhibitedly for his peers' wild applause and considers making a run at it, he is even more furious than before with certain of the same peers. Now that he has openly felt his despair and traced its roots back into childhood, the despair begins to wilt. This crazy hope sprouts unbidden. But there remain facts which fed the despair and are still present. Two colleagues he most wants to impress are not the type that change their minds. Martin cannot recollect their ever having done so. Nor ever having got excited about someone else's original ideas. Martin knows they classify him as unoriginal.

So Martin cannot imagine succeeding in his new project without seeing Wilkinson's face working to hide its dismay or without hearing a tremor in O'Hara's voice. Martin desires and, in anticipation, delights in their pain. He takes savage delight in daydreams of his new book's forcing these two colleagues and other belittlers whom he vaguely imagines to realize in agony how much they underestimated his understanding of the seventeenth century. Fresh energy surges in him. He'll show them! This anger is not frantic as was the anger with which he used to write his first drafts. This anger is placid. But it is at first more frightening, for he intends to carry it out.

Is it moral to act to satisfy such vindictive anger? Is it humanly good? Is it Christian? Jewish? Secular humanist? Existentialist? Justified by respectable ethic at all? Is Martin not lowering himself, acting unworthily of being a person? Is he even being adult? Human? Sane?

My *third* moral question may not seem to be moral, but I believe it is. Even granted, for the sake of argument, that it is morally good for Martin to engage in writing out of the kind of desire and anger he now feels, the question remains: Is it worth it? The chances are against success. The probability is that Martin will fall on his face, lose what esteem he did enjoy, never be read religiously again, etc., etc. His stomach knots each time he thinks of it. He is likely to end up a failure.

Is it courage to go ahead, or senseless rashness? What place should the virtue of prudence play here? What place, faith, whether religious or secular? To live morally, to live in a truly human way, to live as a person is to live realistically, not chasing after pipe dreams. Martin's new project may be courageous, but is it wise? The development of this third question I leave to another occasion. I mention it to place in relief the first two questions.

We, with Martin, will return shortly to these two questions. But let me first give another scene of his story.

Martin is in his office on a bright December morning. It is two years after the morning on which we first saw him. He sits stooped, straightening with care the blank sheet of paper in the typewriter. He straightens up and types:

The Unity of Seventeenth-Century Thought

In the same year, as the sixteenth century turned into the seventeenth, the young men who were to exert the most influence on the thought of their time and our time were all extending their imagination along parallel lines, in a direction unprecedented in the history of Western civilization. The young men included Francis Bacon, Galileo Galilei, William Shakespeare, Jakob Boehme, Hugo Grotius, King James I, Cornelis Jansen, Vincent de Paul, Peter Paul Rubens, and Vasco Balboa.

Martin stops typing. He stares at what he has written. He grimaces, shakes his head, pauses, nods slightly, and types on.

I tell Martin's story no further. There is enough so far to ponder and discuss. I conclude the essay by giving Martin's own ponderings when he goes back over what happened.

II

It is already dark that afternoon when Martin drives the winding, wooded road home. A good day's work behind him! A careful start at his hardy opus.

Why doesn't he feel guilty? The question hooks him merely by curiosity. After six hours of intense writing, the mind yields readily to play. And why doesn't he feel guilty about not feeling guilty? He feels good. Has his therapy led him down the primrose path onto the meadows of "feel-good" morality, oft decried by preacher, social critic and Martin himself? Has he, despite his age, slipped into the ranks of the "me" generation? Where has his old, honed moral judgment gone to?

What does the traditional Christian morality he has held all his life—and believes he still holds—say about his new goals? He is as clear now as when he left therapy a week ago: his aims in his new writing project are human glory and vengeful punishment and not much else. He knows damn well what his old morality says about this. He doesn't care. Maybe he should, but he doesn't. He can't make himself care. He does not have the slightest inclination to consider stopping what he is up to. Or to judge it negatively. Or simply to condone it, or accept it resignedly. He endorses it enthusiastically. It's great, however risky!

What Martin plans, of course, is unobjectionable scholarly work. If it succeeds, it'll advance the field. If it fails, no harm will be done, except to Martin. He could easily give himself praiseworthy purposes for what he proposes to do. But it does not seem worth bothering to find such purposes. He is at peace with what he knows are his two principal purposes: human glory and vengeful punishment.

He did not choose these motives. No, that is not true. He did not choose these desires for acclamation and vengeance. He found out that he desired these things with unbidden, massive and, so far as he can see, undislodgeable desire. That was not a choice, but a fact.

But he chose to act on these desires, to make them his motives for action. On sabbatical now, he devotes the work of each working day to satisfying these desires. He chose to let these two disreputable cravings move into action, to make them his motives for an undertaking likely to last years.

So he did choose his present motives. He could have chosen not to. Driving home, with the carlights furrowing ahead, he again, with spirit, chooses them. Yet must not so deliberate a choice be subject to moral judgment?

This is curious. Martin feels as if he has made a number of moral judgments and they culminated in and justify now his present enterprise and his motives for it. But he does not at first remember a single one of the judgments. Yet he feels extremely "moral" in pursuing his goals. At peace. Even proud, happy. Like a knight cantering forth on a gay, spring morning.

Martin's attitude makes no sense to Martin. He has always scorned moralities based on feeling or "sense" or intuition. He articulated his own morality in steely principles of clear, distinct reason. The principles codified the imperative of his religious faith to serve others. Has he developed implicitly an additional morality of a different kind, which he has not yet explicitly recognized?

Well, he recognizes that his choice to embark on his present writing venture is of a piece with a series of other choices he made, starting that winter day when he abandoned his typewriter. On closer look, the choices do seem generally to have followed some implicit judgment he made of "good" or "bad," "right" or "wrong." These judgments seem somehow akin, of a nature unprecedented in Martin's life. It is all fuzzy and dubious and puzzling. Adding to the puzzle: why do these moral questions about his present life interest him only in a detached, curious, playful way?

Anyway they interest him. What indeed is the nature of this series of moral judgments that he came to one by one, without noticing it? In the following, I condense and collate Martin's musings on the subject on these late afternoon drives, as he lets his mind off the leash and it sniffs happily about in the darkness rushing homeward with him.

Was his first decision to get help based on any moral judgment, however implicit? He does not recall making then any judgment of "good" or "bad," "right" or "wrong." Did he make any rational judgment at all when, unable to get his hands up to the typewriter keys, he lunged for the phone to call Pat? He doesn't remember *thinking* anything. Just picturing days without end when he would never type again.

Terror shot through him. He was terrified of being destroyed as the inertia came over him and into him. He was going under. He grabbed for the first thing at hand: the phone. His impulse does not seem rational or moral, but a reflex of self-preservation. He spoke decisively to Pat because there was only one decision possible. He had no choice. Nothing else to think about. Nothing else to do. All this was false, of course. Two years later, he imagines other things he could have done. But then he saw only one plank floating by.

Pat referred him to Donna. He disliked her and his first sessions with her. He disliked all his therapy sessions. He never got to like Donna much. Anyway, around the third or fourth session, something started to shift in him. The need for a choice emerged. It was of a new kind. It was not the choice whether to continue with the therapy. Martin had already decided to give therapy a few months' trial. That was that. If this decision was a moral one, and it probably was, it was based on considerations and principles familiar to Martin. He wanted to write. He had writer's block, a well known, minor mental illness, like a cold. Therapy was said to succeed sometimes in removing such blocks. *Ergo* he should give it time to work. He would do so.

But in the therapy a different matter for choice began to materialize. He watched it draw near in horror, as Hamlet watched his father's ghost. The vision horrified Martin because it purported to be no ghost, but real; no father, but himself. The real Martin. He did not recognize it. It posed the choice. Was he unwilling or was he not unwilling to believe that this unfamiliar apparition, getting clearer and clearer, session by session, was what it claimed to be: himself?

He was unwilling to believe it because he did not recognize himself. It represented himself as a tragic figure in his twenty years of scholarly writing. Therapy soon widened the picture to show him a tragic figure in his whole life. But, in this brief chapter, we cannot follow the broadening perspective. We stay with the fact that Martin moved in his therapy toward his first novel choice as he confronted a new, tragic picture of himself as scholar and critic. Martin purses his lips and leisurely ponders that confrontation two years later on the road home.

In my first recounting of Martin's story, I described how before therapy he pictured himself writing. First, he would respond to the book or article by excoriating furiously its gaucheries, presumptions, errors, etc. Then he would conscientiously censor his critique to make sure it held nothing untruthful or unfair. Even before therapy, the thought of the two stages made him uncomfortable. He preferred not to think about them. At any rate, his writing ended up admirably vigorous, highly moral criticism. Or so he pictured it.

All the more terrifying then, in the beginning of therapy, was this bad smell, this dumb sense, coming out of nowhere and based apparently on nothing, that his writing, as a whole, was "bad." That he was consistently doing something wrong. That his twenty years of scholarly publication constituted a sustained failure, a moral tragedy. The words—"bad," "wrong," "tragic," "moral"—come two years later, on his peaceful drives home as the sun sets later and later. But they seem to verbalize his dumb terror of two years ago, his terror of shapeless shame and guilt. What do the words mean? The terror is less obscure in retrospect. But Martin, who, after all, as specialist in seventeenth-century European thought, knows a good deal of ethics, cannot at first disentangle the moral issues.

There was nothing bad or wrong about Martin's writing looked at objectively, in itself or in its consequences. Unlike Othello or Macbeth or Lear, he hurt no other person by what he did. He helped a good number. No one could object to the contents of Martin's reviews on moral grounds. No one did, except Arnold Meis, who was not sane. Yet Martin's therapy pressed him to believe he had been doing something terribly wrong by his writing.

Not to recognize one does wrong when one does wrong is further wrong. This caps the tragedy of an Othello or Oedipus. Christian morality always branded this fault. To the extent that one is responsible for this failure in moral recognition, to that extent one sins the sin of pride or self-deception. Knowing his weakness in this respect, Martin always combated this sin with special vigor. He tried hard to be honest with himself, to be humble, as the old phrase went. Renewing this effort in therapy, Martin expected to be on a familiar path, straight and narrow. His dogged honesty led him this time to the outskirts of a wilderness.

It would not have been an extraordinarily hard choice for Martin to admit that some unworthy passion had covertly driven him on. This, too, fitted into his Christian outlook. Could it be that over the years he has been swept by passion to his typewriter, as unaware and helpless as the Moor to Desdemona's bed or Macbeth to Dunsinane? Martin shuddered, but was ready to confess it if it were true. The evidence, however, that his memory reluctantly collected in Donna's back office, pointed in the opposite direction. Towards another kind of tragedy. Another kind of wrongdoing. For a long while, he could not believe it. He refused to believe it.

Two years later, he knows that back then he was too frightened to be willing to believe what the evidence pointed to more and more unequivocally. The emerging feel of self that paralyzed him with fright was the unfolding of the opaque, sinking sense of something wrong that terrified him into therapy in the first place. He was too frightened to admit that he had been right in being frightened in the beginning!

And yet, in the same terror, he knew he had no hope except in the truth. So the same terror that kept him from admitting the possibility of what seemed more and more evidently the truth also kept him sullenly returning to Donna's unanswerable questions, like "What are you so scared of about yourself?" Finally, as the vise closed, in desperation he chose. He chose not to be unwilling to accept the increasingly plausible answer to that question. He chose to look at what growing evidence supported. It disoriented him because he chose to admit something as possibly true which he had never thought much about, which he had never conceived as present in his own life and which he had certainly never judged to be as evil as he now did.

"Martin, what are you so scared of about yourself?" He forced himself to look at the evidence of what had terrified him to the phone two weeks earlier. He pushed aside his theorizing and tried to remember how it was. Some of it was plain. He did not panic because his decisions were no longer being obeyed by himself, though in fact they were not. He did not panic because some blind inner force had overcome his rational control and was now running his life. He had no sense of this happening. No. Something else scared him.

The inability to get his fingers to the keyboard was symbolic. Martin, sitting there like a lump, felt fright so bottomless as he had not since childhood, because he felt he could not act at all. He felt he could do nothing. No irrational power in him had surged into control of his life. He had lost all power. He was going cold. Terror then burst inside him and pumped a spurt of strength to reach for the phone and talk.

To Martin, looking back relaxed from the steering wheel, the terror was melodramatic, overdone. But its core was true. Thank God for the terror! In it, he knew—so obscurely that he could for weeks deny it—that his being too weary to type only climaxed, by dramatizing, a weariness of years of trying to write and failing, despite the flow of essays he composed and published. Only weeks after that winter morning, did he distinctly recall the words that proceeded like a telegraph message in a foreign language through his head as he sat there limp at the machine, "When was the last time you wrote anything?"

So what was at the heart of his terror, driving him simultaneously towards and away from its truth? That he had not written anything for years! In his panic in Donna's office, Martin, stylist par excellence, did not notice the wordplay or paradox. The literal truth enveloped him. He had not written anything for years. He had done nothing. He was terrified.

Martin cured, detachedly remembering Martin ill, can interpret this. Writing for Martin meant a meaningful, satisfying communication to someone else of something important to Martin. But Martin's compositions had long been meaningless and unsatisfying to him, and their contents of little personal importance.

This, of course, is subsequent interpretation. The hour Martin consented to accept this truth, he was too frightened to conceptualize philosophically. He could only conceive and accept this much: he had for many years failed to achieve his goals for writing, whatever the hell they were. In the press of resistant realization, Martin could not recollect what he had meant and dreamt and intended by his writing, but he knew he had not done it for a long time. He had become impotent without noticing. He had been too busy to note he was doing nothing. He wasn't achieving a damn thing of what he wanted to achieve. Just marking time, year after year. Martin chose to believe this fact. He will not recant.

No wonder his writing had been joyless. Only now did it strike Martin as strange that at the completion of his best essays or at the most positive recognition his work received, he had experienced at most only that thin, dull pleasure. A faint relief before turning to his next endeavor. A machine inside him turned out inexorably his printed pages, yielding him no satisfaction in the process. That was a second, connected choice he made: to recognize that in his scholarly work, which took the greater part of all his time and effort, he had been boring himself.

Martin chose to believe these two truths: his scholarly life was ineffectual and unsatisfying. He chose to believe these to be facts of his scholarly life although and because he maintained the judgment which, vaguely, like a fog, had inspired his terror and now slowly took form: these two traits of his scholarly work were bad and wrong and monstrous and must be changed. He went on to make a third choice: to work with Donna, who was getting more and more on his nerves, at changing this.

"Curiouser and curiouser," reflects Martin two years later. If he had discovered that a mighty self-centered passion had secretly motivated him to write and the progressive feeding of it given him secret gratification, it would have shaken him. But it would not have shaken him a tenth as much as to discover instead that no passion had driven him to write and he had derived no gratification from it. The writing functioned mechanically to disguise a life of sterility and frustration. Martin judged this disgraceful and wrong. Remorse filled him. As I said, he chose to dig in and try to change.

These were patently moral judgments and moral choices that Martin made. But of what morality? By what standards? On what principles? I, like Martin reminiscing, postpone any attempt to answer these questions. I continue, with him, to recover the story of his therapy, observing how he continued this new kind of moral judgments and choices.

To put an end to the tragedy of his scholarly writing, he needed to understand its causes. So, as I related earlier, he made himself look closer at the rages with which he first wrote each piece. He forced himself to recall the fantasies flickering as he slashed with his pen and to let the fantasies now flow freely on their own before his mind. Two years later, after countless remembered fantasies have reflowed under the bridge, Martin is amused at his initial horror at what he saw.

You may recall a sample fantasy I reported Martin having in his first stage of writing a review. The author under review and Martin's colleagues knelt around Martin in agonized humiliation as he masterfully exposed them all for their failure to appreciate him. Another fantasy, older but persisting, was not vicious, but equally childish. Author and colleagues danced a jig around Martin, waving his latest review with enthusiasm and delight. Martin's other fantasies while writing were mainly variations of these two. When he first relived them in full consciousness, Martin reluctantly realized that they still represented what he wanted to do with his words. To be passionately acclaimed. To punish those who would not passionately acclaim him.

What made the realization excruciating for Martin? Perhaps it is a question of personality. A different person from Martin, having the same fantasies and feelings, might have stayed horrified by his true motives exposed: his vengeful wrath and his craving for adulation. But Martin soon smiled at his fantasies and the operative desires they expressed. Martin smiled, but not as sultans smile, at his aspirations à la Don Quixote.

The more he got to the bottom of his motives, the more he sympathized with himself. So he dreamed of being celebrated for his contributions! Of punishing those who refused to celebrate his contributions! What was so wrong with that? It could be worse. From the start, amid his embarrassment and self-disgust, he had an odd good feeling about it. These motives had the fresh, unfamiliar feel of reality. They were him. He could live with them. He found himself liking himself for them.

Something else he uncovered at the same time, he could not tolerate. The thought of it still impales him with horror two years later at the steering wheel. His mouth dries. To have extravagant ambitions like Don Quixote is one thing. To pursue all of them as Don Quixote did, that is, only in solitary fantasy, while making irrelevant, ineffectual gestures in reality, is another thing entirely. Some time in his life, his life had slipped into his head and he had been living it there.

Martin resisted as long as he could the realization that he had been doing this for years in his scholarly work. When he finally let himself realize it, the horror buried him. "Horror" was the word Martin used in those days to himself and to Donna. Looking back from the steering wheel at himself stumbling down the stairs after that session, he uses another word: remorse. Remorse filled him on those stairs. Every part of his body was numb with remorse at what he had done to years of his life and the best of his efforts. He murmured out loud to himself, "I will not live this way any more."

We noted earlier Martin's remorse and resolution of amendment when he discovered how ineffectual and unsatisfying his scholarly life was. We see now his new horror and resolve as he uncovers the causes of this busy, joyless impotence. The new discovery altered further his picture of himself. He had exaggerated his demise. He had imagined himself dying mentally, going cold. But in fact he was alive and well and living in fantasy. It was very funny. So funny it increased geometrically the tragedy of his life.

This early stage in Martin's therapy did not spare him a further horror. It, too, was a nice comic touch he had put to his scholarly life. One moment in Donna's office, as he stared at his fantasies, Martin saw two Martins struggling simultaneously to get out through a door wide enough for one. As a result, neither could get out. Stuck in the door, they thrashed and flailed at each other, thus gluing themselves together and keeping themselves stuck in the door. "God!" Martin cried aloud, "I am both Laurel and Hardy!"

Vindictive Martin kept thrusting back the Martin seeking applause. Vainglorious Martin blocked every attempt of his vindictive wrath to achieve its goal. Being Laurel and Hardy was even worse than being Don Quixote.

If, therefore, in his real scholarly life, Martin achieved nothing he wanted and experienced hardly any satisfaction, he was withal "a man of desires," as God called King David. His desires were intense and active. Hidden away in and from his mind in dimmest fantasy, two mighty desires defeated each other alternatively, like the dual pumping of a monstrous machine. More than anything else, as Martin now realized, it was this incessant, indecisive conflict of himself with himself that he had become so tired of he could not type any more. Facing it openly made him only more tired of it. "I will not!" he said.

Martin could imagine himself, with a smile, as an aspirant for the plaudits of an Einstein or a Caruso. He could imagine himself, like the Count de Monte Cristo, as vengeful punisher of those who had treated him badly. He could not imagine himself as one totally turned in on himself. He refused to imagine himself as one who lived a fake, impotent, frustrated life with others because he was engaged in a sterile, joyless, mechanical warfare between his desires, a warfare of fantasy hidden even to himself. Even Don Quixote was at one with himself. Even Frankenstein responded to other people. But refusing to imagine it did not help. He remembered. For, as I said a while back, Martin chose finally to remember as much as he could.

To these successive horrors of his memory, Martin responded, as I have tried to show, with a series of implicit moral judgments and moral choices. They were mostly negative. "This is bad. This is wrong. I must stop it." Of what to do instead, Martin had at that time, no clear idea.

As therapy wore on, however, one vague idea came to him repeatedly. The idea was openly moral and positive. An old Stoic adage ran through Martin's mind those days: "Be what you are!" Martin repeated it most often on stairs: down from bed in the morning, up to class, down from Donna's office, etc. It bore on the operative motives Martin had uncovered in himself. If he was one who irrepressibly wanted to be acclaimed, and to get even with those who refused him acclaim, then let him be! Be Martin! Let himself want these things in full awareness and engagement and in vigorous pursuit of them in reality. Break up the log jam and let himself flow!

It amuses Martin now how he came to pronounce this moral imperative to himself with little, if any, moral reasoning. His judgment that he must be what he is was like a spasm of his intelligence. It was an intelligent reflex before the moral horror of the life he had been leading. That was the evil that therapy revealed: he was not what he was. The new moral judgment, "Be what I am!," constituted the positive image emerging from the negative.

Having nothing better to do, on his drive home, he starts to poke the positive image to analyze critically what moral substance it may really have. Surely he doesn't want to be everything he is. But he does want to be a lover of applause and revenge. He judges this to be a good thing. Why?

We leave Martin placidly probing. What do you think? Is there any truth in Martin's moral judgments? If so, what? Why? Can there be any goodness, truly human or moral, in deliberately wanting to be acclaimed and to get even with those who refuse to acclaim?

*   *   *   *   *   *   *

The story of Martin, like our first two chapters, raises our question, What good can there be in vindictive anger? But all three chapters raise the question obliquely. They use mostly other words and concepts. They intertwine this question with other questions. We need now to face squarely our question.

II
The Question

4

The State of the Question?

"Anger" (*menin*) is the first word of the *Iliad,* one of the oldest, most read stories of Western civilization. Homer announces that he is about to tell a story of anger. For the length of the *Iliad,* 300 pages in my edition, he tells of the anger of Achilles.

Achilles is the greatest Greek warrior of the Greeks and they are locked in mortal battle with the Trojans. Achilles becomes enraged with the Greek king and commander, Agamemnon. The anger of Achilles makes the *Iliad* one of the most painful stories we have in our literature. Its opening lines:

> An angry man—there is my story: the bitter rancour of Achilles, prince of the house of Peleus, which brought a thousand troubles upon the Achaian host. Many a strong soul it sent down to Hades, and left the heroes themselves a prey to dogs and carrion birds, while the will of God moved on to fulfillment.[1]

There will be many other tragedies of anger in Western literature after the *Iliad.* One thinks, for example, of plays like *Medea, The Duchess of Malfi, Hamlet, Othello, The Wild Duck* or, on the boards of our time and place, *Amadeus, Ma Rainey's Black Bottom, The Lie in the Mind* and *The Crucible.* In these plays the tragedy is twofold. Anger does horrible things and is a horrible thing. More accurately: the angry person does horrible things and is horrible himself or herself. It is hard to say which is more horrible: what Achilles, Medea and Othello *do*? Or what, flooded with passion, they *are*?

Our question in this book concerns the latter. It concerns anger itself, not the actions it leads to. We look at the enraged person and ask: What good is there in anger? Ours is a leading question: we look for the good in anger, not for its evil. Yet we mean by "anger" the same thing the writers of tragedy mean generally by the word. We mean what Achilles, Medea, Othello and others feel. We mean the passion to get back at someone, get even, get revenge, punish someone for the sake of punishing, get somebody for what they did to me or mine. How can this be good?

Does not common experience as well as the tragedies make the question ridiculous? Isn't such anger simply bad? Are not the instances of apparently "good anger" turned up in our preceding chapters only exceptional cases where the good resulting from the vindictive anger happens to outweigh the evil of vindictive anger itself? Suppose that by chance, contrary to the actual story, the anger of Achilles and Othello did little harm and resulted in much good. Could we even then say that the anger itself, Achilles' sulks and Othello's blind, murderous jealousy, as Homer and Shakespeare depict them, was something humanly good?

Stop and recall stories of anger you know. Stories of fiction. Of real life. Where you were the object of the anger. Where you were the person enraged. Stories you observed or heard about. Long stories where the anger went on for years. Short stories where the anger died within seconds. Tragedies. Comedies. Stories of irreparable harm done in anger. Stories where little harm and much good resulted.

Meditate awhile and relive these stories. Focus on the anger itself. On the feelings of the angry person. Ugly, unpleasant, regrettable, no? Even when the outcome was good! Painful to recall. Most of the stories, I venture, still sicken or sadden or embarrass us. At best you may judge that on some occasions the anger was not that bad a means to a very good end.

Physical details, when we remember them, still unsettle us even if we knew at the time and know even better now that it was only a tempest in a teacup. The faces of our two friends, their tones of voice and body postures, get us tense when we recollect how one evening for a minute or two they slipped out of control, snapped back and forth at each other, were vicious.

We read earlier two anecdotes where the anger seems evidently good. My fellow discussants pick up and resonate to these two anecdotes more than to any other of the first three chapters. The anecdotes are the fight of

Paul and Luce on the stairs and the exchange between the father and the grown son who comes home late. The outcome of both scenes is happy. But what of the initial passion? The brutal frenzy of Paul and Luce? The sadistic impulse of the father? Surely there is nothing good in this passion itself. The outcome is happy, but is this not because after the violent exchange the two realize that their mutual love is strong enough to sustain and absorb their momentary, regrettable hate?

I add two stories of anger for our meditation. One story is a tragedy of literature. One is a comedy of real life. The first is *Native Son* by Richard Wright. In his rage, Bigger Thomas, young ignorant black of the '30s in Chicago, murders two innocent women. There is not the slightest justification for his killing them. His rage is to kill them. He derives satisfaction from killing them. The reader is horrified by what Bigger feels as much as by what he does.[2]

My second story was recounted to me by my friend, Olaf, who knew I held that anger was a good thing. "Here's something for you, Giles. Couldn't be more trivial. But it might not have been trivial."

"I came into the AA Big Book meeting Sunday night, put my cap on a nice chair by the window, and went and got a copy of the book. When I came back to the seat, a young woman had taken it, having removed my cap and put it on a nearby table.

"I went bananas inside. The woman asked me, 'Is this your seat?' 'It was!' I replied, as I turned away. 'You can have it,' she said quietly. 'No, it's alright,' I muttered and went to a seat on the other side of the room.

"It was absolutely crazy. I went into sheer passion when I saw her take 'my seat'. It was like suddenly going blind. Pure viciousness filled me and only fear kept me from showing it. I could barely utter my five words for fear I'd go out of control and say and do what I'd be sorry for.

"As the meeting started, light began to filter back into my consciousness. I couldn't believe the state I was in. I was shaking. My mouth was working. My body was tense. Furious ideas and images swept back and forth in my mind. It was ten minutes before the awareness of how irrational I was dissipated the madness.

"You claim, Giles, that anger always has some good in it. I don't see a damn thing good about my bout. It was pure insanity, simple unreality. Right at the start, if I had wanted to, I could have had 'my seat' and an apology! What the hell went off in me?

"Part of the insanity was to get carried away about something trivial. But, you know, my getting carried away wasn't trivial. I came close to chewing out that woman. I nearly let her have it. Three-quarters through the meeting, she spoke up, saying quietly, 'I'm only eight hours sober.' She was coming off a drunk! She was undoubtedly in a very shaky state, using all her will power to come into that meeting and take a chair and eventually speak up. All she needed was for me to snarl at her for her to lose courage and leave before the meeting began. I nearly did it. That's anger for you! On the way to destroying somebody!"

Does anyone know of a vengeful or punitive anger, real or fictional, that they did not experience as ugly and frightening? In itself bad stuff? I don't. Yet I ask: Is this anger not also good? I ask this of Olaf's and Bigger's and any anger I know. May it be true that all anger, even the most brutal and sad, has substantial good in it? May it be at times more good than bad?

*　*　*　*　*　*

What do we mean by "good"? At this stage of our discussion we can each mean by it whatever we spontaneously do mean by it. From the beginning, however, we have to all mean the same thing by "anger." The discussion gets nowhere as long as people mean different things by the word. Perhaps the most important and most difficult thing is to get clear what we do *not* mean by "anger."

In our discussion we do not mean by "anger" any of the kinds of anger that are purely constructive. The word, "anger," for example, can mean an impassioned desire to overcome obstacles to change things for the better. In this sense I may be "angry" that my kids don't do better in school or that sales have plummeted in my store or that there are in Rhode Island 3000 children who have no family of their own. I may not be angry at anybody, for I may not know what the cause of the trouble is. Perhaps it is nobody's fault. But having tried to improve things and failed, I know there is something blocking improvement. I get angry at the obstacles. They have to go, for I am going to make things better. Anger in this sense cries, "It's got to change!" We can dub this anger "anger for change," in the sense of "anger for betterment."[3]

Another kind of purely constructive "anger," and therefore another kind of anger which we are not asking about, is an anger which I may have at people who oppress me and deprive me of rights. They treat me unjustly. They deprive me of freedom that all human beings should have in my circumstances. I tried peaceful ways to get them to stop oppressing me. They won't. Passion surges up in me now to strike back at them to make them stop oppressing me.

My fury is against my oppressors, but only because they are on my back and won't get off. I rage to strike back at them simply to knock them off and end their domination. Striking back is the only way I see to do this. If my oppressor stops oppressing me before I hit him, I am no longer angry at him. If I hit him and hurt him but he does not stop oppressing me, I am still angry at him. What I want is freedom to live my rightful life. "Anger," in this sense, cries simply, "Get out of my way!" Feminists and black theologians tend to use "anger" in this sense. We can dub this anger "anger for liberation."[4]

"Anger for change" and "anger for liberation" are rough ideas which can use further clarification. They obviously overlap. Hopefully they are clear enough to identify two kinds of anger which we are not inquiring into in this book. In these two kinds of anger we want to strike back as means to a further, constructive end. We have no interest in striking back for the sake of striking back. It is not our end. If we get our goal without striking back, so much the better! It is not of such purely constructive anger that I ask: "How is it good?"

If I get angry for change or liberation, I do usually face further questions. They are practical questions about my situation. Is the change I want a real improvement? Is the freedom I want a freedom that I in this situation should have? Do I really want it? What or who really blocks my way to the change or freedom I want? What exactly are the obstacles? What is the nature of the oppression? How can I best get what I want? What action is likely to break through obstacles or remove the oppression?

In real life we need to deal with these practical questions. They are important, often difficult, sometimes impossible, to answer. But we do not need to ask a value question about such anger. There is no question that anger for change or liberation has good in it. However mistaken I may be about the facts, it is obviously good for me to want passionately to improve things or to want passionately to have full freedom in equality with other human beings. In the final chapters of the book I will argue that these practical, factual questions that purely constructive anger has to face get light from the more contemplative value question we ask about a much less constructive kind of anger. But it would confuse things to discuss this now.

I do not, therefore, mean anger for change, anger for liberation or any other purely constructive kind of anger when I ask, "What good is there in anger?" I mean by "anger" what Homer meant when he announced what the *Iliad* would be about. I mean the wrath that moves Othello towards Desdemona's bed. It is what ancient Greeks and Christians down to modern times meant when they listed anger among the "passions." They defined "anger" as the passion to avenge or punish. How is this a good passion? That is our question.

Part of the trouble in getting a clear idea of this kind of anger is that there is no single English word for what we want to do when moved by this anger. In Greek there is one word for it, *timoria*. In Latin there is one word for it, *vindicta*. In English we say sometimes "revenge" and sometimes "punishment" when in concrete instances we identify what this anger wants. In colloquial English, this anger is the passion to get back at someone, get even, get someone for what they have done, not let them get away with it, make them pay. Let us bite the bullet and for the rest of the book call this kind of anger "vindictive anger." It is of this anger that we ask what good there may be in it. It is indicative of our modern problem with this anger that we have to refer to it by an unpopular word with negative connotations, "vindictive."

Vindictive anger is not purely constructive. Whether it is in any way constructive is a question we will raise shortly. But vindictive anger is manifestly destructive in its goal. Wanting to avenge or punish, it wants to destroy something belonging to the person at whom it is angry. It wants him or her to suffer some damage, some loss, some pain. The fact that the boy returned my car which he stole is not enough. He must pay for it by being punished! Turks must pay by suffering and death for their massacre of Armenians seventy years ago although the Turks' suffering and death have no further effect.

Destruction is vindictive anger's goal and its only goal. Once the destruction is achieved, anger is satisfied. Only if the destruction is achieved, is the anger satisfied. When we ask presently whether vindictive anger can be constructive, it is to ask whether the very destruction anger seeks can be constructive! We are not asking whether constructive results follow from the vengeance or punishment once it is achieved. This latter question is a more important question. But we are not asking it in this book.

Purely constructive anger wants destruction only as a means. It wants to destroy obstacles or oppression purely as means to its constructive goal: a change for the better or greater freedom. This passion is essentially not destructive because it is just as satisfied if it achieve its goal without any destruction, without damage done or loss inflicted. Vindictive anger has to have destruction. It has to wreak damage, loss, pain on the other. Vindictive anger wants revenge or punishment and revenge and punishment consist in damage, loss, pain to the offending person. Vindictive anger wants this, and nothing more. It is of this anger we ask, "How is it good?"

One can be at the same time vindictively angry and angry with a purely constructive anger. My wife was rushing to buy a lottery ticket seconds before the liquor store closed. A man gathering signatures for an environmental proposal stepped out, blocked her path and addressed her. Without a word Annie elbowed him onto the store window and rushed past. I take her here to be elbowing out of purely constructive anger for change and freedom. "But," she reflected pensively afterwards, "I gave him one last jab after I was already by him." That, I take it, was out of vindictive anger. It was punishment for his blocking her way. This is the kind of anger about which we want to ask: How is it good? But how can there be any good in the impulse behind Annie's final jab?

In the news media every week, almost every day, there are stories of vindictive anger. At least we tend to interpret them that way. Four Sikhs managed finally to assassinate the Indian general who commanded the invasion of their sacred temple in June 1984. Massacres of Sikhs by Hindus and Hindus by Sikhs have continued since. Christians and Muslims alternately explode cars in marketplaces in the others' sector of Beirut, killing and maiming men, women and children. So, too, do Muslim groups warring against each other. The Irish do the same to each other in Northern Ireland. Terrorists explode Flight 103 over Scotland. This I will not forget, for a former student and good friend was on board.

In India, Lebanon, Ireland and throughout the world we imagine that the killers kill partly to throw off what they feel to be undue resistance and unjust oppression. They kill to stop their enemies from oppressing them further. They kill out of anger for freedom. We may be distressed because we believe that in reality such killing adds to oppression rather than freedom. But we understand and sympathize with this motivation and feeling.

But we imagine, too, that some of the motivation of the killers is simply to avenge or punish, regardless of whether it wins any freedom from the oppression of the others, Hindus, Sikhs, Christians, Muslims, Ulstermen or IRA. The killers want simply to get the others for what they have done. To hurt them back. Not to let them get away with it. Just reading it in the paper, detached as we are from these scenes, we feel sick and horrified at this kind of anger.

The two examples of anger I gave at the beginning of this chapter illustrate well our question because in neither, unlike the anger of massacring mobs or murderous terrorists, is there any cover of constructive anger for the vindictive anger. Bigger Thomas' satisfaction after the murder of the white woman does not come from any expectation of bettering his life or any one else's. He has no expectation of gaining any freedom beside that of further agonizing the white community.

So, too, Olaf rages only to make hurtful remarks to the person who took "his seat." He refuses to take his seat back from the polite offender. The anger that takes over both Bigger and Olaf is pure vindictive anger. We see clearly here what in other circumstances is somewhat obscured: the passion to hurt back, regardless of consequences, good or bad.

But getting clear what we do and don't mean by "anger" and reviewing instances of it seem to make our question senseless. The passion repels us.

Swept by anger, does not the human being become ignorant? A vicious, futile animal? Does he not become less than human? Or human at its worst? Surely there can be no good in this.

*   *   *   *   *   *

And yet . . . And yet . . . It takes only a moment for most of us to recall occasions when we ourselves felt anger of this kind and thought that it was good. Looking back at some of these occasions, we still judge it somehow right and good that we felt this way. We still feel that way and are glad we do. Recall your feelings at certain concentration camp commanders, terrorists, rapists, drunk drivers and child abusers who have so far escaped punishment. We still want them to be punished.

We want them punished not merely to deter them and others from doing the same thing again, though we certainly want this. We do, for instance, want to improve the plight of women and gain them more freedom in the future from rapists. But we also want the rapists to be punished simply because "they deserve it." "It's not right that they get away with it" while their victims live no more or live on scarred.

We in Providence, Rhode Island were gripped a few years ago ago by a rape trial up the road. Men had stood around in the Big Dan bar in New Bedford late one night as men one by one raped a woman held down over the pool table. Those who did not rape her made no attempt to stop it or call the police. There was laughter and joking.

The rapists were arrested and brought to trial. Some of them turned out to be family men, respected in their community. Advocates of the men argued that they had learned their lesson by the arrest and publicity. They would not do it again. A suspended sentence would be enough.

Conversations I heard in Providence seethed with anger. The message was clear. Maybe punishing the gang at the Big Dan will improve in no way the lot of women. Maybe it will deter no future rapists. Maybe these guys have learned their lesson and will never rape again. We still want that gang sentenced and sentenced long. It will be horrible if they don't suffer for their crime. It's not right. They should not get away with it, period.

Those of us who read or watched *Fatal Vision* might reflect on how we responded to the father's determination to bring his son-in-law, Jeff, to justice.[5] Did no part of us share the father-in-law's grim passion to avenge the murder of his daughter and grandchildren? Did we feel only that that passion was evil and sinful, albeit human and forgivable? Or in some deep part of us, did we feel that the father-in-law was right and his rage was ours, tightening our throat?

The other night I watched on NBC television a real-life scene recorded by hidden camera and microphone. A completely unoffending black man protests a white policeman's illegal search of him. His protest is purely verbal and polite. The policeman, not knowing his actions are being recorded, takes the black man by the neck and pushes his face through a plate glass store window. He then takes him the other way and smashes his face down on a car trunk.

Throughout the day fantasies raged through my head imagining the policeman's agony when confronted by the public record of what he had done and by his realization that he was going to suffer for it. My fantasies gave me bitter satisfaction. I know I will not be fully satisfied until the policeman is actually punished one way or other. I feel right in so feeling. My feeling is a good human response.

The examples I just gave of apparently good anger involve punishment by law. We can easily think of examples that do not. On a park path designated for walkers only, a cyclist whizzed through and missed by a hair a two year old child running onto the path from behind a bush. My friend, the mother, leapt into her car, pursued the cyclist, caught up to him where he stopped. She laid him out in lavender.

If my friend's feelings were like mine, sitting beside her in the car, she was not trying to make sure the young man never did anything like this again. That thought had not yet occurred to her. She simply wanted to make him suffer for nearly killing her child. As we drove back, my main feeling, beside relief that Donnie had not been hit, was satisfaction that my friend had told the idiot off. I felt proud of her. I still feel this way.

You can recall similar experiences with similar feelings of your own. If we reflect critically on such experiences, we still judge that in some cases it is right and good that we felt and feel these vindictive, punitive feelings.

Yet, I submit, you, like my discussants and me, find it hard to explain why you believe it right and good. When we reach for pertinent concepts and principles, we have none at hand. Why? Because our modern moral mentality is confused and evasive on anger. When we think about anger, we, children of our culture, think about it automatically in a confused, evasive way.

This is why throughout this book I multiply examples of vindictive anger which we spontaneously approve. I keep spiralling back to ones we have already considered. We need to mediate them again and again. To evade our culture's evasion. To keep the real thing before our eyes. We need to exert ourselves to do so although this passion is a common one of our time and culture. It is for the reader to judge whether in the book we spiral in deeper, like a corkscrew, or just go around in circles.

We moderns feel the same "vindictive" anger as past generations of the last three thousand years. Like them, too, we judge that at times it is good to feel this way. What is different is that we moderns usually judge so only implicitly or vaguely. We have trouble articulating any value judgment. If we do, the judgment is usually neither clear nor thought out. Our culture fogs in our vindictive anger.

The dominant formal ethic of our present Western culture condemns vengeful punishment. Susan Jacoby writes: "The taboo attached to revenge in our culture today is not unlike the illegitimate aura associated with sex in the Victorian world. The personal and social price we pay for our pretense that revenge and justice have nothing to do with each other is as high as the one paid by Victorians for their conviction that lust was totally alien to the marital love sanctioned by church and state."[6] The Victorians laundered for the forefront of their minds the good love between man and woman so that sexual desire and pleasure had no place in it. We, for the forefront of our minds, cleanse our idea of good anger of all desire for vengeful punishment.[7]

The price is high. The Victorians had no clear concept of good loving sex. We have no clear concept of good vindictive anger. The price is also ridiculous. One has to deny the real thing that one feels. We smile at the unreal, flowery language, images and concepts of Victorian lovers. And lovers in our time? As Victorian spouses thought of their love as having nothing to do with sex, spouses of our culture think of their love as having nothing to do with fighting. They see fighting as simply a failure in love. As opposed to love.

That these blinders are common in our culture is confirmed by a recent corrective trend. Counseling and self-help books state what is obviously true. Good fighting is essential to a successful marriage. The couple must learn to fight well or their love will die. Bad fighting destroys love. Good fighting feeds it. It is part of it. I wonder: Is there any other period of culture, Western or Eastern, where husband and wife or parent and child need to be encouraged to fight with each other?[8]

What first drove me, and still most drives me, to ask how vindictive anger is good is my experience of the angers of intimacy. My attention is gripped by the flow of vengeful or punishing anger back and forth between adults who live together or regularly spend time together. I am obsessed by the fights open or disguised, of parent and grown child, husband and wife, couples in other relationships, siblings, relatives, work associates, close friends. I see the love between the various pairs. I see between the two who love each other a rhythmic, vicious punishing of each other, a to-and-fro getting back at each other, a giving each other what he or she "deserves," a "showing" each other. Vindictive justice is demanded and carried out, back and forth, day by day. This commonplace, ugly pheno-menon is where I start digging.

For some pairs, the tireless punishing and getting even ends up by wear-ing away their love. The fighting is corrosive and evil. For other pairs, the tireless punishing and getting seems even to be part of the love and to feed it. The fighting seems to have a lot of good in it. It seems at times to be good loving. I tried to evoke such experience towards the end of chapter 1.

This can be true not only of habitual warring of intimates but also of a single fight. Who in the cinema hall does not come to realize that some-thing good happened in the violent physical fight of the characters played by Shirley MacLaine and Anne Bancroft in *The Turning Point* and of the characters played by John Wayne and Victor McLaglen in *The Quiet Man*? Somehow they have come closer together personally and peacefully in the very fight. Who has not had some experience of an out-and-out furious fight, whether physical or verbal, that made things better afterwards be-tween the two? My fellow discussants conspicuously identify with Paul when he, in "One Moment of Love," finds his fight with Luce to have been his one and only moment of love in the day past. The "good fight" may be the exception, not the rule. But it is a common exception.

Even those wise enough to encourage us to fight occasionally with those we live with wear often the same blinders. They depict the fighting with real anger censored out of the picture. Much counselling and self-help prescription describe good fighting as an assertion of one's own feelings and a listening to the feelings of the other. That's not what my wife and I have in mind when we get madder and madder at each other. The careful assertion of "where I am" and attentive listening to the other are fine and good. But that's not fighting. If they're telling us to fight, they should know what they're saying. Does anyone know of an experience which they would call a fight and in which no vindictive anger was felt?

It is often better not to fight. Perhaps most often. Careful assertion of my feelings and attentive listening to the other work better in most situations and serve love better. But they are not to be confused with fighting, with love active in vindictive anger. They are not to be confused with the lunge I feel to get back at you, to get even with you, to make you feel pain. And, it is true, many couples need to fight with each other or their love will die.

I do not carry through this lunge if I "get my anger out" by simply shouting, "I am angry at you!" "I'm pissed at you!" says the therapist, modelling for his client. "I am bullshit!" But if I say that to my wife, I'm declaiming my anger, not carrying out its thrust. I am playacting. I'm not even expressing my anger as it is. My anger does not move me to tell you I'm angry. It moves me to make you feel pain.

Truer to my feelings is to say, "You took my eye; I am going, lover, to carve out yours." I get my anger out when I stab with my verbal knife. Stab and stab again. Lovers know—I appeal to your experience—that such niceties can occur regularly and destroy a good loving relationship. But we know, too, that they can occur regularly and nourish a good loving relationship. This is one reason why we ask the question, "Could it be that there is some good in anger?"

The therapist, expressing his anger as being "pissed" or "bullshit," believes he is daringly defying cultural convention and expressing a raw emotion. True, by his shocking words he does defy a minor convention, but what shocking words he chooses conform to a more serious cultural convention. He chooses metaphors that are euphemisms for what must not be said. They must not be said, for the metaphors stand for urges to hurt the other person. Both metaphors misrepresent, too, since "pissed" and "bullshit" image the angry person as passive or inert whereas anger is a drive to do something. Finally, the two metaphors image as matter for excretion and the sewer what would be more aptly imaged as coursing blood. These metaphors are all the more misleading if it turn out to be true, as I will argue, that vindictive anger for all its evil can be an intrinsically good component of personal and interpersonal life.

*   *   *   *   *   *

There is also the obvious, curious fact that in certain ways inconsistent with their declared value system people of our culture openly indulge vindictive feelings. Perhaps the culture permits it as safety valve release. In any case, few object. Almost everybody takes it as a good thing. Others join in.

Take humor, for instance. Black and yellow diamond-shaped signs multiplied a while ago in the back windows of cars. They say "BABY ON BOARD!" Or "MOTHER ON BOARD!" The other day, Alicebelle spotted, "EX-HUSBAND IN TRUNK." I imagine a woman having and relishing murderous feelings about her ex-husband, though she has no intention of acting on them except by this sign. We relish the feelings with her. We assume there is nobody in the trunk.

You who enjoy comics, look at this week's. You chuckle perhaps at *Garfield, Peanuts, Andy Capp, Momma, Beetle Bailey, Funky Winkerbean, Hagar the Horrible, Dennis the Menace?* Or perhaps you prefer to smile at some *Fabliaux, The Miller's Tale, The Reeve's Tale, Twelfth Night, Die Fledermaus, The Mikado, etc.* Comedy is good stuff, no? Human life without this kind of laugh and smile would be wanting. But what do you laugh or smile at in this humor?

Is it not often the comeuppance you take pleasure in? Do you not delight in the comeuppance delivered Garfield, Lucy, Andy Capp, Momma, Sarge, the coach, Hagar, Mr. Wilson, the carpenter, the miller,

Malvolio, Count von Eisenstein, Pooh Bah, etc.? Do you not relish the merited revenge or punishment delivered these heavies? But to enjoy merited revenge or punishment is to feel one's vindictive anger satisfied. Are you not then feeling and indulging this anger in fantasy as you identify with the agents of justice in the comedy and enjoy uninhibitedly their eminently fair evening of the score?

True, my eagerness and joy in Sarge's getting what he deserved have an innocent detachment which real-life anger never has. But is it not otherwise the same as my fury the other day at my boss and my exquisite pleasure when he went ahead and made an ass of himself before his boss and his boss reamed him? If real-life passion for vengeance and punishment is all bad, why do I have no scruples about enjoying it lustily in humor? Some of my discussants have no taste for this sort of comedy. Why do I feel sorry for them? As if they were somehow handicapped?

This kind of comedy is good stuff! It needs no further justification. It does not gain its main value by good aftereffects which it has on you. It may well have good aftereffects. This laughter may render you more relaxed afterwards and able to work better or be gentler with others or whatever. But the laugh is worth it, we know, even if no further advantage happens.

We rightly approve, relish, display our laughter. That means we rightly approve, relish and display a certain vindictive anger of ours. True, the passion and pleasure of our anger on these occasions is playful, unreal, fantasy. But there must be something good in this passion and pleasure. What is it?

Laughter at a comic evening of Gilbert and Sullivan is not, I submit, a mere letting off steam of lower instincts. Your smile and laugh are precious elements of good human life. Sharing a comic strip with one you love is one of the loveliest things in life. Enjoying with Shelly the latest comeuppance of Hagar the Horrible is special. So, too, savoring with Lewie the fate of Tom, the piper's son.

"There's nothing worth the wear of winning/Save laughter and the love of friends." Belloc who wrote the lines surely laughed heartily with his friend, Chesterton, when he first read to him his gaily avenging poem against "dons who dare attack my Chesterton."

We know all this. Do we know why it is so? It violates the morality of our culture to get back at somebody just to enjoy their pain. It contradicts the values and ideals we hold for real life. How can a passion be completely bad in real life yet thoroughly good in play or fantasy? Can it be that there is some good in it in real life, even though it is also bad?

Not only in comedy do we relish uninhibitedly vindictive passion. With our culture's approval and encouragement, we enjoy serious stories where vindictive anger triumphs, and, to our mind, rightly so. At least some of us walk away satisfied from reading or viewing dramas of the triumph of just vengeance or punishment. I think of—to pick at random artistic and popular—*Hamlet, Othello, The Bacchae, Count de Monte Cristo, Little Red Riding Hood* and other *Grimms' Fairy Tales, The Purloined Letter, The Virgin Spring, Soft Skin,* and *Breaker Morant.* I think of the majority of the detective and spy stories which I and my friends consume.

The lightness of comedy is not here. How is it that we approve innocently the satisfaction we feel at Hamlet's stabbing his father's murderer or at Iago's being led off to be tortured.? We might not approve such stabbing or torturing in real life. But we approve and are grateful to Shakespeare for making us feel this punitive satisfaction. Why?

Aristotle says that there's a purgation of passion in tragedy. Perhaps. Perhaps looking back at the passion the artist evoked in us, we do feel some horror or embarrassment at what we felt. But if it was a purgation, we do not judge it as similar to a bowel movement or throwing up indigestible food. We appreciate that our being carried away by the passion was somehow in itself a valuable, worthwhile experience.

* * * * * *

In brief, we recall experience of various sorts where we felt vindictive anger and, to our best judgment, the feeling was good. Our culture permits and even encourages some of this experience. But the culture offers no clear, incisive value judgment on the anger. When our culture thinks about good anger, it leaves out of sight the vindictive kind. It has no concepts or principles for good vindictive anger. To probe critically our experience of good vindictive anger, we need concepts and principles as tools. Since our modern culture provides none, we must look elsewhere.

Notes

1. Homer, *The Iliad*, Book I, transl. W. D. H. Rouse (Edinburgh: Nelson, 1938; New American Library Mentor printing), p. 11.

2. Richard Wright, *Native Son* (Harper & Row, Perennial Library, 1966 [1940]) p. 101.

3. Barbara Deming advocates this anger in *"On Anger"* and *"New Men, New Women"* (New Society Publishers, 1982); the two essays appeared originally in *We Cannot Live Without Our Lives* (Grossman, 1974).

4. Cf. James Cone, *Black Theology and Black Power* (Seabury, 1969). Adrienne Rich, *Of Woman Born* (W. W. Norton, 1976) speaks for the most part of anger in this sense. Occasionally she means by "anger" the narrower sense of the word which I am about to define and will use in this book.

5. The TV film was based on Joe McGinnis, *Fatal Vision* (Putnam, 1983).

6. Susan Jacoby, *Wild Justice: The Evolution of Revenge* (Harper & Row, 1983), pp.12-13. This book complements mine from a historical and social scientific perspective.

7. That modern culture evades the issue of possible good in vindictive anger is a main thesis of Jacoby's book and Carol Zisowitz Stearns' and Peter N. Stearns' *Anger: The Struggle for Emotional Control in America's History* (University of Chicago, 1986). The paucity of modern literature on vindictive anger supports the thesis. The Stearns' offer evidence repeatedly to belittle Carol Tavris' claim that modern culture glorifies vindictive anger and encourages uninhibited expression of anger (Carol Tavris, *Anger: The Misunderstood Emotion* [Touchstone 1982]). I agree with Tavris that a certain therapeutic trend in our culture does encourage indiscriminately that one "get out" vindictive anger. The trend, however, does not glorify or even esteem the anger. The trend is not concerned with what might be good in the anger itself Knowing this good, I argue later in the book, helps limit and control the expression of anger. Moreover, this trend is limited and countercultural. As Willard Gaylin argues in *The Rage Within—Anger in Modern Life* (Simon & Schuster, 1984), the expression of anger is increasingly unacceptable in our civilized world and this causes

tensions and problems that are increasingly difficult, if at all possible, to deal with.

8. Cf. Daniel Goleman, "Want a Happy Marriage? Learn to Fight a Good Fight," *New York Times*, February 21, 1989, pp. C1, 6. According to one source Goleman cites, the idea that couples should be encouraged to learn to fight by certain rules in order to strengthen their relationship has lost the popularity it had among marital therapists in the 1970s. The idea, however, is found to be true by recent studies, one by John Gottman, psychologist at the University of Washington in Seattle, and one by Howard Markman, psychologist at the University of Denver, as Goleman reports in detail.

5

Anger of Aristotle?
Anger of Christ?

How can there be good in this lust to hurt another? How can there be good in the melee of rage inside me for which "bullshit" and "pissed off" are euphemisms? What good, if any, is in vindictive anger?

Can we shake off some of our cultural conditioning, move closer to our raw experience of vindictive anger, look at it as it is, and see what good, if any, is here? To do so, we could use some concepts to point to this or that aspect of the experience. But though most mainstream philosophy and theology of the late twentieth century West make much of experience, none that I know of focuses on the experience of vindictive anger. Like our contemporary culture, contemporary Western thought, whether Christian, Jewish or secular, avoids the question of good vindictive anger.

Even contemporary ethicists do. In my discussion of the question with other ethicists, I find none who has done any sustained thinking about it. I find none who want to do any! "Important question, Giles! Little's been done on it. Go to it!" they exclaim as they walk away. I would be grateful to learn of published ethical work of our time on the anger that seeks avenging or punishing justice. I find little such work. What I do find is mainly negative. It makes no sustained effort to determine if there be anything intrinsically good in this passion.[1]

The evasiveness and confusion of our modern moral mentality on vindictive anger contrast with some moral traditions of other cultures. One moral tradition of Greek antiquity was clear and incisive about the goodness of anger. This ancient cultural tradition continued in subsequent Western cultures, Judaic, Christian and Islamic. Even in our current Christian and post-Christian culture, we hear this tradition now and then. Though an aged alien among us, its voice rings out on occasion with startling vigor, says what is taboo, and adds to the confusion.

This long-lived cultural tradition of the West holds that vindictive anger is in principle good. It is good because its object, vengeance or punishment, is, in principle, a good thing. This tradition does not rate high the actual moral quality of human lives. Human beings do not for the most part act morally. The anger which individuals feel is usually more bad than good. The revenge and punishment which angry persons seek are in fact much more often wrong than right. But, this tradition maintains, vindictive anger is essentially good, for vengeance and punishment are essentially good. Anger, like revenge and punishment, is bad only when misdirected, which it commonly is.

A moral tradition of a culture is much more than a philosophy. It is a whole moral mentality of a community. A moral tradition lives on in customs, practices, rites, beliefs, attitudes, songs, stories, etc. But philosophy does it service. Philosophy expresses the mentality in clear and distinct ideas. Philosophy, as Hegel put it, grasps the mind of its time in concepts. Since we need concepts for our discussion, we turn to a philosophy that was one of the first to put into concept this Western moral tradition of the goodness of vindictive anger.

The philosophy originated with Aristotle in the fourth century B.C.E. Aristotelian thinking had vast influence in the West. It penetrated other intellectual traditions such as the Platonic, Stoic, Roman, Neoplatonic, Hebrew Biblical, Judaic and early Christian. Even in twentieth-century Western philosophy, some thinkers arousing discussion draw on Aristotle.[2] We will draw on Aristotle as systematized by Thomas Aquinas. Thomas, teaching in Paris 1600 years after Aristotle taught in Athens, built his Christian anthropology and moral theology with ideas of Aristotle.[3]

Aristotelian ethics declares without hesitation that anger, the passion for punishment and vengeance, is essentially good. Not all human passions are essentially good. Envy, for example, is not. Under no conditions is it good or virtuous to feel envy.[4]

Aristotelian reasoning is straightforward, reflecting the Greek cultural tradition. Anger, the passion for punishment and vengeance, is good in itself because punishment and vengeance are good in themselves. More precisely, anger is good because it is the passion for *just* punishment and vengeance. Anger is essentially good because it is a passion for justice.[5]

That violent impulse, this foggy urge to hit back, is, say Aristotle and Thomas, a lunge of the person, both mind and body, for justice. When one has hurt the offender enough, one's anger is satisfied because one wanted justice and one got it. True, anger impels one more often to act unjustly because anger's impulsive rush clouds judgment and thus pushes one to act on false assumptions. But all that anger wants is justice. It is good to want justice. In this respect this savage lunge to punish or avenge is essentially good!

We moderns may have trouble with this theory but when we get angry we think this way. In our passion we think like Aristotle! As we deliver vicious blows or cutting words, we are likely to say to ourselves: "I'm just giving her what's right." "He's getting what he deserves." "We're paying them back for what they did." Bigger Thomas felt that by killing he was able to "fulfil a debt to himself."[6] "Right," "deserts," "paying back" and "debt" imply justice of some sort. We usually do not think out what this justice is we're talking about. We prefer to forget about the whole thing once our anger dies away.

Aristotelians stay with the phenomenon and think it out. They share the general moral understanding of the West that justice is equality. There are different kinds of justice as there are different kinds of equality that should exist among human beings. There is commutative justice, for example. I sell you something. Justice demands that you pay me equal value. There is distributive justice. Justice demands that the state divide goods among its citizens in an equality of proportion according to merit.

The angry person wants another kind of justice, another kind of equality. Somehow vengeance or punishment can make things equal. This is a peculiar kind of justice, a justice consisting solely of pain and loss as somehow equal payment for evil done. It is sometimes called "vindicatory justice."

We moderns concede that the vindictively angry person wants and, if successful, gets a certain equality. He wants and gets an eye for an eye! We concede, too, that the surge of his wrath makes him want this equality as "justice." We, at least we liberals, can think of him only as deluded. Surely, eye for an eye is not true moral justice. Yes, Bigger Thomas by his murder of innocent women "evened the score," but was that an equality of justice?[7] The Aristotelian replies that it is. The angry person is right. The equality he seeks, the eye for an eye, the evening of the score, is true justice. This is true even if the action he intends to do in order to get this justice will not achieve it, but will in fact be unjust.[8]

Not only Aristotelians, but practically all moralists of the Western tradition, Greek, Roman, Jewish, Christian and Muslim, maintain that vindicatory justice is true justice. Vengeance and punishment can be deserved. When it is, it is right and just to seek to bring it about. One may, under circumstances, be obliged to bring it about. It is virtuous to desire to effect merited vengeance and punishment, to bring it about and to find satisfaction in doing so. Thomas calls it the virtue of "vindicatoriness" (*vindicatio*). One who has this virtue tends habitually to avenge and punish justly, as the situation calls for and right reason judges.[9]

Western moralists knew how dangerous this idea of justice is. Human beings invoke it to justify grave wrong, flagrant injustice and irreparable harm. One of the seven deadly sins is "anger," wrongful acting out of anger.[10] Since the moralists have a low opinion of the moral practice of "the many," they lay down stringent limits for the licit carrying out of this justice. They restrict it generally to competent authority. But what challenges our modern thinking is that the moralists take for granted that just punishment or vengeance is genuine justice. It is morally good. It restores due human equality.

What makes Aristotelians unusual among traditional Western moralists, and what distinguishes Thomas Aquinas from preceding Christian thinkers, is Aristotle's and Thomas' praise of the *passion* of anger. They affirm not only the intrinsic value of vindictive justice, the rational choosing of it, and the deliberate willing of it. They affirm also the intrinsic value of the passion for vindictive justice. Aristotelians can value positively the passion of anger because they, unlike most other schools of traditional Western ethics, see intrinsic value in natural human passions. There is thus a virtue of feeling anger as one should which is distinct from the virtue of acting on anger. The former virtue is the habit of passionately wanting vengeance and punishment where appropriate. The latter virtue is the habit of carrying out appropriately vengeance and punishment.[11]

Moralists of other Greek traditions agree that vindictive justice, the object of anger, is just and good. One may rightly choose to enforce it. One may be obliged to do so. But many of them, preeminently the Stoics, maintain that anger itself is not good, for it is a passion. Passion is never good. All passions are bad because passions are by nature unstable, uncontrollable and blind.

Passions, the Stoics acknowledge, happen at times to support good moral action. But they are not necessary for such action. They are always unreliable. They do on the whole far more harm than good. Strong will, directed by right reason, is all that is needed. Only out of rational understanding and by rational choice, not from passion, should one pursue vindictive justice.[12]

Aristotelians, contrariwise, affirm that many human passions are essentially good. They are integral to every good human life. A human being is not completely virtuous if he does not feel these passions. This includes the passion of anger, though, like all good passion, virtuous anger must be a mean, not felt too much nor too little.[13]

It exceeds the limit of this book to discuss what was really the issue between Aristotelian and Stoic on the nature and value of human passion. Historians do not agree what Aristotelians and Stoics each meant by "passion" (*pathos, passio*), and to what extent, if at all, they really disagreed. Thomas anticipated some modern scholarship in suggesting that the disagreement may have been mostly verbal. Stoics may not have condemned human passion as sweepingly as they seemed.

We will use the concepts of Aristotle because the position which we want to propose in this book and test by our experience is that not merely vindictive justice but also the passion for that justice, the passion of vindictive anger, is good. Aristotle provides concepts useful for this, particularly as they are systematized by Thomas Aquinas. We will not presuppose that the Aristotelian concepts are true. As Aristotle and Thomas did, we will test them by appealing to ordinary experience. I will argue that key ideas of Aristotle and Thomas Aquinas on anger are verified in experience. They thus illumine the experience. I will bring in eventually concepts that are not of Aristotle or Thomas in order to identify more clearly than they did the nonrational interpersonalness of the passion of anger.

* * * * * *

But vindictive anger is surely not Christian! When we broach the question of the goodness of vindictive anger, discussants reply frequently, "Perhaps pagans, like Aristotle, saw such anger as good. Christ didn't. Anger is a sin. Christians are supposed to turn the other cheek. Jesus said so."

Discussants who make this observation seem not to have read the New Testament in a long time, if ever. The Gospel according to Saint Matthew, for instance, resounds throughout with the vengeful, punishing anger of Jesus and his Father.[14] Pier Paolo Pasolini renders faithfully their thunderous wrath in his film, *The Gospel According to Saint Matthew.* John the Baptist in announcing Jesus warns the Pharisees and Sadducees to flee "the wrath to come." "His winnowing fork is in his hand, and he will clear his threshing floor and gather his wheat into the granary, but the chaff he will burn with unquenchable fire" (*Matthew* 3:7, *Revised Standard Version*).

The wrath to come which Jesus will bring, after his death, is the merited avenging punishment by God, his Father:

> Afterward he sent his son to them, saying, "They will respect my son." But when the tenants saw the son, they said to themselves, "This is the heir; come, let us kill him and have his inheritance." And they took him and cast him out of the vineyard, and killed him. When therefore the owner of the vineyard comes, what will he do to those tenants? (21:37-40)

Jesus makes clear repeatedly what the Father will do to those who kill the Son or reject him. He will cast them into eternal fire, into outer darkness, where they will weep and gnash their teeth. Read, for example, 3:12; 8:12; 12:30-32; 18:8-9; 22:13; 25:30, 41-46, and parallel passages in *Mark.* The epistles of Paul, too, ring with God's punishing, avenging anger, past, present and future, e.g. in *First Thessalonians,* 2:16; 4:6; 5:9 and *Romans,* 1:18-2:11; 5:9; 9:14-33. The early Christian Church condemned as heretical the proposition that Jesus' words could be understood of temporary, purifying punishment leading eventually to the salvation of all.[15]

What of Jesus' injunctions to "turn the other cheek"? Some exegetes argue that in light of the text and the historical situation Jesus could not have meant this as a universal rule nor could he have unconditionally condemned retaliation.[16] In any case, to turn the other cheek is his injunction for human believers, not for the divine judge. God will not turn the other cheek on the day of judgment. After commanding his followers, if one strikes them on the right cheek, to turn to him the other cheek, too, Jesus states the reason for loving your enemies: "so that you may be sons of your Father who is in heaven; for he makes his sun rise on the evil and the good, and sends rain on the just and the unjust." The reader of the Gospel knows well that the Father will not continue this evenhandedness on the day of judgment. He will give then the unjust the punishment that they deserve. The just present at the judgment will, one presumes, applaud. Read *Matthew,* 5:20, 46-48; 7:19-23; 11:20-24; 12:36-37; 13:37-43, 49-50; 16:25-27; 23:34-35.

Jesus rails at length against the scribes and Pharisees:

> But woe to you, scribes and Pharisees, hypocrites! because you shut the kingdom of heaven against men; for you neither enter yourselves, nor allow those who would enter to go in.
>
> . . . blind guides, straining out a gnat and swallowing a camel . . you cleanse the outside of the cup and of the plate but inside they are full of extortion and rapacity . . . . You are like whitewashed tombs, which outwardly appear beautiful, but within they are full of dead men's bones and all uncleanness. . . .
>
> . . . You serpents, you brood of vipers, how are you to escape being sentenced to hell? Therefore I send you prophets and wise men and scribes, some of whom you will kill and crucify, and some you will scourge in your synagogues and persecute from town to town, that upon you may come all the righteous blood shed on earth, from the blood of innocent Abel to the blood of Zechariah the son of Barachiah, whom you murdered between the sanctuary and the altar (23:33-35).

Jesus' own anger, therefore, is at times "vindictive" as we have defined the word. For a modern Christian or modern Jew or, for that matter, modern nonbeliever, the words of Jesus that may ring most admirable in their vindictive anger sound as if they were spoken quietly:

> Then he will say to those at his left hand, "Depart from me, you cursed, into the eternal fire prepared for the devil and his angels; for I was hungry and you gave me no food, I was thirsty and you gave me no drink, I was a stranger and you did not welcome me, naked and you did not clothe me, sick and in prison and you did not visit me." Then they also will answer, "Lord, when did we see thee hungry or thirsty or a stranger or naked or sick or in prison, and did not minister to thee?" Then he will answer them, "Truly, I say to you, as you did it not to one of the least of these, you did it not to me." And they will go away into eternal punishment, but the righteous into eternal life (25:41-46).

Can a modern reader avoid feeling as one's own the avenging anger of Jesus if one imagines at the Lord's left hand slumlords, warmongers, self-centered rich, rapists, child-abusers, sexists, racist lynchers, etc.? One can feel as one's own Jesus' anger even if one imagines oneself standing surprised on the left.

My Christian or postChristian discussants declare often that while vindictive anger is permitted and encouraged in the "Old Testament," it is done away with and replaced by love in the New. No such thing! True, Jesus forbids those who believe in him to be angry or, even more, to act in anger. But that is not because Jesus sees anger as bad and wants only love. Anger is good but it is God's prerogative, not humans'.

Anger is forbidden Christians not because it is too bad, but because it is too good for them. Vengeance is forbidden Christians only because it is God's alone. Belief in Christ is belief in the coming judgment. "Vengeance is mine!" says the Lord of both New and Old Testament. A believer can only assume that the anger with which God damns unrepentant sinners for eternity is a form of His love for them. He is Love and can do nothing but love.

Jesus made it clear that Christians should share God's anger. They should not be angry on their own, but they may and should be angry with

God's anger. This is virtuous "zeal." Christians understood this from the beginning. They should share in anticipation God's attitude at the final judgment towards those who died unrepentant. God wanted human beings also in this earthly life to carry out his punitive justice. He "who is in authority" should punish wrongdoers, even to the extent of taking their lives. God delegated his authority to human beings, Christian or not, to punish with just anger.

Christians linked the neighboring texts of Romans: "Repay no one evil for evil . . . never avenge yourselves, but leave it to the wrath of God . . ." for he who is in authority ". . . is the servant of God to execute his wrath on the wrongdoer." Christians may not avenge themselves but, if given authority, are called to carry out God's punishing, avenging anger.[17]

Down through the centuries Christians claimed often this delegation of divine authority, e.g. to massacre Jews on a Crusade to the Holy Land or to burn heretics at the stake. Today, high from a church tower in the center of Munster, West Germany, hang still the cages in which orthodox Christians once hauled up Anabaptists to starve to death before public gaze and approval. That Christians were admonished not to feel or carry out their own anger, undoubtedly increased their enthusiastic sharing of God's anger, their "zeal," in numerous instances like this. The anger of a Christian, like the compassion of a Christian, was wrong only when it was not a participation in God's.

We live in a different time and a different culture. Not many of my Christian discussants are convinced that God actually puts sinners in hell for all eternity. Of those who are convinced, fewer claim to understand why. All Christians, I trust, are ashamed of the Christian cries of righteous anger as they slaughtered helpless Jews or tortured to death sincere dissidents. We are glad that capital punishment is no longer in Christian cities an occasion for crowds of spectators enthusiastically relishing and celebrating the event. Such celebration, incidentally, still took place regularly in London in the early nineteenth century.

We of the waning twentieth-century West have gone to the other extreme. Rarely does anyone of our time approve by name vindictive anger or just vengeance or punishment for its own sake. When they do, they are usually those who consciously resist modern ways and return to traditions of the past. Denizens of our culture, at least of the "more educated" strata, tend to condemn in principle vindictive justice and anger. When one calls something "vindictive," one means it's bad. With contemporary culture, the word has taken on a negative connotation.

Perhaps our modern extreme is the truth. Why should we turn to learn from this moral tradition that exalted vindictive anger and vindictive justice as divine and, under the guise of delegation, performed atrocities century after century? I cannot come up with a single historical incident of this tradition in which I would justify the vindictive anger righteously carried out. Moreover, Christians of the past readily accepted God's punishing anger toward offenders because they imaged God principally as supreme monarch and judge. Most of us moderns, believer or not, cannot imagine a worshipable God that way.

What if one imagines one's God as loving parent? Or as lover of each individual person? What if one cannot believe a loving God could send definitively into eternal torment one he loved? Is it then still inconceivable that a punishing anger might be a moment of divine love? Might it be never the final moment, but a frequent, recurring one, nonetheless? Might, with this modification, Christian scripture and tradition suggest how anger can make part of love?

Humans have to imagine God in human wise. If not as monarch or judge, then perhaps as parent or lover. Parents and lovers fight with their children and loved ones, and vice versa. Could it be that this tradition, for all its errors and excesses, had a clearer insight than our culture does into the goodness of vindictive anger as recurring, appropriate phase of love? So, too, the Jewish and Muslim tradition?

One need not be religious believer to adopt this suggestion for our inquiry into the goodness of anger. Even if all religious faith be illusion, it may express truths about the human condition. Even if there be no God, religious believers may in making God to their own image reveal realities about themselves as humans. They may project existing human values onto their image of God. They may reveal realities of being human that are precious though dangerous and frightening to face in themselves. Believers can dare to disclose these human realities to themselves by putting them safely in divine love and in the believers' limited, secure participation in that love.

And if their faith be true, and their God exist and love in anger as in other modes . . . ?

*   *   *   *   *   *

Recall our quandary, expressed in the preceding chapter. In our explicit morality we condemn vindictive anger At least we cannot bring ourselves to justify it. Yet we feel it strongly at times and on those occasions judge our feeling is right. We want the rapist to be punished independently of any hope that it will help him to amend his life or better the lot of women in any way. We hope such things more passionately than we rage. But our rage to punish this man is not dependent on any hope of further good.

We felt deep satisfaction when the Massada finally killed on the street the man who had masterminded the massacre of Jewish athletes at Munich. We felt this satisfaction even if we had little hope it would discourage Arabs from future terrorism. We rejoiced when in *The Color Purple* Celie finally felt something. She wanted to put ground glass in Albert's glass of water. Neither we nor Shug wanted Celie to put the glass in the water. But we were delighted that she felt this vicious anger. It was better than anything she had felt for years. It was better mainly because Celie was likely to move to stronger, less destructive emotions. But her anger was a step forward, even if she took no further step.[18]

When we read of the raped woman, the Massada assassination and Celie's urge, their anger grip us. When we recall the incidents now, anger grips us again. We cannot shake off the conviction that such anger is good. But we cannot explain or justify it. We look bewildered at a secret flow of our life and of our selves. We do not understand it. We do not understand why we are convinced that it is good. We have no modern ethical concepts to put our conviction in.

In the present chapter, we considered ethical concepts of anger from tradition, Greek and Christian. From Chapter 8 on, we will follow this lead. With the help of Thomas Aquinas, Aristotelian Christian philosopher, we will try to find concepts true to our dark flood of anger. Ideas of Thomas, I will argue, fit the experience.

But Thomas' ideas are not enough. We will need to forge other ideas, too, to express more adequately our experience of anger. These further ideas are implied by certain contemporary black and feminist writers. But I know no writer, religious or secular, of past or present, who has articulated these ideas explicitly and applied them clearly to our question of the intrinsic goodness of vindictive anger. This, we will try to do!

In the next chapter, however, I do not yet offer these ideas to answer our question. I only urge once more the question. You are tired of my urging the question? I presume to imitate Socrates as Plato describes him in the earlier dialogues. Socrates was wont to start discussion with fellow Athenians he met about the city. He asked them something about what they were doing. He did nothing, for the rest of the conversation, but press this single question. The Athenians put Socrates to death because he refused to stop pressing his questions on them. On the other hand . . . .

Notes

1. This is my criticism of the books of Carol Tavris and Willard Gaylin cited in the preceding chapter.

2. E.g. Alasdair MacIntyre, *After Virtue: A Study in Moral Theory* (University of Notre Dame, 1981) and *Whose justice? Which rationality?* (University of Notre Dame, 1988); Stanley Hauerwas, *Character and the Christian life: a study in theological ethics* (Trinity University, 1975); Martha Nussbaum, *The fragility of goodness: luck and ethics in Greek tragedy and philosophy* (Cambridge University, 1986); William A. Galston, *Justice and the Human Good* (University of Chicago, 1980); James D. Wallace, *Virtues and Vices* (Cornell University, 1978).

3. Thomas deals with anger systematically in his *Summa Theologiae,* I-II, 46-48; II-II, 108 and 156-159. The texts of Aristotle which Thomas commonly invokes are in the *Nicomachean Ethics,* I, 13-III, 5; IV, 5, and the *Rhetoric,* Book II.

4. E.g. *Summa Theologiae,* II-II, 158, 1, following *Nicomachean Ethics,* II, 6.

5. E.g. *Summa Theologiae,* I-II, 46, 2, 4 and 6; II-II, 108, 4 and 157, 6. The Aristotelian ethic of Thomas is presented in detail in Chapter 8.

6. *Native Son,* p. 101.

7. P.155.

8. "Eye for an eye" can be misleading. The equality of just retaliation is an equality of proportion, depending on the persons involved, e.g. free or slave. Moreover, an unjust aggressor who was the first to begin should suffer more than he inflicted, for he was wrong in starting it as well as in what he did (*Magna Moralia,* transl. St. George Stock (Oxford University Press, 1915), 1194a37-b2).

9. *S. Th.,* II-II, 108.

10. II-II, 158, particularly 6.

11. II-II, 157. Thomas notes, after Aristotle, that this virtue, as the habit of keeping the mean in feeling anger, has no proper name. The virtue is called therefore "meekness," which literally means the lessening of anger. This is appropriate since humans tend much more to feel too much anger than too little.

12. E.g. Lucius Annaeus Seneca, *De Ira,* in Seneca, *The Moral Essays* (The Loeb Classical Library, Harvard University Press, 1985).

13. E.g. II-II, 157; *Nic. Eth.,* II, 5 and 6; IV, 5.

14. See 3:7-12; 5:20; 7:13-14, 19-23; 8:10-12; 10:14-15; 11:20-24; 12:30-37; 13:24-52; 15:13-14; 16:27; 18:5-9; 21:12-13, 33-41; 22:11-14; 23; 24:45-51; 25:26-30, 41-46.

15. See the edict of the Emperor Justinian to the Patriarch of Constantinople *Enchiridion Symbolorum,* eds. H. Denzinger and A. Schonmetzer, S. J. (Freiburg: Herder, 1963), #411, p. 142.

16. Richard Horsley, "Ethics and Exegesis: 'Love Your Enemies' and the Doctrine of Non-Violence," *Journal of the American Academy of Religion,* LIV, 1 (Spring, 1986), pp. 3-31; C. H. Dodd, *Gospel and Law: The*

Relation of Faith and Ethics in Early Christianity (Columbia University, 1951), pp. 46-63.

17. *Epistle to the Romans,* 12.14-13.7; *Deuteronomy,* 23.35. Cf. *S. Th.* II-II, 108, 1 & 2; 158, 1 & 3; I-II, 47, 1.

18. Alice Walker, *The Color Purple* (Harcourt Brace Jovanovich, 1982).

6

Practical Point to the Question?

If you should arrange a discussion of the value of vindictive anger, I warn you. Your discussion partners won't want to discuss it. You will have announced it as the subject of the discussion. They will come to discuss it. They won't discuss it. They don't want to. They will resist talking about the value of vindictive anger. This happens every time I begin a discussion of the subject.

My discussion partners keep turning the subject to the value of more constructive kinds of anger. They will talk about the value of anger for change, yes. The value of anger for liberation, yes. They doggedly resist talking about the value of vindictive anger.

Or yes, they will talk about vindictive anger. But they will not talk about its value. They will not discuss whether there is any good in it. Yes, it is worth getting clear how normal it is. How human. Even how healthy. But not how good! Perhaps how good some of its consequences may be? As for Celie or for Paul and Luce. But not how good the anger itself is. How personally valuable in itself. This, they will not discuss. Something keeps their minds from fixing on this question.

The resistance is instinctive, unintended, hardly conscious. It is a result of the evasive and confused mentality of our culture regarding vindictive anger. But, as I slowly realized, my discussion partners may also have a valid reason for their disinclination to talk about the question. They don't see the point of it. Why look for good in vindictive anger? To what end?

This is natural human resistance to any new question brought up. A truism of Western thought is that the crucial step in thinking is asking the new question. It is also the most difficult step. This is why it is uncommon. Not only Socrates, but Aristotle and Hegel, Teilhard de Chardin and Pascal, among other thinkers, affirm this. Human beings ignore much because they do not ask the right question.[1]

It is not enough to know a proposed question. To know a question is not to ask it. To ask the question for ourselves is strenuous. We need a motive for doing so. Something must stir our intellectual inertia and move us to ask seriously this question.

My discussion partners find no strong enough reason for asking about the value of vindictive anger. Nothing moves them to do so. They know the anger and fear it. They have experienced it in themselves and others. They remember its ugliness and destructiveness. They know what Carol Tavris insists on. The trendy principle, "It's good to get out your anger!" is much more often false than true. Getting out our anger regularly does harm, often grave.[2]

The last thing my discussants want to do is to encourage anybody, including themselves, to feel more vindictive anger. More such anger in the world will, they fear, lead to more vengeful or punitive acts and words. Such word and action may occasionally be justified, as with rapists or concentration camp criminals. But people need no encouragement to act this way. They do it more than enough.

Why did they come to the discussion? Most seem to have come in the hope of finding a way to defuse or control destructive anger so that it would explode less often in hurtful word or act. They hoped to get ideas of more constructive kinds of anger. Getting clear what good might lie in vindictive anger seems in no way conducive to this goal.[3]

The question may be of interest to speculative minds, my co-discussants would concede. After reviewing experiences such as we saw in preceding chapters, most discussants will concede that some vindictive anger may have some good in it. It is undoubtedly a fascinating puzzle to construct a theory on what this good is. But is it worth the trouble? This theorizing has no use or effect in real life. If anything, it is likely to encourage, not discourage, destructive words and actions. My co-discussants, perhaps because they are Americans, insist on a *practical* point to the question.

Curious! Motives which Aristotelians, like Thomas Aquinas, give for inquiring into the goodness of anger are the same as motives my discussants have for not wanting to inquire into it. As we noted earlier, Aristotelians assert flatly that the anger people feel is generally excessive. It leads generally to wrongful harm. Seldom is the destruction that anger does outweighed by any good it achieves. Knowing this, Aristotelian ethicists set strict limits to acting in anger. Like my reluctant discussion partners, and like all moralists of the West, the Aristotelians want to lessen the vast amount of immoderate, cruel, unjust anger which they witness around them.

But unlike my discussion partners, Aristotelians believe that the most hopeful way to lessen this unjust anger is for people to learn what just anger is. Vindictive anger can be moderated and be just both in itself and in its execution. There is a golden mean that can and should be aimed at in angry feeling and action. If people know this mean and strive consistently to achieve it, they will act far less angrily than they normally do.

The prevalent vice which the Aristotelians see is too much anger, not too little. To curb this excess, they want people to understand what makes anger good. One who understands what is good anger will understand what it is good for and what it is not good for. One can then in most situations understand that it is better not to act on one's angry impulse.

Similar, as we saw, is the motive of traditional Christians in extolling anger. They extol anger in order to curb the angry deeds of humans. Anger, vengeance and punishment is the Lord's. Human beings can act only on His anger. The Lord's delegation of execution of his anger takes mainly the form of law and authority. This drastically limits occasions for vengeance and punishment. Thus, as for the Aristotelians, to know the goodness of anger leads to acting on it less.

When my discussants overcome their initial resistance and they and I finally work out an idea of what can make vindictive anger good—such as the ideas I will argue for in this book—we never conclude that people should act angrily more often than they do. On the contrary! We come to the same conclusion as the Aristotelians and Christians of the tradition. One who knows what is good about the passion of vindictive anger, will carry it out less often than people generally do.

My discussants and I and this book end up with few situations, real or imaginary, where we would advise the angry individuals to go ahead and carry out their vindictive anger. Most of the time the situation is such that even if the feeling of vindictive anger be good, the action to carry it out is wrong or counterproductive. Vengeful punishment has most of the time further consequences whose evil outweighs whatever good it might do immediately.

My discussants and I can imagine some situations where we would approve an individual's acting on vindictive anger. But in almost all these situations the circumstances justify the action from another point of view besides that of vengeance and punishment. The critics whom Martin in Chapter 3 will humiliate will also learn something about the seventeenth century. Our anger wants the rapist and child molester and concentration camp commander to be severely punished. But the heavy sentence, we hope, will serve also to deter others from similar crimes. We hope, too, that the offenders themselves will learn something from their punishment. Our anger is not motivated by and does not depend on this hope. But the belief and hope by themselves justify the action independently of our anger.

But does not this, too, justify my discussants' initial resistance? Vindictive anger may have good in it, but one can rarely justify acting on it. When you can justify it, you usually have, and depend on, other justification for acting this way. An ideal of a golden mean of vindictive anger simply doesn't determine our decision to act. Perhaps in ancient Athens the ideal helped moderate anger. But it is neither used nor needed today. Why bother to ask about the value of vindictive anger? What's the point of the question?

*   *   *   *   *   *

Sometimes, to show the practical point to our question, I draw analogy with other human passions. How many of your sexual impulses in a given week do you believe you should have acted on and satisfied? For many of us at many times of our life, it is a small percentage of these impulses, no? At any given moment there can be all sorts of reasons why we judge it better not to act on our perfectly good sexual impulses.

The person we have in mind is not presently interested. The locale is not conducive to making love. The other person's spouse is given to violence. Our spouse, who is not the person we have in mind, is given to violence. We believe in marital fidelity. We are very hungry. The person we have in mind is upset or absorbed in something else. We have other things to do. Etc., etc. Yet though we judge it better not to carry out most of our sexual impulses, few educated people of our time would draw the conclusion that there is no point in trying to appreciate the goodness of our sexual impulses in themselves.

Similarly, how many situations can you think of where it would be good to act exclusively out of sexual passion? With no other interest in your partner? My discussants and I are perhaps idealists, but when we have sex, we like to have sex with friends. (Aristotle and Thomas Aquinas claim that marriage is a perfect and most natural friendship.) When we have sex with friends, we have usually other good aims along with that of satisfying our sexual passion. Yet we may still want to understand better the value of sexual passion.

Counselors and mental health people say that persons who engage in excessive or harmful sex are more likely to have a low esteem of their sexual feelings. Those who prize their sexual drives are not among the most active sexually. Because they prize the drives, these men and women are more at ease with them and freer to face them and see how they can wisely and fruitfully be satisfied. Moreover, if I believe my sexual feelings are valuable, important parts of me, I am more likely to want to be careful and fulfill them only in an appropriate, worthy way.

That this be true of my sexuality suggests by analogy that it might be true of my vindictive anger. One can lessen promiscuous sex by teaching the value of sex. Might one lessen wanton revenge and punishment by making clear whatever goodness revenge or punishment has in itself? Similarly, the fact that moralists of the Western tradition insisted on the goodness of this anger in order to lessen its active expression does not prove they were right. But it suggests that they might be.

"Might be" does not dispel the resistance of my discussants. Perhaps the comparison with sexual passion is too abstract to be convincing. My discussants still do not sense a practical point of the question for them-

selves. So they can not bring themselves to really ask the question. We
mill around in discussion getting nowhere.

In desperation, I asked myself one day what is the point of the question
for *me*. How have I got into this? Why have I become curious about the
value of vindictive anger? I realized that practical considerations sucked
me into the question, and still draw me on. They are practical in that they
suggest how the answer to the question could affect real life. Perhaps I
could draw my would-be discussants into the question by narrating how it
has hooked me.

This works. It breaks the resistance of at least some of my discussants.
We go on to have fruitful, exciting discussions of the question. Let me
therefore tell the reader some of the practical considerations that led me,
and still lead me, to ask about the value of vindictive anger. Perhaps it will
draw you to ask this question and thus be able to join the discussion.

* * * * * *

First of all, I became aware of the frequency with which people act out
of vindictive anger but do not face the fact that they do so. We seem
ashamed to admit we feel this way and act with this motive. We slash
away at our victims under pretense of some other purpose. The result is
often tragic or comic or both. Chapter 1, "Blaming for Blaming's Sake,"
collects experiences of this kind.

If we admitted to ourselves that this anger were our true motive, we
could better judge whether we want to act this way. We cannot admit it
because we believe vindictive anger is a shameful motive to have. But
suppose it is not? Suppose vindictive anger can, at least sometimes, be a
good motive? If so, we need not be ashamed of being moved by it. We
can more readily acknowledge it. We can then see clear to judge whether
we want to act on it in the present situation. Is it appropriate here? Will it
not do more harm than good?

A student came to my office and complained that my criticism of one of
his papers was too severe. I read my comments. They were harsh. The
words and tone implied that the student had done completely thoughtless
work. I remembered being worked up when I wrote the criticism. My
scrawl was even more crabbed than usual.

I reread the original paper as the student sat by my desk. The paper had defects but was far from thoughtless. On the contrary, it showed more thinking than most papers do. The student developed a line of thought which I strongly disagreed with, though it is followed by respected scholars.

My criticism was unfair. I had no doubt now that it was determined by vindictive anger at some of these scholars, who had dismissed in print my own position. My criticism was not determined by the objective quality of the student's paper. Long before Freud, Aristotle noted what everyone knows: anger blocked from its original object slides easily over to other objects where it does not belong.

If at the time of my first reading the paper I had asked myself why this paper got me worked up, I would not have been able to detect the emotional vindictiveness at work in me. I was unwilling to admit I had vindictive feelings, for I held them to be despicable, childish, etc. I was, therefore, unable to realize that my criticism did injustice to the objective quality of the paper and to its author. Freud and Aristotle saw it: when we act for purposes hidden to ourselves, we cannot see our actions for what they are. We thus cannot direct our actions to the purpose we consciously choose to have.

If, like Martin in "The Critic," I had become at peace with my vindictive anger, I would have been readier to detect it at work. I could, then, have seen how unfair it was to take it out on the student, who had offended me in no way. I could then have made my criticism fit the objective quality of the paper. Of course, that would have raised the question, as it did for Martin, of whether I might then want to go after the scholars who were the real objects of my anger.

Being vindictively angry without admitting it does sometimes no harm to the the ones we are angry at, but great harm to others in the situation. I took part in a meeting of a coalition campaigning against a proposed state constitutional amendment to prohibit all abortion except to save the life of the mother. We were planning a public presentation of arguments against the amendment. One argument proposed implied that anyone concerned for the life of the fetus opposed choice by the pregnant woman. No one at the meeting seemed to really hold this. Those proposing the argument were evidently overcome by anger at the extreme pro-lifers and were lashing out at them. They wanted to make them look despicable by whatever means.

With the anger I had no problem. But I was very troubled by the fact that the aim of our presentation was not to ridicule extreme pro-lifers but to influence the large number of Rhode Islanders who had not yet made up their minds how to vote. Most of these people were concerned both for the life of the fetus and the choice of the woman. The proposed argument might alienate them and move them towards voting for the amendment. In fantasy the argument flogged the extreme pro-lifers and put them to flight. In reality it might serve the pro-lifers by pushing some undecided voters over to their side.

One could not discuss the counterproductiveness of this argument with those who proposed it for they could not focus their minds on it. Its possible counterproductiveness did not interest them, though they thought it did. Their real motive for proposing the argument was not its possible effect on the election. It was a need to punish publicly the hard core opponents of the women's cause. Yet their liberal idealism, which looked down on vindictive anger, could not let them recognize that this was their motive. If they had recognized it, they would have withdrawn the argument. Fortunately calmer heads prevailed and the argument was not used. The presentation ended up being realistic and constructive. It may have helped the amendment's being voted down by 65% of Rhode Island voters.

It was, therefore, a practical consideration that started me wondering whether vindictive anger might be a good human passion. Because people today believe it is a bad passion, they tend to deny it when they feel it. Consequently, they act on it without knowing that they do. They act blindly. Unnecessary harm results. Sometimes serious harm.

But suppose one knew that vindictive anger was in some respect a good passion. If one knew this, one would be less afraid and more ready, when one felt the anger, not to deny but to acknowledge it. One could then decide whether one wanted to act on it or not. One could judge whether acting on one's anger served the other purposes one had. One would often, perhaps most of the time, judge it better not to act on the anger. Much harm would be avoided.

It is, therefore, of practical use to ask: Is vindictive anger in any respect a good passion?

* * * * * *

The question is urged on me, too, by a second fact which I have observed. Another thing can happen to those who come to believe that vindictive anger can be good. Not only are they freer to recognize when they are angry and thereby better judge their motives and more wisely choose their actions. They now can also let themselves feel more fully the anger they have. They roar to their own amazed consciousness. Hearing themselves roar can be an experience which they find precious, momentous in their lives. In "The Critic," one of my first essays, I struggled to identify this gain. It became clearer as I heard discussion partners tell of their experience and as I read angry fiction and poetry.

Melanie, dark-haired, short, plump, sat through the entire semester of my anger course without speaking. Towards the end of the course, she handed in, as her weekly paper, the following true story. I abridge it, but use her words.

> I lost my virginity five years ago when I was in high school. Four of us went for a picnic in the woods. The boy with me was a friend of my boyfriend. We drank rumcokes and I was soon lying down barely aware of what was going on. The other couple wandered off. The boy raped me. I had drunk too much to speak or move. I didn't even care. I had no feeling as he did it.

> I got home somehow. When I sobered up, I felt dirty, guilty, upset. I bled for twelve hours. Whenever I thought of it since then, I felt the same way, though less and less keenly. After listening these weeks to the anger expressed by authors and other students in the course, I thought again of my rape and for the first time, last week, I got mad. I got furious at Rob. I punished him in fantasy in a dozen ways. In daydream I confronted him, embarrassed him, humiliated him, accused him before others. I even struck him physically!

Rob has been long out of my life. I do not know where he is. When I was raging last week, I had no interest in finding him. If I ran into him, I don't think I'd have done any of the things I did to him in my fantasy. It wouldn't be worth the bother. But I'm glad I did it in my heart. I don't do it any more. I'm satisfied. I feel whole.

Melanie profited from learning that vindictive anger can be good. She had learned it from the theory of the course. She had learned it more profoundly from the personal experiences shared by authors we read and by fellow students. Learning that vindictive anger can be good enabled her to discover her own anger at being raped. She felt it then to the full. To feel it to the hilt and act it out in fantasy was painful, upsetting, overwhelming, satisfying and valuable. Melanie now "feels whole."

Alison, another student, put similarly her gain from discovering her anger at her father: "I found out I was larger than I thought." Melanie and Alison rejoined a part of themselves. It bewilders them still. They like it and are proud of it. They smile at it wryly and share it serenely with others. For practical reasons, they have no intention of getting revenge or punishing the persons at whom they are angry. They have better things to do. But coming to feel their anger and prizing it, they judge one of the best things that happened to them. They feel whole. They know they are larger than they thought. It was able to happen only when they began to suspect that anger of this kind is a good thing.

A person can gain the same thing from discovering his anger even when he regrets what he did in that anger. He can cherish and prize the passion while feeling remorse for the action. As we finish the last page of *Native Son* and stare ahead, we see how this can happen.

Bigger Thomas murdered two innocent women. On the last page, Max, Bigger's defense lawyer, staunch liberal, compassionate supporter of Bigger from his arrest on, takes final leave of Bigger. All Max's efforts in the trial and in appeal of the death sentence have failed. Bigger will be soon put to death.

Bigger's final words to Max express a discovery we have seen Bigger struggling towards for a long time. The words shock us as they shock Max.

"I didn't want to kill!" Bigger shouted. "But what I killed for, I *am!* It must've been pretty deep in me to make me kill! I must have felt it awful hard to murder. . . ."

Max lifted his hand to touch Bigger, but did not.

"No; no; no. . . . Bigger, not that. . . ." Max pleaded despairingly.

"What I killed for must've been good!" Bigger's voice was full of frenzied anguish. "It must've been good! When a man kills, it's for something. . . . I didn't know I was really alive in this world until I felt things hard enough to kill for 'em. . . . It's the truth, Mr. Max. I can say it now, 'cause I'm going to die. I know what I'm saying real good and I know how it sounds. But I'm all right. I feel all right when I look at it that way. . . ."[4]

Max, terrified, says "Good-bye," gropes for his hat like a blind man, feels for the door, keeping his face averted from Bigger, and leaves the cell. Outside the door he acknowledges tersely Bigger's final messages without turning to look again at Bigger. But so skillfully has Wright prepared the reader over 400 pages that we agree with Bigger and feel what he feels, although we feel also the repulsion that Max feels.

Bigger *is* all right. He is all right for the first time in his life. He knows his murders were wrong, but knows, too, that the anger out of which he murdered was good. It was wrong to kill Mary and Bessie but it was right to feel his anger hard enough to kill. Waiting alone for his execution, Bigger is all right, for he now, regretting his act of murder, feels clearly and fully, with pride and peace, what in his rage he murdered for. The drama of the final section of the book is Bigger's struggling towards, nearing and finally reaching unity of himself and his feelings.[5]

Some of us, unlike Max, continue to look at Bigger. We resonate with his remorse and loneliness and pain, but also with his new pride and peace with himself. Like Alison and Melanie, he rejoices at joining a part of himself he had never known. Like them, he finds this larger self to be good. The joy of it enables him to face with serenity the bitter end of his life.

For Bigger, as for Alison and Melanie, this joyous discovery of their larger self came only after they had begun to believe, for the first time, that their vindictive anger could be a good feeling. It is Max above all who teaches Bigger this, though Max is not able to deal with the outcome, when Bigger experiences for himself its truth. Bigger's, Alison's and Melanie's process urge on me and my discussants our question, "How can vindictive anger be a good feeling?" If it be good, others could share the gain of Melanie, Allison and Bigger. If not, their achievement is delusion.

These reflections give practical point to our question, but also show how difficult it is. In Bigger, we see our question in the flesh. How can there be so much good in Bigger's vicious fury when it is also so evil? Bigger becomes convinced it is that good. As we feel with him at the end, we are inclined to say, "Yes!" But how could the original murderous feeling be in any way good? In what respect? What was the good thing his rage made him kill for? We will look more closely at Bigger when in later chapters we try to answer our question.

* * * * * *

People gain often a third thing when, coming to believe that anger can be good, they become free to feel their own anger. They share the anger. Because they hold, however uncertainly and vaguely, that their feeling is good, they are readier to share it with others for their empathy and support. Bigger's smile in the last line of *Native Son* is bitter not only because he is going to die but because no one, not even Max, will listen to him. Wright, we imagine, wrote the novel so that some people would listen to his anger. Wright wanted other men, especially white men, to feel his anger with him. That he succeeded must have yielded him grim satisfaction, a not negligible personal gain amid his pain and loss of being black in America. It was even greater gain for the white readers who listened and felt with him.

Certain women poets, too, share richly their vindictive fury. Susan Griffin writes in "BITTER":

> bitter
> I want this to be
> my first "bitter poem."
> this poem
> is for every child
> who starved

during an eloquent speech
about hunger.

this poem is written
instead of
jamming a hand through
glass or down
some man's throat;
an ugly poem
marred by
ill-will,
achieving next to
nothing . . . [6]

Griffin writes in "THE FROZEN SEA":

. . . You think this is just
a poem, but it is not.
It is the sound of an axe.
I want you to hear that I am tired.
I want you to hear that I am no longer
reasonable. Hear my
footsteps as I enter the bank
and think for two brief seconds
of holding it up. Hear the pages
turn in the bookstore where for
two brief seconds I consider
throwing the book,
across the room. Hear the
rush of soundlessness on
the telephone wires
while my mind hatches
obscenities. Two seconds
can be so
long, I am sus
pended in two
se
conds,
my toes blue with rage,

the top of my head
hot with weeping,
I shudder as the axe
comes down, what
will you do with me
when you hear the blow
where will you put me then.[7]

In "1971":

. . . there was nothing to do
but drive the car there
where the woman
we had met the night before
(who wanted help) waited
in a
telephone booth;
outside a man had said
he'd beat her up.
I brought my screwdriver, truly
I wanted to hurt him,
I wanted to strike him with my fists
and see him bleed
for the dead baby
for the tears in her voice
for this woman,
because she needs
and is being told not to
need, I would have liked
to see him bleed,
and not consider
who he is
who is he? [8]

In none of the three poems does Griffin decide to strike the persons at whom she rages. She writes a poem instead of jamming her hand down a man's throat. She writes a poem that despite her disclaimer is only a poem, not an axe. She writes how she wants to strike at a man without considering who he is, but her last words are, "Who is he?" Moreover, there is little chance that the kind of men she writes against will read what she writes. Neither she nor any other feminist whom I have read advocates actual revenge or vengeful punishment of men.

Alice Walker admires an old curse-prayer that Zora Neale Hurston collected in the 1920s. The author is a colored woman cursing white men for their enormous crimes against weaker people. Walker marvels at the precision of her anger, the absoluteness of her bitterness, her utter hatred of the enemies she condemns. Walker feels deeply with this "curse prayer by a person who would readily, almost happily, commit suicide if it meant her enemies would also die. Horribly." But Walker chooses to pray not a curse, not a hope for satisfaction from the grave, achieving revenge. Walker chooses rather to pray "only the hope that my courage will not fail my love." She chooses to hope that "*justice can stop a curse*." Walker writes the essay to share with her reader her "cursing" feelings whose fulfillment, she makes clear, she will not ask nor hope for.[9]

I take Griffin and Walker to express anger they personally feel. I take them to prize their anger for all its pain and the pain it responds to. I take them to prize the anger because it is a right response to the pain they rage against. They prize their poetry or prose for the same reason. So, too, do readers prize it. Black and feminist writers feeling and sharing their fury achieve "next to nothing," but it is something! I urge the reader to read, or re-read, angry poems of Marge Piercy, Judy Grahn, Robin Morgan, Adrienne Rich, Audre Lorde, and Ntozake Shange, and other poems of Susan Griffin and Alice Walker.[10]

Their readers certainly gain if they are ready to understand and feel with them in their poetry. When I read their text, I gain. I resonate with their wrath. I taste some of their sore satisfaction. I join respectfully the murderous fury they feel and express at brutal abuse. The next to nothing they achieve is something, for them and for me! I am grateful. I am privileged.

On the face of it, it is damn' peculiar. We approve and resonate with this individual's passion to get revenge. We would disapprove and be horrified by their actual getting it. We noted this when speaking of *Color Purple*. With Shug, we want to stop Celie from putting ground glass in Albert's throat or slitting his throat as she shaves him. But after her bleak, apathetic life so far, it is a momentous step forward that she wants to do something like this. Her rage lifts and cheers our hearts—even though we pray she will not do what she now wants to do.[11]

The rage of strong women who had been abused by men drew me further into the labyrinth of my value question about anger. These women have the strength to rage against their rapists, beaters and other oppressors. These women do not lie weeping. They do not put up with the abuse in sullen despair. They rise in anger.

Their anger, by itself, moves us who hear their voices to marvel and admire. It gives hope for human beings that individuals pinned down by the more powerful can at least in gut and word strike back. By so doing they have already started to stand up and throw off the oppression. But even if they go no further, they have gained something. I, philosopher, cry: "What have they gained?" Perhaps we others can gain it, too.

Once they felt and shared their anger, the poets I read, like Celie, manifestly went further. Their discovery of their rage, its appropriateness and its "beauty," liberated them. Anger felt fully and shared with others moved them beyond their anger. This proudly affirmed and openly shared rage to avenge and punish energized them not to avenge or punish, but to confront men and act pragmatically to lessen the abuse and injustice they suffered at the men's hands. Susan Griffin and Adrienne Rich illustrate this from their own life.[12]

In later chapters we will discuss this peculiarity of vindictive anger. When fully felt, esteemed and shared by the angry person, the anger tends to move the angry person into action and passion that is not vindictive, but principally and powerfully constructive. This gives further practical point to our question.

The brunt of the present chapter is simply that the very experiencing of one's vindictive anger, prizing it and sharing it are themselves valuable in real life. But they are rare in our culture, for our culture resists them. People often need to be encouraged to move towards and open themselves to such experiential knowing, prizing and sharing of their vindictive anger. They are so encouraged when they begin to glimpse that such anger is not all bad and may have considerable good in it. This gives immediate practical point to our question, "What good is there in this repulsive passion?"

Notes

1. Recent researchers into women's ways of knowing note how one determines what one will know by one's positing of the question. To freely and flexibly form questions is key to fruitful knowing. Mary Field Belenky, Blythe McVicker Clinchy, Nancy Rule Goldberger, Jill Mattuck Tarule, *Women's Ways of Knowing. The Development of Self, Voice and Mind* (Basic Books, 1986), pp. 133-140.

2. Carol Tavris, *Anger: The Misunderstood Emotion* (New York: Touchstone, 1984).

3. Carol Zisowitz Stearns and Peter N. Stearns trace as a widespread phenomenon of human culture the resistance to face and deal directly with human anger. *Anger: The Struggle for Emotional Control in America's History* (University of Chicago, 1986).

4. *Native Son*, pp. 391-2.

5. See pp. 256, 288-289, 323, 332-3, 335-6, 383, 385-391.

6. Susan Griffin, *Dear Sky* (Berkeley: Shameless Hussy Press, 1971), p. 3.

7. *Let Them Be Said* (Oakland: Mama's Press, 1973), p. 37.

8. Pp. 50-57.

9. Alice Walker, Only Justice Can Stop a Curse," *In Search of Our Mothers' Gardens* (Harcourt, Brace Jovanovich, 1983), pp. 338-342.

10. E.g. Marge Piercy, "A just anger," *Circles on the Water. Selected Poems* (Knopf, 1985), p. 88; Judy Grahn, the poem which has no title but begins, "I have come to claim/ Marilyn Monroe's body/ for the sake of my own" and "A Woman Is Talking To Death," *Work of a Common Woman* (St. Martin's, 1982), pp. 31-32, 113-131; Robin Morgan, "Letter to a Sister Underground" and "Monster," *Monster* (Vintage, 1972), pp. 58-64, 81-86; Ntozake Shange, "with no immediate cause," *Nappy Edges* (St. Martin's, 1972), pp. 114-117; Adrienne Rich, "The Phenomenology of Anger," *The Fact of a Doorframe* (Norton, 1984); Audre Lorde, "A Poem For Women In Rage," *Chosen Poems—Old and New*, pp. 105-108; Susan Griffin, "I Like to Think of Harriet Tubman" and "A Woman Defending Herself Examines Her Own Character Witness," *Made From This Earth* (Harper and

Row, 1982), pp. 263-265, 275-276. Note Griffin's subtitle in *Woman and Nature. The Roaring Inside Her* (Harper & Row, 1978) and pp. 175 ff. I am indebted to T. L. Hill, Dana Cherry and Jennifer Drake for showing this writing to me.

11. Alice Walker, *The Color Purple* (Harcourt Brace Jovanovich, 1982).

12. Susan Griffin, "Introduction," *Made from this Earth,* pp. 9-20; Adrienne Rich, *Of Woman Born* (Bantam, 1977), pp. 1-22.

7

The Right Attitude Towards Anger?

Recently, in an Ethics section of the annual convention of the American Academy of Religion, I read Chapter 3 of this book, "The Critic." I concluded with the leading question, "Might not Martin's attitude to his vindictive anger be justified?" In the ensuing discussion, one theologian responded, "Yes. It is important for us Christians to accept our dark side. To accept all our humanness. To accept all our selves."

The response angered me. My internal reaction was violent: "You missed the point!" All I said was: "You're right. But doesn't Martin do more than 'accept' his feelings? And doesn't he do so because he experiences them as not just his dark, human self?"

My interlocutor's response is a common Christian one. With a Christian of moral principle and sensibility (as Martin was described to be), the most positive attitude towards vindictive anger that most Christians can conceive of taking is to accept it. Christians follow here, not traditional Christianity, but contemporary culture, for, as I indicated above, traditional Christianity held that vindictive anger was essentially *good*. The appropriate response to what is good is something more than mere acceptance.

In discussion after discussion my respondents, Christian, Jewish and nonbeliever, like the AAR theologian, understand Martin as simply "accepting" or "owning" his drives for vengeance. This is the attitude which they take me to mean by "justified." As they often put it, they can conceive of vindictive anger at best as "OK" or "alright" or "normal."

But the attitude which I ascribe to Martin is more positive than acceptance. He "likes himself" in his desire for vengeance. He "wants to be a lover of applause and revenge. It's a good thing." His project to get glory and to punish his closedminded critics is "great, however risky!" It is this more positive attitude towards his anger that I suggest can be justified. This is what my discussants find difficult to conceive as a possible answer.

My discussion partners have reason for their difficulty. There are at least two conceptual problems here. What positive attitudes can one take towards feelings anyway? And what attitudes more positive than acceptance, can one take towards feelings that we certainly experience as ugly, revolting and indubitably evil? What attitude, more positive than mere acceptance, could we conceive of taking towards such feelings? In what follows I try through a concrete illustration to solve these problems and to get clearer what positive attitude to vindictive anger I propose.

*   *   *   *   *   *

Ella is dean of a small college. She lives with husband, two children and elderly mother. Scarcely a day passes when she doesn't feel violent, angry impulses to lash out at her mother and the president of the college, to make them suffer as they make her suffer. Children and husband provoke her relatively little.

Both mother and president treat her badly. They put her down, humiliate her, embarrass her. She longs to do the same thing to them, to get back at them. But she has learned by experience that it makes things worse to act on these impulses of hers. If she does, she often succeeds in making mother or president suffer. But she makes herself feel worse and improves not at all their treatment of her. They often respond by treating her worse. Her striking out in anger at them just compounds the mess. She concludes that it is irresponsible for her to strike back at her two oppressors. She no longer does it.

Ella tried vainly for years to correct or ease her situation. With the help of counseling, she tried assertiveness, communication, negotiation, confrontation, etc. To no avail. She cannot correct or ease the situation. She does not want to leave her post at the college. She does not want to ask her mother to move elsewhere, for she loves her mother. She cannot improve the way president and mother treat her. So she lives with vindictive, vicious urges and lives them out only in dramatic fantasies as she drives to and from work or when she tries to get to sleep at night. Our question is: what attitude ought Ella have to these feelings of hers?

Our fictional paradigm is in a pure state, not likely to be found in reality. I describe Ella as feeling anger because of completely unjustified treatment of her, which she in no way occasions. There is absolutely nothing she can do to make it better or less bad. So she does absolutely nothing about it. Her fury is totally frustrated and kept inside her. I have to imagine her sharing her fury with her husband or close friend, but she takes no action to carry out in any way, direct or indirect, what her rage drives her to do. As I say, Ella is pure paradigm, unlikely to be found in reality.

"Acceptance" is too neutral a concept to characterize adequately the attitude that Ella has towards her vindictive rages against mother and president. I imagine her attitude towards her rages as more affirming than mere acceptance because I imagine her as a mature human adult. "Acceptance" does adequately characterize her attitude towards unchangeable circumstances of her life that provoke her anger. She "accepts" the endless passive aggression of her depressed mother and the untiring phoniness of the college president. It is adequate, too, to say that she "accepts" the daily humiliation by mother and president that fuels her anger. But she does more than "accept" her vicious rage. Her attitude towards her fury includes "acceptance" but it is a more positive attitude than the word "acceptance" by itself denotes.

Why is "accept" an inadequate concept here? Not false or impertinent, but inadequate, incomplete? Well, the word "accept" has a generic sense that gets specified in its various uses. Ella accepts that she is diabetic. She accepts that she is a tall woman. She accepts that she has excellent administrative ability and mediocre teaching ability. She accepts that she has committed herself to a full time career, marriage and the raising of two boys. She could conceivably abandon career, husband and sons, but she has to accept the fact that she has committed herself to them.

In all these cases, the word "accept" means the same thing: Ella wills decisively to live with the particular fact in question. She could choose to rebel internally against the fact. She could choose to ignore it. Instead she chooses to live with it.

Yet in each of these cases, the word "accept" means also something different. The attitude designated by "acceptance" is the same, but also different in each of the cases. Contrast Ella's "acceptance" of her diabetes, of her tallness, and of her administrative ability. Contrast her acceptance of her career and her acceptance of her family. Not merely are the realities accepted different. The very attitude we call "acceptance" is specifically different in each case, though it is also generically the same.

None of the realities we have thus far imagined Ella accepting—diabetes, ability, family, etc.—is itself a feeling. Let us look now at different feelings which she has and which we could say she "accepts." Again, we can describe her attitude in each case as "acceptance" because all these attitudes have a basic similarity. But they also differ significantly. Ella accepts the fact that she is easily moved to pity. She accepts the fact that she gets envious at times. She accepts that she gets days of depression. The depression lasts rarely more than a day, but the sense of hopelessness that then crushes her paralyzes her so that she can do hardly anything at all.

Ella accepts, too, her passion for buying and wearing new clothes. And her passion for theatre. And her passion for friendship and her intense enjoyment of friends. "Acceptance" can aptly be used to describe all these attitudes of Ella towards particular feelings. The attitudes differ among themselves but in all of them one element is the same: Ella wills to live with these feelings.

She wills to have the feelings because she wills her life and they are irremovable elements of her life. Of course, she cannot avoid living with them. She has no choice. But we all know that it is far from automatic that one accept, that one will to live with, what in fact one cannot avoid living with. (You, reader, may wish to challenge my definition of "acceptance" as the will to live with this or that. It could be a fruitful discussion, I think.)

As Ella knows, the particular feelings of hers I listed—compassion, depression, love of friends, etc.—can be lessened or increased by events in her life or actions she takes. It is also conceivable that emotions that seem irremovable might one day disappear from her life. A friend of hers, regularly depressed, stopped taking drugs, got some counselling, and four years later claims he has not had a depressed day in a year.

Ella tried various tactics against her envy and depression. But the feelings still recur, and strongly. Eventually Ella decided to take them as permanent aspects of herself and to live with them and their consequences. She "accepts" them, under protest, but with a firm will. She wills to be alive, to be herself, and wills these feelings as necessary concomitants.

Ella's attitudes towards her feelings which I listed so far can all be called acceptance, but fall into two classes. Ella wills firmly to live with her envy and depression, but does not will these emotions for their own sake. If it ever became possible to get rid of them, Ella would will mightily to do so. She wills them only because they are inextricable parts of her self and life. But her compassion and her passion for friendship, she wills for their own sake. If it became possible to be rid of her compassion and her passion for friendship, she would not.

I list now three other feelings that Ella "accepts." Her attitude to them does not fit into either of the two classes we just recognized. The attitude she has towards these three feelings seems to me to come closer to the attitude I imagine Ella to have towards anger. Ella accepts that she misses sorely her oldest child, Tillie, who three years ago was killed by a drunk driver. She accepts that she is terrified of death. She accepts that now and then she gets attracted to a man who is not her husband, though she is content with her marriage and holds no truck with adultery.

What is Ella's attitude towards these three feelings? She wills to live with them, yes, so we can say she "accepts" them. But there is something more. She wants somehow to feel them for themselves though all three are painful. She endorses them. She prizes them. She is glad to feel them, somehow proud of feeling them.

Ella prevents these three feelings from leading her to do anything she would regret. She prevents them generally from leading her to do anything at all. (I'll note below some minor exceptions.) Without any intent of acting on these feelings, Ella still wills to feel them for their own sakes.

Though therefore Ella is somehow glad to have these three painful feelings, she is not glad about the events that cause two of them. She wishes with all her heart that Tillie was still alive. At this moment of her life, she wishes there were no possibility of herself suddenly dying. On occasion, she even wishes she were not married or there was no commandment against adultery. But Tillie is dead, Ella could be killed crossing the street to lunch, and she is a Christian in a Christian marriage.

In light of these facts, Ella wants to keep mourning for Tillie and fearing violent death and being attracted to men to whom she is not married. Her attitude to these feelings is conditioned by the facts. But it is not conditioned by the impossibility of getting rid of the feelings. If some drug could remove any of these three feelings, she would not take it, though she might be tempted to.

Why wouldn't she? Why does she want these feelings for their own sake? She cannot articulate why, even to herself. Since I imagine Ella as pure paradigm, I imagine her as completely virtuous and morally wise. But following Aristotle and Thomas, I assume one can have perfect moral wisdom and yet be unable to put it into clear and distinct ideas, much less into words. I imagine it is so with Ella.

In the face of Ella's inarticulateness about why she prizes these three feelings, let me cite Dietrich Bonhoeffer's expression of his attitude towards an analogous feeling: his vain longing in prison to be with those he loved. He ached to be with his fiancee, Maria, his best friend, Eberhard Bethge, and his elderly parents. His longing was agony, but he prized it, was glad of it, and willed to feel it for its own sake, given the facts of his life. He wrote to Eberhard who, at the Italian front, longs for his wife and child:

December 18, 1943:

> When a man enters on a supremely happy marriage and has thanked God for it, it is a terrible blow to discover that the same God who established the marriage now demands of us a period of such great deprivation. In my experience nothing tortures us more than longing. Some people have been so violently shaken in their lives from their earliest days that they cannot now, so to speak, allow themselves any great longing or put up with a long period of tension, and they find compensation in short-lived pleasures that offer readier satisfaction.

It is the ruin of all intellectual fertility. It's not true to say that it is good for a man to have suffered heavy blows early and often in life. True, it hardens people for times like ours, but it also greatly helps to deaden them. When we are forcibly separated for any considerable time from those whom we love, we simply cannot, as most can, get some cheap substitute through other people—I don't mean because of moral considerations, but just because we are what we are.

Substitutes repel us; we simply have to wait and wait; we have to suffer unspeakably from the separation, and feel the longing till it almost makes us ill. That is the only way, although it is a very painful one, in which we can preserve unimpaired our relationship with our loved ones.[1]

December 25, 1943:

First, nothing can make up for the absence of someone whom we love, and it would be wrong to try it; we must simply hold out and see it through. That sounds very hard at first, but at the same time it is a great consolation, for the gap, as long as it remains filled, preserves the bonds between us. It is nonsense to say that God fills the gap; he doesn't fill it, but on the contrary, he keeps it empty and so helps us to keep alive our communion with each other, even at the cost of pain.[2]

* * * * * *

Let me recapitulate, using Bonhoeffer's words along with my paradigm of Ella, to distinguish different positive attitudes I can have towards my feelings. When I say that I "accept" certain irremovable feelings which I have, I can mean one of three things.

At one extreme, I mean that I will to have the feeling, for its own sake, unconditionally, no matter what the facts of my life. Ella wills in this way to have her passion for friends, her need for friends. Even if she be thrown into prison for life, she still wills to be the kind of person she is, "powerless trembling for friends," to borrow words again from Bonhoeffer.[3] Her will to always want friends is in good part spontaneous, most of the time, implicit. But when she reflects on it, it is also her ratifying, unconditional choice. She wills it all the more absolutely because she believes it is God's creative will working in this need of her being.

When, however, I say Ella "accepts" certain other feelings, such as envy or depression, I mean a different attitude. She wills to live with these feelings so long as she can't get rid of them. These feelings have shown themselves to be undislodgeable parts of her life and she sees no way to get rid of them without dying. She does not will them for their own sake, but wills to live with them because she wants her life. As I said, this will is her decision, her choice. It is not automatic. Many fail to make such a decision and choice about the unchangeable elements of their life.

Her "acceptance" of feelings like envy and depression is more positive than willed rebellion or even willed indifference. It is willed resignation to the feelings as well as willed determination to use them to good ends when she can, e.g. to get laughs out of her own inner pain or to sympathize more sensitively with others who are depressed or envious.

Ella wills all the more to live with feelings, like depression and envy, because she believes God wills her to do so. She "accepts" the feelings in the same way He does. Since she cannot eliminate them, He must will them as He wills her other ineradicable defects and deficiencies. He could eliminate them but wills not to. He wills rather that she live as she is, a sometimes envious, sometimes depressed person. She joins her will to His living, saving, incomprehensible will of her sinful life.

I skirt here the quicksand of the theological problem how God wills evil. I take it that in the Christian context God does, in some sense, will evil, though not for its own sake. So, too, does Ella. If this seems too strong, it is enough for my purpose to say that Ella wills to live with her envy, whether or not one can say she wills the envy itself.

The word "acceptance," therefore, can designate two different attitudes of will towards a feeling. Ella "accepts" her love of friends, that is, she wills for its own sake and unconditionally to have this recurrent emotional need. She wills to have her passion for friends no matter how her life turns out. On the other hand, Ella "accepts" her recurrent depression in willing to live with it conditionally, i.e. only so long as it is undislodgeable from her life, which life she unconditionally wills. She certainly does not will her depression for its own sake.

The word "acceptance" can designate a third kind of attitude towards one's feelings, an attitude that falls between the two I have just stated, an attitude which is acceptance and much more. An example is Ella's attitude towards her grief for Tillie. I center now on this attitude because I want to ask, for the rest of the book, whether the attitude one should have towards his or her feelings of vindictive anger is like this third kind of attitude.

In part, Ella wants desperately not to grieve for Tillie. She hates her grief. Part of her resists that grief more violently than she resists her envious feelings. She experiences her grief, as her loss of Tillie, to be an ugly, sickening evil that has befallen her. She wishes with all her heart that Tillie were still alive and not to be grieved for. That longing for the impossible is the core of her grieving.

But Tillie being dead, Ella also wants unconditionally to grieve for her. If some drug or therapy were offered her that could eliminate her grief, she would refuse, without hesitation. Her passion for Tillie is complex and intricate but set like stone, living stone. It is her deliberate will to miss Tillie always, no matter how her life turns out, until she dies.

Ella wills her grief for Tillie for its own sake as she also wills for its own sake her passion for friends. She does not will her envy for itself. On the other hand, her will to grieve and her will to live with her envy are similar in that in both cases she wills to live with ugly, sickening, evil feelings only because of facts beyond her control.

Ella wills her grief for Tillie for itself. If it has any psychological advantage for her, she is not interested. Her belief in life with Christ after death seems to her strangely irrelevant in this respect. Why does Ella will to grieve for Tillie? Ella cannot say. As I said earlier, we imagine Ella as perfectly wise, virtuous and philosophically inarticulate. Bonhoeffer's formula speaks for her: she wills her longing for its own sake because it is the only way to keep her relationship with Tillie. Grieving *is* a relationship with the missing one. Ella cannot be with Tillie except in the hurting.

Ella's rocklike conviction and deliberate will generates or strengthens other feelings about her grief. She feels good about feeling her grief. Her longing for Tillie is always agony, but it gives her a certain satisfaction, a certain contentment, that she can be with Tillie at least in painful memory and yearning.

Ella cherishes her grief. It is terribly ugly but it is also beautiful. There is good in its evil. She is proud and glad that she does not forget Tillie, but lives with her in bleak aching and regret. She has none of these positive feelings about her envy and depression. She imagines that God, too, is glad that she still misses Tillie. He is surely not glad about her feelings of envy and depression, though He wills them, too.

The different attitudes of Tillie towards her envy and towards her grief affect what she does when she feels them. When she is aware of feeling envy, she does not deny it or try immediately not to feel it. She doesn't believe this would work. She is likely to smile ruefully at herself for feeling this way or to gently gibe herself about it. She turns her attention then to other things, trusting the feeling of envy will sooner or later pass.

When Tillie comes to Ella's mind and she begins to ache, she does often turn her attention to other things, for she wills other parts of her life, too. She wants her grief to take only a proportionate part in her life. On occasion—now it's about every month or two—she lets herself go and thinks of Tillie with mixed pain and pleasure, sometimes reliving memories, sometimes leafing through photos, sometimes imagining what she and Tillie would do if Tillie were there alive. These moments, never long and becoming less frequent, are prized and precious to Ella, though so painful that she shares them only rarely and with her husband. She feels her grief more personally and fully and intensely than her envy.

*   *   *   *   *   *

The chapter is at its end. I made a billowing detour illustrating three different attitudes with which which we can "accept" a feeling. I did so to make clearer both our question about anger and the answer which I am now about to propose to our question. Another way of asking what good, if any, there is in vindictive anger is to ask what attitude we should take to it. I will now begin to offer evidence that a person's attitude towards vindictive anger should be more than mere acceptance.

Our attitude to vindictive anger should be similar to Ella's attitude towards her mourning for Tillie. We should want and will our anger for itself and unconditionally, though we feel bitter pain at the unchangeable fact at which we rage. Though part of us hates and resists our anger, we should want and will to prize our anger, should be glad of it and be proud of it. Ella's grief helps by analogy to make this intellectually conceivable. In the remaining chapters of the book, we pore over experience to see whether it be true.

Professional ethicists will detect that I make two terms convertible: "what is good in itself" and "what should be willed and prized for itself." If, at least for the sake of discussion, they accept the convertibility of these terms, they may want to be more precise in what they mean by "good." Some will mean by our question: What, if anything, is there in vindictive anger that is *worthy* of being willed for itself, prized for itself, etc.? Other ethicists will mean: What, if anything, is there in vindictive anger that we human beings *basically, naturally strive for* and therefore should will and want for itself, prize, etc.? In discussing the goodness of vindictive anger to the extent that we do in this book, I find this further precision unnecessary. Whether one mean one or the other by "good" or whether one simply abstract from this further precision does not seem to affect our working out of an answer. I suspect that most of my discussants and I mean both these things.

Notes

1. Letter of Dec. 18, 1943, *Letters and Papers from Prison*, enlarged edition, ed. Eberhard Bethge (Macmillan, 1972), p. 167.

2. Letter of Dec. 25, 1943, p. 176. Cf. J. Giles Milhaven and Terrence Reynolds, "Human Longing in the Later Theology of Dietrich Bonhoeffer," *Thought*, forthcoming; Terrence Reynolds, *The Coherence of Life Without God Before God: The Problem of Earthly Desires in the Later Theology of Dietrich Bonhoeffer* (University Press of America, 1989), and "Dietrich Bonhoeffer's Encouragement of Human Love: A Radical Shift in His Later Theology," *Union Seminary Theological Review*, XLI, 3 & 4 (1987), pp. 55-76.

3. From the poem, "Who Am I?" p. 348.

III
An Answer

8

Take Me Seriously!

We can begin now to answer our question. What good, if any, is there in vengeful or punitive anger? What, if anything, in such anger should be willed and prized for itself? Looking for ideas, we examine the answer of Aristotle, as systematically developed by Thomas Aquinas. The reading of experience is Aristotle's. The systematic coherence is Thomas'. We turn to Aristotelian ethics because the moral thinking of our own time and place about anger is confused and evasive.

Thomas systematizes out of his "faith seeking understanding." His faith looks for understanding by bringing in human experience and intelligence. Our sole test of Thomas' answer is our experience, scrutinized by our intelligence. It is not Thomas' sole test, but it is a test which he continually applies. We want to keep comparing what he says to our concrete experiences of vindictive anger. They can be instances referred to in earlier chapters. They can be your own experiences, personal or vicarious.

Where Thomas Aquinas asks whether "anger" (*ira*) is good in itself, he means usually vindictive anger: the rage to wreak vengeance or punishment for its own sake.[1] It is the same as we mean by "anger" in this book. When Thomas asks whether this anger can be good "in itself," he asks, in Aristotelian wise, whether it may be not just a good means, but desirable for itself. His answer, however, is not simple, for he tells us that this anger is in itself both bad and good.

When the anger we feel is appropriate to the present situation, the bad in the anger serves its good and is outweighed by it. When this happens, the anger is on the whole good. It can and should be willed for itself. This is human anger as God created it. Thomas strives to see why the Creator "saw that it was good."[2]

Recall Thomas' ethic as we saw it in Chapter 5. Anger is essentially good because it is the passion to bring about just vengeance or punishment. Anger is always essentially good because it is always essentially a passion for justice. Our anger, despite its goal of justice, moves us often to do what is unjust or otherwise wrong in the present situation. Then our passion is concretely and morally bad. It is unjust and reprehensible. At other times our anger not only intends justice but moves us in fact to do what is truly just in the real situation. Then our passion is concretely and morally good, just and praiseworthy.[3] Well aimed anger is essential to good human life. There is a distinct virtue of feeling appropriately angry and a distinct virtue of acting appropriately on one's appropriate anger.[4]

Thomas endorses thus the common parlance of our time as well as his. Angry men and women use generally synonyms rather than the word "justice." "We only want to give them what they deserve!" "It's not right that they get away with it!" "It's not fair!" "We have the right to get even!"

For Thomas, our cry of "Justice!" as we rage is not hypocrisy or rationalization. When we get angry, we do want justice. Thomas knows, however, that, though "essentially good," most human anger in actuality is concretely and morally bad. Most of the time what we rage to do in the particular situation is not really just. The moral evil here is the corruption of what, even when corrupted, remains essentially a good passion. In our worst anger, we still seek justice. But we seek it very badly. This is a typical tragedy and horror of human evil. Aristotelians see the same fate for all good human passions. They hold all along the line a low opinion of the moral life of the "multitude." Anger, however, says Thomas, is one of the least sins because, even at its worse, it seeks so high a good: justice.[5]

So high a good is the goal of human anger that human beings need to exercise their human reason in order to seek it. They can desire only what they know. In human beings, according to Thomas, only their reason knows justice. Their senses do not. Many human passions may seek a goal determined by reason, but they need not. With no help from reason I can desire and enjoy food or sex or sleep. Without help from reason I can hate, turn from and be pained at extreme cold or hard blows. Sense knowledge suffices. But I cannot get angry at you unless I have reasoned that you wronged me and that it is therefore just that I punish you. That is what anger is all about. Only reason can draw that conclusion.[6]

Humans do on occasion get angry without exercising their reason. They feel on these occasions simply as brute animals do. Their rage comes solely from "natural instinct" reacting to sense perception. This instinct is indeed determined by reason: God's reason. But human anger generally arises because of the human being's rational perception of injustice whereas human passion for food or sex never arises because of the individual's rational perception of its goal: the good of self-preservation or procreation. Such passion arises from instinct determined by Divine Reason which intends the preservation and procreation of humans.[7]

Reason's conclusion may be only dimly conscious or implicit. The reasoning that produced it may be even more so. But this exercise of reason is what sets off and grounds the bodily passion of anger. We may, of course, reason badly. Human reason is thoroughly fallible. The surge of angry passion can from the beginning cloud reason. Errors are possible at several points in the reasoning process that gives rise to anger. Did Peter say what I thought I heard him say? Did he mean what I thought he meant? Was the remark really uncalled for and unfair? Does it merit punishment or vengeance? And even if affirmative answers to these questions be all correct, I may still err in concluding that it is right for me to get even with Peter in the way I plan to.

What interests our inquiry, however, is that Aristotle and Thomas assume that the reasoning that gives birth to anger can be correct. The conclusion by reason that it is right and good to punish this individual in this way can be true. How can it be true? How can it be right and good for me to make you suffer simply because you did me wrong?

We feel this way. We do at times want to make someone suffer for what they did to us. In the heat of this feeling we usually believe on some blurry reasoning that it is right to do this. But can the "reasoning" stand up to analysis? Are not Aristotle and Thomas merely rationalizing a primitive, irrational urge that we all have? Is this urge not in fact an animalistic drive which we human beings inescapably inherit?

We must accept these cravings as part of being human. But can reason or any other mode of objective knowledge find grounds to judge them "good" or "right" in any real sense? To judge them to be "good" in any personal or interpersonal sense? Have not we of the West learned something since Thomas' time? Do not we rightly take the word "vindictive" to mean something thoroughly bad?

* * * * * *

This objection may seem to gain force if we follow Thomas as he traces in experience what is this "rationally determined justice" that we in anger consciously strive for. In anger we want to hurt the other person. We want not merely to do them objective harm. We want them to feel it. We want them to be in pain. Anticipatory pleasure seeps into our pain as we begin to rage and foresee our hurting this person.

We imagine him or her wanting not to suffer but be unable to prevent it. They suffer against their will. We imagine them knowing that they are suffering for what they did to us. All this is essential to what we want in anger. It is what we strain to bring about. If we succeed in bringing it about in reality, our pleasure of anticipation swells into pleasure of execution. It climaxes, explodes and satisfies us. We move on then to other things.[8]

In experience anger contrasts with hate. She who hates someone wills only evil for that person. She wills the person's suffering simply for the sake of the person's suffering. Such hatred is always wrong. But she who rages in anger at someone wills evil to that person for the sake of some good, namely justice. She wills the person's suffering because it is just.

This means that anger, unlike hate, wants something completely individual. I can hate a kind of person, e.g. all politicians or all of a certain race or nation. Aristotle's and Thomas' example is: all thieves. But I am never angry at a kind of person. I am angry only at individuals. I am angry at him or her who wronged me. The justice that I seek in my fury has to be exacted from the individuals who did me injustice. It's only on them that I will have revenge. I will be satisfied only if they suffer punishment. Anger is even more individual in that my offenders must know that I am the cause of their suffering. To satisfy my anger, they must know that it is for my sake they are being punished. By whatever agency or agent, it is I who now make you suffer.[9]

Hate, therefore, may not move me to do anything to the person I hate. If it does, it is only as a means, not an end. Hate is aversion, a turning away, a desire to be rid of someone. I don't want to have anything to do with the hated person. I do something to them only so that I won't have to do anything else to them. If Thomas is consistent in his statements about hate, the hater wills the hated one's suffering for its own sake only because this suffering is the person's destruction. It is the hater's being rid of this person. But if I rage at you, I want to do something to you simply because I want you to experience this happening to you. Your experiencing it is my goal. Only if you do, is my anger satisfied.

The passion of anger is thus a passion to relate myself in an individual mode to another individual or other individuals. But do I not get angry at injustices done to others? Yes, I do this by virtue of another natural passion's igniting my anger. It is the natural passion of human beings to love others as themselves. This victim I see of violent injustice becomes another self for me. I identify with her or him.

Parents get angry at poor teaching of their children. Americans get deeply angry at terrorist murder of Americans abroad, as on Flight 103. We experience it as somehow done to ourselves. We can get angry at wrongs done any human being, because we love naturally all humans and identify with them. Thomas, like Aristotle, speaks here of the human tendency to "identify" with others. They speak for instance of willing the other's good as "another self."[10]

Thomas helps us, I submit, to recognize in retrospect how intensely interpersonal our anger is. As my discussion partners often put it, these persons must have meant a lot to me that I wanted so much to get back at them. I was certainly not indifferent to them. In some sense, I cared very much about them.

The interpersonal quality of anger seems to make it all the more objectionable. It makes anger revolt and frighten us the more. It shows even more how evil it is. When I am mad at you, I want something intensely interpersonal and intimate. I want me to hurt you. I can be satisfied only by the simple fact that I—hurt—you! Yet Aristotle and Thomas claim that my desire here is basically "rational." It corresponds to reality. The interaction I want *is* due the other. For all its evil, it *is* essentially good.

How? Thomas, following Aristotle, offers an answer by pointing to causes of anger and of its absence. What gets us angry? What fails to get us angry, or makes us cease to be angry? Looking at experience, we will find, I submit, that their observations are obviously true. They describe ac-

curately experience familiar to us. But if we bring their observations to
bear on our question, they throw surprising light.[11]

*   *   *   *   *   *

What according to Thomas causes our anger? First of all, our pain.
Our anger never arises unless we feel pain. When we are angry, we are in
pain. It is always emotional pain. It is always physical pain, too, or at
least physical disturbance. Our hearts pound, our breath comes short, our
hands may shake, our lips may resist our efforts to speak.[12]

What pain makes us angry? Pain at what? It is not merely that this person wronged us in the sense that he did us harm that we did not deserve. It
angers us little if the individual did it unintentionally, not knowing that his
action would harm us. If it was intentional, it still angers us little if he was
swept by passion into doing it. He was so distraught with grief or terror
that he could not help striking out at us. If we are convinced that he in-
jured us purely out of ignorance or passion, it tends to anger us little. We
are likely to desire compensation, but not punishment or revenge. If compensation is made and punishment is still possible, we are inclined to not
punish but pardon the offender.

What gets us really angry is someone deliberately wronging us. Knowingly and by choice, they do us wrong. It is because we perceive them acting this way that we become furious. It is the deliberateness of their
wronging us that enflames us.[13]

Why does this wound and infuriate us? Whether my clothes have been
damaged by pure accident or deliberate intent, the damage done me seems
the same. Yes and no. It depends what you mean by "damage." The
deliberateness of the wrong infuriates me because it expresses the offender's contempt for me. Aristotle and Thomas affirm this as an evident
fact of experience. My discussants have little trouble verifying it, usually
to their surprise, in much of our experience of anger. Yet it is a new idea
for most of them as it was for me.[14]

The idea seems so obviously true in experience that we can miss the
peculiarity of it. Imagine parents raging at an auto driver who killed their
four-year-old child. At what exactly do they rage? Not at the killing by
itself, though the killing devastates them. They would not be angry at the

driver if the child had raced out unexpectedly in front of the car moving properly and at moderate speed. They rage at the driver because they believe that he one way or another could have avoided hitting their child.

They rage at the driver because he hit the child because he chose to risk hitting the child. He chose to drive at 60 down a residential street. Or he chose to have so many drinks for the road that his reflexes were in slow motion. Or perhaps he chose simply to take his attention off the street in front of him. What is so wrong and infuriating about these choices? He could only make such a choice because he had little concern for any child possibly running onto the street. He had little concern for their child. He did not kill their child out of ill will. He killed their child because she did not mean much to him. It is for his contemptuous killing of their child that the parents want him sentenced to a long term in prison.

Wrong done us can arouse various passions in us. But we are enraged, Aristotle and Thomas say, only inasmuch as we see ourselves dealt with contemptuously. That is, we feel treated lightly, as of little worth or importance. Two women discussants, independently in different discussions, used the same words in a similarly bitter tone to epitomize something of the atrocity of their rape: "He treated me like a piece of meat."

Contempt by itself is not the cause of anger. My anger is not caused merely by the internal attitude of others towards me. It is their expressing their contempt, their doing something contemptuously to me, that sets me on fire with anger. It is their acting contemptuously towards me that convinces me it is good and just for me to make them suffer. We have no one English word for contemptuous action in all its forms. I will use the word "slight" for lack of anything better. The Latin word translated, *parvipensio* (etymologically: "weighing as little") and the Greek phrase, *oligoria,* (etymologically, "making little") are more general and inclusive than "slight." Many of Aristotle's and Thomas' examples imply a more serious contemptuous action than "slight" denotes in English. For instance, sinners arouse God's anger because by their sin they act in contempt of him.[15]

To get a better idea of this "sole cause of anger," let us look at some examples. The first is mine. The rest are Thomas', mostly derived from Aristotle, and rendered more concretely by my imagination. I put in quotation marks the actual synonyms Thomas uses for "slight," because the variety of terms brings out the breadth of what he and Aristotle perceive as contemptuous treatment.

The anger of my friend, Al, at his real estate agent rankled him for weeks. The agent had pressured Al into selling his house for less than Al believed he could have got if he had waited a bit. I explained to Al that according to Thomas he was not bitter because the agent deprived him needlessly of $30,000. What infuriated Al, Thomas would say, was the thought that the realtor went about getting him to lower his price, knowing she could get him down, treating him as an easy mark, patsy, negligible person, etc. "Exactly!" Al cried.

"Slight" can take a broad variety of forms. We suffer misfortune and someone is glad about it. We are furious at this person. Is it not because they will us evil? Yes, but that enrages us, claim Aristotle and Thomas, because of something else in their ill will. They fail to take us seriously. To be glad about our misfortune, they must "care little" (*parvum curare*) about our good or evil. They must take us as unimportant. I slip on the icy walk, shoot up upside-down to crash on my shoulder, lie stunned, fearing I have broken my back. I look up and see a passer-by doubled in laughter. I am enraged. One can construct more serious examples.[16]

Human beings are angry at those who "despise what they are very interested in" (*maxime student*). Why? Consider an example. They who are extremely interested in philosophy are angry against those who despise philosophy. Why? Those who express their scorn for philosophy, say nothing directly about the philosopher's person. They do not hinder the philosopher from philosophizing. Why get angry? Because human beings consider what they are interested in, e.g. philosophy, to be a good of theirs. To despise it is, therefore, to despise them.[17] A parallel example appears in the Bible: How can the Lord be "exceedingly angry with His people"? Human beings cannot hurt God. What, then, is he angry at? God's people did not harm Him, but despised Him in His commandments.[18]

Someone prevents me from doing what I want to do although she gets no advantage from so preventing me. My boss regularly passes over my proposals and requests. I believe she has no particular reason for doing so. I get angry not because I perceive her as malevolent towards me but because she shows she "doesn't care much (*non multum curare*) for my good will."[19]

We are irritated when people forget us. They obviously take us lightly, for one keeps in memory what one "thinks much of" (*magna aestimamus*). We are annoyed with someone who tells us bad news. She obviously "thinks little of us" since she's not afraid to cause us pain.[20] We become more angry if the person we verbally attack remains silent. His silence "makes little" of our anger.[21]

All "slights," different though they be, anger us, says Thomas, because they belittle our "excellence" (*excellentia*). A "slight" always belittles some particular quality or possession or aspect of the victim. Our wealth if we are rich or our speaking if we are a public speaker is said to be "worthless" (*nullo digna*). A slight does not merely deny that we have outstanding wealth, speaking ability or whatever be the good quality in question. If the denial be due to ignorance, it does not greatly anger us. It is not a slight. It is not contemptuous action.[22]

Only if we believe that the person denying that we are excellent orators knows that we are excellent orators, do we feel slighted. We become annoyed or enraged. We feel the same way if we believe that the person denying that we are excellent orators does not know whether we are or not. In both cases, our slighter wants to diminish the esteem we receive for oratory, regardless of whether or not we are excellent orators. They "don't care about" our oratorical excellence. It is this not caring which angers us. We find this same cause of anger if we are especially angry at friends when they don't help us.

On the other hand, if we manifestly excel in oratory or in whatever quality of ours is being slighted by some individual, we tend not to be pained or angered by the slight since it will scarcely lessen the general esteem we receive for this excellence. Correspondingly, we get very angry at the slight if there can be suspicion that we do not excel in the quality at issue. We get angry, not at some positive evil that the other person does us, but at what they in acting deliberately fail to accord us or deliberately try to lessen: esteem of others for us. All our anger in every instance arises from another's refusal to give us "honor" for our "excellence."

Excellence (*excellentia*) for Thomas, unlike the modern English "excellence," swerves in meaning between the good quality we actually have and its social recognition. "Excellence" for them is broader, too, in that it includes any kind of being good (or better) at or in something. The hierarchical world of Thomas so impresses my discussion partners that they tend to take him as meaning superiority whenever he says "excellence." But superiority is, for him, only one subspecies of excellence. This should be evident from the examples of Thomas cited above as well as from others I have not cited. For instance, we get angry when friends neglect us or people tell us bad news gratuitously or forget our names. We get angry not because they are not caring for us more than they care for others. We get angry because in what they do or do not do they show no or little care for us.

These Aristotelian ideas of the cause of anger are not completely coherent nor universally true nor perfectly systematized, even by Thomas. Thomas is aware of this, as is evidenced by his frequent qualification, "for the most part," "more angry," "less angry," "especially angry," etc. Thomas knows that experience is much more complex and varied than reason can describe. But the panoramic view he provides is, on the whole, recognizable in experience.

The view is also startling in what it suggests for our question. If "slight" be the cause of anger, then the goal of anger, the goal of wanting to make the offender suffer, must be to make up for the slight. The goal must, therefore, be to gain counterbalancing esteem. This goal is not what one expects. At least it is not what I expected when I started the inquiry. It is not what my discussants expect. This flood of fury in me, convulsing my body, blinding my reason, dissolving my control, seeking frantically to make the other suffer, is nothing but a lunge of my being to be esteemed!

Thomas says so explicitly. Experiencing ourselves to be treated contemptuously, we react in passion to get what the contemptuous treatment denied us. Thomas uses various wording to express various aspects or forms of this goal: esteem, honor, respect, being "cared about," "thought much of," "judged worth much." Looking over his examples and wordings, we can sum up anger's goal in modern terms as: to be taken seriously. What got us angry was the other's failure, while acting in our regard, to take us seriously. Our anger is our responding passion to make her or him now take us seriously by forcing them to feel our avenging or punitive action on them.

This is why anger does not have a proper pleasure.[23] Our anger rises and swells, Thomas says, only to achieve a good we would normally have otherwise gotten. Anger's satisfaction, therefore, is simply the satisfaction of that appetite which was deprived of this good. It is our appetite for esteem of our excellence. The satisfaction of our anger is, therefore, in our getting taken seriously for the excellence we have. This is all we wanted by the vengeance or punishment we roared for. This alone is what satisfies us if we do succeed in making the offender suffer.

Thomas confirms and clarifies this goal of anger by recalling a common occurrence when we cease to be angry although we were treated contemptuously and have not yet got revenge or punished the offenders. "We are not angry with those who confess and repent and are humbled; on the contrary, we become gentle with them." They calm our anger because they now seem not to despise us, but rather to "make much of us" by their confessing, repenting and being humbled. Anger tends to cease here because we are no longer hindered in getting the good we want. We are getting it once more from those who hindered it. The goal is that they make much of us. The Latin for "make much of" is *magnipendere*, to weigh as great or much. It is literally and etymologically the contrary of "slight," *parvipendere*.[24]

Thomas' explanation fits the tradition, Christian and other, in which the sinner voluntarily does penance for his sins. One thinks of certain fasts, Christian, Jewish and Muslim. One thinks of the "necessity" for Jesus to suffer and die on the cross. However modern theologians explain it, believers of the tradition believed that voluntary human pain could somehow make up for offenses against God. It lies beyond the limits of this book to discuss this concept of atonement. But the reader could profitably keep it in the back of his or her mind as they read the rest of the book. Is such an idea merely primitive and childish and therefore devoid of moral or genuinely personal value? Or does the idea, however much it need purification and integration, reflect a real value in interpersonal experience?

In any case, it follows from the commonplace occurrence to which Thomas refers that anger is a dispensable passion. It tends to fade when I get taken seriously as I should and do want to be. Correspondingly, anger is a desperate passion. It is a passion of last resort. I do not get angry unless all my other passions and actions have failed to make me or keep me duly esteemed. I am now taken lightly, as of no importance. Then arises this lust to be taken seriously by inflicting pain only because the other available means of getting taken seriously have failed. This lust arises from my last hope and a final daring. I hope and dare to try to be taken seriously by this person at least inasmuch as I make him or her suffer. Furthermore, I feel this rage only when I suffer pain at being treated as of no importance. I do not get angry at slights if I am happy and enjoying myself so much that I feel no pain at this individual's making little of me.[25]

It is not surprising then that under favoring circumstances anger cedes to other passions and phases itself out. More accurately: an enraged person can, under favoring circumstances, become less angry because she or he now feels more satisfying passions and pleasures. The passion of anger is good in itself, but also evil and essentially less good than other passions which naturally and satisfactorily replace it. This insight of Thomas into vindictive anger becomes crucial when, as later in the book, we discuss with liberal activists, particularly feminists, the practical usefulness for oppressed people of knowing the intrinsic goodness of vindictive anger.

*   *   *   *   *   *

The ideas of Thomas sketched above open a door where there seemed to be only a wall. If the ideas are true to experience, then the dark, physical, violent passion of anger is thoroughly personal and interpersonal. The smoke-filled inferno of our fury sweeping outward to make someone suffer is a thrust of our being to be made much of, taken seriously, esteemed, for the worth we have. If this be true, the door opens to a promising inspection of other passions to see how here, too, passion and interpersonal may fuse. I have in other writings attempted a parallel inspection of our passion for pleasure.[26]

In the present book, however, we stick to the passion of anger. We stay staring at the commonplace experience. We lust to make the other suffer because he caused suffering either to us or a loved one of ours. Why do we so lust? I trust that most readers will, like many of my co-discussants, see there is some truth in experience to the Aristotelian answer. It is evident, I submit, in most examples we imagine or remember. Yes, we lust to make the other suffer because we feel that in their very suffering at our hand they will take us, or the loved one, seriously as they failed to do in the past. Whatever else may be true of anger this seems to be generally true. I recommend that the reader go back over experiences of anger and meditate what this comes to in experience.

If you agree, if only hypothetically, with this assertion of fact, we can return with sharper focus to our question of value. How, if at all, can such passion be good in itself? How, if at all, can we want it for itself, prize it, and be glad we feel this way? Even if it be true that we make someone suffer in order to make them take us seriously, it does not sound good at all. What kind of "taking seriously" is this? What good is there in one person "taking seriously" the other in that the other forces her or him to suffer?

Notes

1. Thomas does at times use the word *ira*, not for what we label "vindictive anger," but in a more general or more constructive sense, e.g. *Summa Theologiae*, I-II, 46, 6; II-II, 108, 1.

2. The following account of anger is based on Thomas Aquinas, *S. Th.*, I-II, 23, 25, 46-48; II-II, 108, and 156-159, and Aristotle, *Nicomachean Ethics*, II, 5-7; IV, 5; VII, 6-7 *Rhetoric*, II, 2-3. I provide specific references selectively below. Either the older Blackfriars English translation of the *Summa* or the newer McGraw-Hill one is usable. Translations which I give are mine.

3 *S. Th.* I-II, 46, 2, 6 and 7; 47, 1; 48, 3; II-II, 108, 4; 157, 3 and 6; 158, 3.

4. II-II, 157, 1.

5. II-II, 158, 4.

6. I-II, 46, 4, 5 and 7; II-II, 156, 4 and 158, 1.

7. I-II, 46, 4 and 7; cf. I, 78, 4.

8. I-II, 46, 1, 2, 6, and 7; 47, 4; 48, 1; II-II 108, 4.

9. I-II, 46, 1, 2, 6 and 7; 47, 1; II-II, 108, 2; 158, 4.

10. I-II, 47, 1; 48, 2; II-II 108, 2; cf. I-II, 27-28. That love is the source of all the passions, and virtuous love is the source and "form" of all the virtues: I-II, 46, 1; II-II, 23, 7 and 8.

11. Thomas treats of the causes of anger and of its absence in I-II, 47, Aristotle in *Rhetoric,* II, 2 and 3.

12. I-II, 25, 1; 47, 3; 48, 1, 3 and 4; II-II, 158, 4.

13. I-II, 47, 2.

14. I-II, 47.

15. I-II, 47, 1 and 2.

16. I-II, 47, 1, 3 and 2, 3.

17. I-II, 47,1, 3.

18. I-II, 47,1, 1.

19. I-II, 47, 2, to 3.

20. I-II, 47, 2, to 3.

21. I-II, 47, 1, to 4.

22. I-II, 47, 2-4.

23. I-II, 25, 1.

24. I-II 47, 4. Anger is one of the five principal passions that arise only when a desired good is being hindered, e.g. I-II, 23, 1 and 2; 25, 2.

25. I-II, 23, 3; 25; 46, 1.

26. E.g., "Sleeping Like Spoons," *Commonweal,* April 7, 1989, pp. 205-207; co-authored with Terrence Reynolds; "Human Longing in the Later Theology of Dietrich Bonhoeffer," *Thought,* forthcoming; "An Experienced Value of Marital Faithfulness in *Dubin's Lives," Journal of Religious Ethics,* Winter, 1983-84, pp. 82-96; "Sex and Love and Marriage," *National Catholic Reporter,* January 13 and 20, 1978; "Thomas Aquinas on Sexual Pleasure," *Journal of Religious Ethics,* Fall, 1977, pp. 157-181; "Christian Evaluations of Sexual Pleasure," *Selected Papers, 1976, of the Society of Christian Ethics,* pp. 63-74.

9

To Feel Pain Can Be Good

Our anger is a passion to be taken seriously for the excellence we have. So says Thomas Aquinas, following Aristotle. I agree, appealing to the numerous examples in the book and the reader's experience. This is the phenomenon, the experience of anger. In most cases where we say someone is "angry," we can see that the angry person, we or someone else, is striving to be taken seriously. They want vengeance or punishment as a way of being respected, taken seriously, made much of. If you are not convinced, grant it for the sake of discussion. We will try to make the concept clearer as we look more closely at the experience.

Does this explain how anger is good? It connects with the Aristotelian perspective on justice. Aristotle and Thomas claim that anger is a passion for justice. Driven by anger we lunge for what is our right and has been denied us. We see now what the right is: to be taken seriously for our excellence, to receive due honor and esteem.

The brute sweep of anger in individuals is their gut insistence on a right of theirs, their right to be taken seriously. The individual may hold an ethic or morality that denies there is such a right. But his fury gives the lie to his ethic. In his passion the individual insists on being taken seriously as his right. Or that others be taken seriously as their right.

Does our passion tell the truth? Is what our anger thirsts for really its right? Do we have a right to be taken seriously? And if we do, do we have a right to punish and avenge in order to get taken seriously? What kind of a right is this? What basis does it have? The questions open an inviting road for our appraisal of anger.

In what follows, however, I follow a different, parallel route. I prefer not to get into a problematic of rights and justice. I stay with our problematic of good and evil. I will on occasion indicate how what I

137

propose complements and fits with the Aristotelian idea of anger as desire for justice.

Return to experience. Watch ourselves straining to strike back so that we or others be taken seriously. Is this striving and straining something good, to be willed for itself, to be prized for itself? Well, my first response is affirmative. What I strive and strain for is good, so striving and straining for it must be good, too. I cannot deny that on a basic level I want myself and those I love to be taken seriously for their real excellence. That they be taken seriously is clearly something worthwhile and valuable for itself. It is, therefore, a fundamental human good.[1]

I cannot help but admire this thunderous passion of mine to get this good. I must exercise extreme caution, for anger is so explosive it gets easily out of control and wreaks great harm. But I cannot help but prize my foggy, brutal lunge of rage inasmuch as it is a mode of mine of reaching for something good and important and necessary: that I and those I love be taken seriously for the excellence we have.

Something else follows. Anger must be a kind of love. Love is wanting good for someone. In their anger the angry person wants for someone this fundamental human good of being taken seriously. If the angry person wants herself or himself to be taken seriously, it is love of self. If I want it for other persons, then my anger is love for them. I want them to have the good of being taken seriously.

A further thing follows. Anger is not only love of the victim. It is also love of the offender. The empassioned lunge of anger is not only for the good of the angry person or of others with whom that person identifies. Empassioned anger is a lunge, too, for the good of the offending person, the object of the anger. In seeking to punish him or wreak vengeance on him, the angry person seeks his good, loves him!

The angry person seeks that the other take her seriously for the excellence she has. Surely it is a fundamental good of human life that one take others seriously for their true excellence. An individual's life is lacking if she fails to take seriously the people she deals with. To make her take me seriously is good for her. It is a way of loving her.

Is all this mere wordplay? We will take up shortly objections to this reasoning. But let us first imagine it to be true. Forensic specialists announced a while ago with "reasonable scientific certainty" that the skeleton dug up in Brazil was of Josef Mengele, "demon doctor" of Auschwitz, known for his hideous medical experiments on hundreds of dwarfs, cripples and Jewish children. His son, Rolf Mengele, recalled, "He could never understand why anybody could think he should feel guilty for wanting to get rid of what he called unworthy lives."

Many grieved that Mengele died in hiding and was never arrested, brought to trial, sentenced and punished. Our question is: might it have been better *for him* if he had? Might he have gained something truly good for him? Might he not have sensed, in being imprisoned and with his punishment looming before him, that the victims of his medical experiments are not as negligible as he thought? Suppose that he senses now, if only for purely selfish, pragmatic reasons, that the lives of those long dead victims are more important than he thought? Because of them he now suffers in terror. He takes them seriously now, for the first time. Is he now better or worse off than if he had died undisturbed in his Brazilian village? If better, then those who caught and punished him in order to make him feel this, were in fact loving him. They desired what was good for him.[2]

No one can deny that when I rage at you, I lunge to grab you in an intense, interpersonal relationship. I want to make something very intimate happen between you and me. If, as we suggest, the intimate relationship I want in my rage is that you here and now take me seriously, then I want something good for you as well as for me. My thirst to punish or take vengeance on you is love of you! To realize this is to realize that I love more than I think I do. This, I believe, is the most fertile hypothesis (eventually, conclusion?) of the whole inquiry of this book. We love more than we think we do.

That anger is love follows, too, from the Aristotelian description of anger in terms of justice, referred to above. After all, we in our fury want to give the offender only what he deserves. We want only to treat him justly, to give him the justice he might not otherwise get. It is good for a person to get what he deserves, to be treated justly. Our passion, therefore, is for his good as well as ours. We want his good, too. We must, therefore, love him.[3]

*   *   *   *   *   *

Wait a minute! There's something wrong in this thinking. However logical it may be, does it not contradict the actual experience it purports to describe? Look at a man or woman when their anger blazes in them. You call it love of self, but it is nothing but raw passion to reach out and make another suffer. You call it love of the other but it is pure glee at cornering the other and skewering her. At the height of our fury we have no interest in any benefit which our victim might gain from the agony we inflict feverishly on him. What gives us complete satisfaction is when we inflict pain on the offender with his full awareness and over his frantic resistance. This is love? This terrified, unwilling agony is good for the offender, regardless of further consequences?

This is a solid objection. We have met it in various forms a number of times in the book. It is a basic objection to my whole argument for good anger. We are finally about to tackle it directly. But, first, recall quickly some distinctions which bring out the precise force of the objection.

If revenge be good, this does not mean that it is always *on the whole* good. If anger be a kind of love, this does not mean it is always *on the whole* good love. Like other human loves, anger can be under circumstances more bad than good. It can, therefore, be good in some respect, but be on the whole bad. It can have some good in it, but be on the whole bad. In the murder scene, Shakespeare makes clear that Othello does love Desdemona and that love has some good in it, but this makes only more horrible the evil of his passion as a whole. Even if all anger be in part good love, we can responsibly prize and encourage our anger only in those situations where our anger is on the whole good, or only for the part which is good.

Anger is, on the whole, not good love, but bad when it is excessive. The punishment the angry person wants to give may exceed in proportion the wrong the offender did. Anger, too, is on the whole bad when it is based on error. The offender may not have done what the angry person believes she did. I cannot responsibly encourage myself to feel anger that is excessive or based on error.

Finally, recall what we have noted more than once. It is true of anger as it is of passions generally. Even in circumstances where anger be on the whole good, not bad, it may still be bad to act on it. The better the passion be, the more careful one should be in acting on it. We referred to sexual passion as an analogy of this.

To say, therefore, that anger is love is simply to say that the thrust of anger has always some good in it. It is always good in one respect. Anger's thrust is always good even when it is much more bad, as when my anger is excessive or based on error. It is always good for me to want passionately to be taken seriously by you for the excellence I have. It is particularly good if you refused to do so in the past. For you to change now and take me seriously is good for you and me. Anger, therefore, in its thrust is always good. It is good even when it is more bad than good, and thus on the whole bad, morally bad.

These distinctions only sharpen the objection made above. It is precisely this "good" thrust of anger that cannot be really good. The essential thrust of anger, as we recognized, is not merely that the other person take me seriously. I rage to make the other take me seriously precisely *in making him suffer against his will*. That is all I want. The objection stands: how can *this* be in any respect good and loving?

We turn the lens to get still sharper focus on the point of the objection. We recall further distinctions. Thomas and Aristotle can provide some of them. First, to make a person suffer solely for the sake of making them suffer is bad. It is not anger either. A passion whose thrust is solely to make the other suffer or to harm the other is not anger, but a kind of hate. It is also evil, inhuman, brutish. It is not what we are talking about.[4]

In anger I want to make you suffer not solely to make you suffer, but to make you suffer *as you made suffer me or others I love*. Why? Here we make a connection we have not yet made and which Aristotle and Thomas only imply. I want to make you suffer in order to bring you back down into an equality with us, an equality which you destroyed. In making us suffer, you took us lightly, treated us as of little worth. You slighted us. We cannot undo the harm you did us, but as we make you suffer, you do in some way, however inadequate, take us seriously again. You experience us as, at least in some respect, ones to be taken seriously. You experience us thus as we indeed are equally with you and all human beings: to be taken seriously for our worth. It is true that anger has no further goal beyond making the other suffer, but neither does it want the other's suffering merely for suffering's sake. Anger wants suffering that makes victim and offender equal once more in the offender's restored or new respect for the victim.

This is why the angry person, as we saw, wants a thoroughly individual punishment or vengeance or getting back. He does not want merely that the other suffer, but that he, in his own name or the name of others, by himself or through others, make the other suffer. It is because we make you suffer that you cannot help taking us seriously.

Now, Dr. Mengele, in your agony, your panic and despair and shame, you will do something you have never been able to do. You will take seriously the long dead individuals with whom you experimented playfully and treated as of no importance. You will take them seriously with sinking stomach and tightened throat and strangled breath as you hear the judge on their behalf lay the death sentence on you. You will finally take them as human beings who are in some elemental way equally as important as yourself.

This offers a plausible phenomenology of at least some of the experience behind the concept of "vindicatory justice." As we saw, all justice is defined by the tradition as equality. Different kinds of justice, e.g. commutative justice and distributive justice, are different kinds of equality due between human beings. Just vengeance and punishment reestablish one kind of due human equality. Though the tradition may not have seen it clearly, it would fit to say that in undergoing vengeance or punishment the offender changes his attitude and to some extent takes the victim as seriously as himself, as equal to himself in importance. In any case, for our discussion, I submit that it describes accurately our experience of anger to say we want, by inflicting pain, to make the other change his attitude and take us as equal to him.

*   *   *   *   *   *

This, of course, does not meet the objection. If anything, it strengthens it. "Obviously, as I writhe in the pain, physical or mental, that you inflict on me, I take you seriously. But what kind of a 'taking seriously' is that? Certainly not a good kind! It is not the good kind of taking seriously that I refused you. Not the kind of being taken seriously that a human being on full reflection and deliberation wants. It is not the kind of being taken seriously that is due equally to all human beings.

"Your 'taking seriously' is loftily abstract and you reason about it and apply it to all concrete instances as if the reality were always the same. But my 'taking you seriously', my agony as I stare helplessly up at you raining down blows, is not something that satisfies you in your humanity. Certainly not a "fundamental human good" for you or me. Why do you think our civilization dropped the idea of 'vindicatory justice'? And if Mengele can be brought by confrontation, conviction and sentencing to finally take his dead victims seriously, this should happen, not by the sheer pain he suffers, but by his being made to see clearly the evil he did and regret it.

"True," the objection continues, "the feelings you describe towards Mengele, rapists, and their ilk are feelings we do feel. They are natural human feelings. We should accept them. We need not be ashamed of them. We need only take care that our actions be determined by other purposes.

"But we must not approve these feelings. Certainly not prize them as you do. Certainly not deliberately want to have them for their own sake. Not be glad if one has them. This feeling is not at all like Ella's grief for Tillie. Look closer at real life experience of this "taking seriously" that anger thirsts for. Your examples all have uncommon contexts that distract and give a romantic glow. Look at some other, more typical instances of this anger.

"Look at the 'being taken seriously' that real life anger often wants and gets. Read the papers. Remember that it is usually in anger that wifebeaters beat and childabusers abuse. Imagine the woman cornered alone in the night, unable to ward off the punches and kicks of the man as he gives her "what she deserves" for her sharp words to him. Hear the child screaming at the "punishment" which leaves him bruised and bleeding. This is good? Loving?

"Turn to TV. Feel what the Sikhs whose burned corpses lie there in the railroad station must have felt as Hindus took vengeance on them for the assassination of Indira Gandhi and set fire to their living bodies. Or feel— much less tragic, but still revolting—with the English soccer player leaving the playing field, doubled up by a kick in the groin from a spectator. Yes, the woman takes seriously her batterer, the child his abuser, the Sikh his murderer, the soccer player his assailant. But this kind of "taking seriously" is not a fundamental human good. It is not good in any respect. It is completely evil.

"Moreover," the objector persists, "you miss an important fact. Look again at the TV screen. Two men come up behind the spectator who kicked the soccer player. They knock the spectator flat. They kick him. As you quaintly put it, he now takes seriously the soccer player. Granted, and what are you feeling now as you watch? Do you not feel, along with more nausea and horror, also a certain satisfaction? 'That will show him!' you murmur interiorly. Your satisfaction feels right and good, you say. This is good anger, you say. It fits the conceptual schema you have erected. But isn't the feeling curiously familiar? Haven't you already met this feeling earlier in this incident?

"Similarly, relive the grim, vindictive joy you felt when you read in the paper and see in the photograph the wife-beater or child-abuser standing before the judge and hearing his sentence of five years. 'That will show him!' Isn't there something *deja vu* here, too?

"In these feelings of yours, which I, objecting, confess I share, we experience the pain of the punished offender as satisfying, as what we want him to feel. I buy your description of fact. We experience it as good. Why? Because it will show them! Now they'll know how important their victims were. They made a mistake in treating this wife or child or head of state as negligible persons. Now they'll take them seriously.

"But what of this vague familiarity of the feelings? Don't you remember? These feelings were pretty much what we imagined the spectator felt as he raced forward and kicked the unsuspecting player. Somehow the player had affronted, made little of the spectator's team. Now the spectator had evened the score. That'll show him!

"Our anger, eager for and satisfied by the humiliating punishment of the wifebeater or childabuser, feels right and good to us. His anger as he beats his wife feels to us horribly wrong and evil. But in the actual feeling what difference is there between his and ours? In our consciousness are they not essentially the same? He felt he was giving her what she deserved. 'This will show her!'

"If we just recall the phenomenon, the feeling we felt, was it any different from that of the assailants setting the still living Sikh on fire? They were showing the Sikh that Gandhi was worthy of more respect than he had given. And for all our disapproval of the mass killings, did we not fantasize with satisfaction how the assassins of Indira Gandhi must react to the murder of hundreds of their fellow Sikhs? 'That will show them!'

"We start by feeling with the victim. Once we are enraged, we are in fact feeling with the assailants. The anger sweeping us is in consciousness the same feeling that swept the assailants at whom we are angry. We have been sucked into the flood of their sewer. In seeking to punish the atrocity, we imitate it.

"By our anger we continue in our heart the chain reaction of anti-personal violence. We strike at these men, in reality or fantasy, with the same passion that drove them to strike at their victims. Imitating the blows of these violent criminals may on occasion be justifiable as a necessary means to lessen such violence. Feeling the same way they did is evil. Normal, natural, at times inescapable evil, but still evil, completely evil.

"All these instances are real life anger in action. True, in their agony, these victims 'took seriously' their assailants. But this is sleight of word. Can anyone reliving the experience and reflecting carefully assert that they want for themselves or others the passion for this kind of being taken seriously? That they prize the passion for itself? Are glad they have it? Could anyone besides a rationalistic philosopher playing with words affirm there was anything good here?"

* * * * * *

I believe so. A philosopher could who, far from rationalistic, was ready to face nonrational interpersonal life. But the philosopher need recognize two truths, which were recognized also by traditional Western rational thought. In human life some of the best things are at the same time very evil and some of the worst are at the same time very good. Indeed, the worst evil in the world is evil in the best. The worst sin of all was the sin of the angels.

Secondly, nothing in the world is purely evil. All human evil has some good in it. Evil must have good to live off, for evil is nothing but corruption of good. Where there is no good being corrupted, there can be no evil. When all good is destroyed, the evil ceases to exist, for there is nothing left that can be corrupted. The worst human evil, say, sheer envy or hatred, is evil not only for what it does to the good of its victims. Its evil is also what it is doing to what remain as good qualities of the envier or hater.

Augustine and most other thinkers of the West found this position implied by the Bible. All that exists is created by a good God. The thinkers, Christian and Jewish, drew on ancient Greek metaphysics to confirm and explain the position. Everything, as long as it exists, is basically good for nothing finite can exist except inasmuch as it participates in divine reality and goodness. Whether or not we accept the Biblical interpretation or the metaphysic, let us pore further over our experience of anger with the working hypothesis that the evil in it may be fused with its good. In some cases the evil may outweigh the good. In others, the good outweighs the evil.

A recurrent roadblock to discussion of the value of passions is the inability to take this as a working hypothesis. It amazes me how many discussants cannot stop presupposing that horrible evil must have no good in it. They presuppose often that it is disrespectful to those who suffered horribly if we ask what good there may have been in their suffering. These discussants are incapable of looking at an evil passion and asking if there is any good in it.

Our hypothesis is the opposite. Evil is horrible precisely for what it is: a corruption of good. We reverence the suffering of victims if, to understand and appreciate their suffering, we are willing to experience what corruption of what goodness was forced on them. The despair in the eyes of starving children, for instance. The terror in the eyes of those who have been beaten and expect to be beaten again soon. The despair and terror would not horrify us as much if it were not that we experience that these are still good, worthy persons who despair and panic. In our experience, the preciousness of a child fuses with its despair. We sense the dignity of the battered in their very terror. The despair or terror of a dog does not agonize anything near as much. Whatever be the truth of all this as generality, let us test it on the viciousness of anger.

If we scrutinize squarely the "taking seriously" that anger demands, we see evil. The inflicting of intense pain, physical or mental, on a person against their will is something that we, from the depth of our being and on careful reflection, do not want. We do not want it for ourselves or for others. The question is: can it, at the same time, be something that we, from the depth of our being and on careful reflection, do want? Can it be good as well as evil? If so, the next question will be: can the good at times outweigh the evil, so that it is at times, on the whole, good? Do we then, on the whole, want it despite its evil?

To answer these questions, we need first to recapitulate ways in which anger is necessarily linked with evil and is evil. First of all, anger is a response to some evil that has already happened. I am angry only because I believe that I or someone else have been treated badly. In the religious traditions of the West there can be good, justified anger only in fallen earthly life. There is no anger among the blessed in heaven, for nothing bad happens there. No one wrongs another. No one slights another. There is no justification there for punishment or vengeance.

It is no different with many secular moderns today. They work for a world without injustice. They work, therefore, for a world that will give no occasion for anger as it will give no occasion for vengeance or punishment for punishment's sake. They work for a world without anger. Anger has no part in the vision drawing them on. This is why a fine thinker and leader like Barbara Deming can see no good at all in vindictive anger. It betrays the vision. We must be honest about its presence in us, she concludes, and struggle to purge ourselves of it.[5]

If therefore on reflection we disagree with Deming and want our anger for its own sake, we can want it only conditionally. We want it only if someone was badly treated. We do not want it in the ideal world which we, too, dream of. If anger is good and we will it for its own sake, it is only because there are rape, concentration camps, child abuse and other wrongs that cry for vengeance or punishment. If Celie's and Bigger's murderous anger is good in itself, it is so only as response to the way they have been treated. No one claims that vindictive anger is so good that it has a place in ideal human life.

Secondly, pain itself is evil. Suffering itself is evil. The religious traditions of the West insist that, on earth, suffering will at times be also good for the believer. Believers will in certain situations want to take pain on themselves or inflict pain on each other. But only on earth. In the

Kingdom there will be no pain nor suffering, for there will be no evil There. The tear will be wiped from every eye.

No one I know, believer or nonbeliever, denies that pain itself is evil. I will try to bring out this experienced evil below in terms of a baby's experience. But our question is: how, if at all, can this evil be also something good? How can pain be still something we want for itself?

Thirdly, if pain is evil, it is all the more evil to inflict pain on another against that person's will. And that is the essential thrust of anger. No one arguing for the goodness of some anger can deny that even the "best" anger remains evil inasmuch as its essential thrust is to cause pain, to make the other suffer. It is all the more evil because anger's essential thrust is to inflict pain, make the other suffer, against that person's will.

Anger thus, in itself and in its context, is always evil. The objection we have been wrestling with insists rightly that in fashioning our fine concepts of good anger we must keep our eyes on the experience of the evil present in all anger. Evil seethes at the core of all anger whether of Sikh or Hindu, wifebeater or sentencing judge, this or that spectator of soccer, you or me. It is the horrible evil which—I understand, though disagree—Barbara Deming and others committed to non-violence will do no more than tolerate as unavoidable evil.

*   *   *   *   *   *

I am arguing, of course, that we should not only tolerate our anger for all its evil. We should not merely "accept" it. We should at times want and will this evil reality of ours for itself. We should will and deliberately want it for itself when it is, as it is at times, more good than evil. It is then on the whole good and we can prize it despite its evil. We then can and should encourage it.

I do not want to belittle the evil in all anger. A few paragraphs below I will try to bring out, even more than I just did, the evil of inflicting pain on another against their will. But to assess clearly the evil of inflicting pain on another, as well as the possible goodness of so doing, we need first to reflect on pain itself. What is pain in our experience? Can some pain be more good than evil? Can it be on the whole good despite its evil?

Forget about anger for the moment. Forget about inflicting pain. Think just about pain. Consider examples of pain caused by no human being. Instances of such pain, blamable on nobody, are among the most atrocious evil we know. The pain of the child dying slowly of disease, in conscious terror and feeble frenzy. The long, drawn-out pain of those starving in drought areas. The pain of the family of victims of landslides, earthquakes, etc. The pain of the autistic child or the child born with useless arms and legs. The pain of those with incurable mental illness who in moments of lucidity know how ill they are.

Such pain is evil. Yet to feel this atrocious pain may under circumstances be more good than evil. How? Well, it can be good at least for someone else who does not have to feel the pain but chooses to do so. Reflecting on my own experience, I am surprised to see that at times I *want* to feel pain at another's pain. I want even to feel the very pain he or she feels.

I want to feel the pain of the starving. I want to feel the pain of the victims of earthquakes and landslides I see on CBS News. I want to feel the pain of the distraught mentally ill man who walks up and down Thayer St. I want to feel the pain of a bereaved colleague at the wake of her mother.

In all these instances, I want the pain for itself. I want to experience pain, the pain of the other, inasmuch as I can share it. I know implicitly that this pain is good for me. I want to feel it. I want to feel it more than I do. It pains me that I feel this pain so little. I am glad inasmuch as I do feel it.

It is, of course, a truism of our time that it is good for me to feel the pain of suffering people I meet. Who would dare deny it? "Empathy" is in. Is it so clear why it is good? It is clear why it is good for me to know rationally the pain of others and the evil of it. This knowledge can make me deliberate what I might, or even should, do about it. But I don't have to feel the others' pain in order to know it and its evil and to decide to try to ease their pain.

What is so good about feeling their pain? It is good, of course, if it does strengthen my decision to ease the pain in some way. But there is more to it than that. Feeling the others' pain is good, something I want, even when I am already doing all I can to ease the pain or when there is nothing I can do to ease their pain. What does feeling their pain add to rational knowledge of the pain and the already firm decision to do whatever I can about it?

It was one thing for me to inform myself and then judge and vote that my city should allow this lean, grey, bent, ill-smelling figure, this mentally ill man, and others like him, day after day to move up and down Thayer Street with his heavy bags and outstretched begging hand. It was a similar thing for me to decide whether or not to give him the change he asks. It is a third, different thing when one day, as I happen to look into his eyes, I feel unexpectedly something of his pain. What is this third thing that happens to me?

I feel a little of the soreness of his confusion, hopelessness, fearful, bewildered hope. What's good about my feeling it? I feel an ugly, dirty feeling that I believe no human being should feel. The pain I feel now is pretty much the kind of pain I always figured he felt. It does not give me any new idea of his suffering. Feeling his pain gives me no new beliefs about him, changes no old ones. It does not add to my rational knowledge of anything. It does not move me to do anything I have not been doing. Why do I want it? Why am I glad I now feel it? What's good about it?

I am not trying to whip up the reader to feel more pain with suffering people you meet. I hope you do, but that's not my present intent. I am trying rather to point to the perhaps unsuspected riches that pain for all its evil can have in a world filled with pain. I point at the moment to the riches of feeling the pain of others.

It is not riches for the man on Thayer St. I wish someone could alleviate his pain. I know no one who can. Something in me, passing by him, wants to share that pain. I cannot make it happen, but on the rare occasion when it happens, I feel richer for it. With him I feel choked, numb, depressed. I am glad I feel this way.

The reader knows such riches. You experience them perhaps often. Suffering is all about us. I point to your experience and ask you: What are these riches? What in our pain in these experiences makes it so good as well as so evil? What do you think? Here, as throughout the book, I invite you to form clearer ideas of what you already know.

What do *I* think? I think: the pain I feel this moment on Thayer St. is good, something I want for itself. The pain is atrocious but I am glad to get it. How can this be? My pain here is good because it is not simply pain but *pain with and pain at.* The pain I unexpectedly feel on passing the mentally ill man is good because it is my pain with another's pain and pain at another's pain. It links me with that person in a new way.

If you can put up with more abstractions: this pain is *being with* another person in a singular way. It is not that my pain moves me to, or enables me to, be with him. My pain *is* my being with him. It is *interpersonal.* I could call it union, fellowship, intimacy, communion, relation, touching, etc. It is all these things, but the words carry sweet overtones. There is nothing sweet about my sudden ugly feel of the horror of his existence. I will call it a "being with." Crude English befits crude experience.

I do not wish to exaggerate. But neither was this trivial. It was only a passing moment. I did not follow it up. I rhapsodize about it now superficially. But for this moment I was with this man. That's the fact. I was with him as I had not been before. It did him no good. I saw no response in him. But it was good for me. As I reflect on it, I see this is a kind of being with people that I want. I want it reluctantly perhaps, secretly perhaps, determinedly, yes. I want more of it.

*   *   *   *   *   *

Can we track down more of the interpersonal character that pain can have? Besides pain at the pain of others, there is another kind of pain that at times is evidently good. Despite its agony we will it for itself, are glad we feel it. It is the pain of loss. The pain of loss can sometimes be good for those who suffer the loss. The loss is not good for them. The pain is. Once we have lost one we loved, feeling the pain of that loss can be good for us. In other words: it can be good for us to feel the pain of longing for those we no longer have.

How may the pain of loss for all its agony be good? We implied an answer with Ella and Bonhoeffer though we did not bring out the aspect of pain. If the loss is irreversible, our suffering the pain of it may be the best way of being with the ones we are separated from. Feeling pain at their absence, letting ourselves at times long for them, may be the realest way of still being with them. When Bonhoeffer could be with Maria, Eberhard and his parents in other ways, e.g. when they visited him in prison, it was infinitely better than the anguish of longing. But when he was placed in what seemed to be and eventually was final, definitive isolation, the best way to be with them, the way, therefore, that he wanted and held onto, was horrible, rending longing.

As we saw, part of Ella does not at all want to grieve for Tillie. Part of her resists that grief far more violently than she resists her depression or envy. She experiences her loss as the worst evil that has befallen her. She wishes with all her heart that Tillie were still alive and not to be grieved for. That longing for the impossible is the core of her grieving.

But Tillie being dead, she wills unconditionally to mourn for her, simply for its own sake. If some drug or therapy were offered that could eliminate her grief, she would refuse, without hesitation. Her passion for Tillie is live and intricate but set like stone. It is her deliberate, unconditioned will to miss Tillie always, no matter how her life turns out, until she dies.

So Ella feels good, too, about feeling her bitter grief. Her longing for Tillie is agony, but it gives her a certain bleak satisfaction, a certain dull contentment, a certain thin peace. She can be with Tillie at least in memory and in the anguish of yearning. Ella cherishes her grief. It is ugly and beautiful. It is evil and good. Ella is proud and glad that she does not forget Tillie, and that she lives with her in aching and loss.

Pain is not a result of the longing of Ella and Bonhoeffer. Their pain is their longing. Their longing is brute pain at the absence of those they love. The agony that Bonhoeffer wills to feel is simply to want to be with Maria and Eberhard and his parents, to want this in the awareness that it is impossible now and may never be possible again. Similarly, Ella. This very agony is the minimal being-with possible, but it *is* that.

Pain is not a faceless coin we human beings have to pay in order to be in spirit with those we have lost. Pain is our being with them. We are with them in feeling the pain of longing. It is often the way we are most with them.

Pain is opaque. We see nothing in it. The more we feel it, the more it closes out light. But pain can be a grabbing. In letting ourselves be swept by our wanting, needing those we have lost, we hold them again, however inadequately. The wanting, the needing, is the holding. To feel pain at the absence of loved ones is somehow to have them present. It is not logical. I do not think it is intelligible. It is a fact of experience. It is sad fact, which can be more good than evil only when there can be nothing better in the particular situation.

Pain can be night in which we hold those whom we cannot see and who are not there. That is why Ella and Bonhoeffer take time and effort to feel the pain that is longing. To take time regularly to mourn for vanished people is not necessarily masochism or neurosis. Its ache and horror can yield the satisfaction of being for a moment with ones we love and can never be with in a realer way. It is little satisfaction, but much better than none.

The point is important for grief. Much in our culture discourages our feeling grief, whether it be pain at dead loved ones or pain at losing all our life and world by our own coming death. The point is important for other passions, and not only anger. As I shall try now to show, pain, crushing, atrocious pain of real life, is often, in a number of ways besides grief, a being with one we love. The pain is more good than evil and we want it only when there is no better way of being with the one we love. It is more bad than good when, for instance, there are better ways. But, whether more good than bad or more bad than good, atrocious pain is often a being together with someone. It is a being together unique to pain. It is not reproducible outside of pain. Nothing else does what it does for us.

* * * * * *

Despite the preceding considerations, my discussion partners continue to have difficulty in recognizing how pain itself can be a being with the other. They recognize it in grief, but they tend otherwise to see pain as self-contained, enclosed. Let us, therefore, look at other ways in which pain itself is interpersonal. Let us look at the pain, not of grief, but of fear.

Yesterday, I yelled at my daughter. She got so furious she stormed off in silence after my speech, slamming the door behind her. Her anger was perhaps not as great as it appeared since she did not forget to leave her son behind for my baby-sitting. But for an hour or two, I felt oppressed, dark, hurting, though I wasn't clear why.

When the cloud began to lift, I saw, with surprise, one thing that was part of my hurting. I was afraid I had lost my daughter's love. I had been too harsh. She would no longer love me as she had. The fear was anguish, numbing, blinding for me. To see the fear helped the cloud lift further. The fear was groundless. I knew it would take much more than this spat to weaken her love for me.

As the cloud drifted off, I felt curiously pleased with my fright that I had lost her. Proud of it. It was crazy but it meant I loved her more than I thought I did. It showed me something of me that I had not known. My love for her was such that for no good reason it became terror of losing her love. I was glad. I hoped I would continue to be gripped on occasion by these pangs. It felt like a richer love to feel the pain of this seismic, unrealistic terror.

Aristotle, Thomas Aquinas, and others identify fear as a phase of love. Fear, the pain at the prospect of losing a precious reality, is a shape naturally taken by love of that reality. If one loves something, one naturally fears to lose it. All passions, says Thomas, arise out of love, for all passions, however negative, derive ultimately from anticipatory pleasure at some good and consequent desire for that good.[6]

This may be true and yet it may still be possible that this recurrent fear of mine is excessive. Does it crowd out other, valuable elements of love for my daughter? Is my fear of losing my daughter's love so powerful that it cramps and weakens my whole relationship with her? My relationship with my wife? With the other people in my life? If so, my fear is more bad than good. It is on the whole, not good, but bad. I do not want that.

Ella and Bonhoeffer had to ask similar questions about their longing. Did their longing interfere with the rest of their life? Bonhoeffer became convinced of the opposite. He became convinced that if he let himself on occasion feel fully his pain of longing, he had then a freedom and energy at other times to feel and do the many other things he wanted to feel and do. The ultimate criterion of the whole goodness of any single passion is how it fits into the individual's whole life.[7]

We will return later to this larger perspective. We want now to stay close to a particular passion itself, anger, and continue to ask, in abstraction from everything else in the person's life, "How is it good in itself?" Since anger is a passion that arises in pain and moves to inflict pain, we have made our question, for the moment, narrower still: "How can pain itself be good?"

Return to my fear of losing my daughter's love. We saw that it is pain that is good in itself. The next question is: Why? To answer this question we use again our umbrella concepts. Why do I want to feel this pain of fear concerning my daughter? Because the pain is *pain at*. This is what makes it a precious phase of my love.

It is pain at the prospect of losing something precious. The prospect happens to be unrealistic, a delusion, the prospect of here and now losing my daughter's love. At the moment, there is no prospect of losing this precious reality. It doesn't matter. I still want the pain that results. I want the pain simply for itself.

Why? Because the pain itself is one way of *being with* this other person. Being pained at losing her love is a way of being with my daughter. There are other ways, better and worse, but this is one way. I want to be with her this way, too.

The umbrella concept of "being with" serves our purpose of pointing to a quality of pain that is verified in many other instances and is often valuable. In pointing, we select and oversimplify. We point with word and concept at one obscure, wavering aspect of confused, ambiguous, infinitely complicated consciousness. But, I submit, this concept pointer helps us pick out some things that are there and are truly good. It can thus guide and encourage me to feel what I want to feel.

In truth, my pain at the mentally ill person's pain, Ella's pain at her lost child, Bonhoeffer's pain at separation from loved ones, and my pain at the prospect of losing my daughter's love are good in themselves. I want such pain for itself not merely because I believe it will move me to act any differently than I would have. I usually believe this, but not always. But I want to feel this particular pain because it by itself is a connection with the other person. In my conscious life it brings the two of us together even though he or she knows nothing of it.

To bring out further how varied can be the "being with" that pain is, I mention two other examples. I experience twinges of pain during the day at the thought of the enthusiastic reception which a rival's new book has received. I experience pangs of pain at the thought of my wife down in

New York City trying to make a big sale and turn her business around. I call the first pain envy. I call the second concern.

I don't like having the first feeling. I don't want it. If I could, I'd get rid of it. It binds me to my rival but I don't want this kind of union with him. It illustrates that "being with" is often more evil than good. It is often on the whole bad. It can be grossly evil and little good. Consider the "being with" that the rapist wants.

I like the second feeling. I'm glad I feel it, uncomfortable though it is. It binds me to my wife 180 miles away. I judge the second feeling to be in itself more good than evil, on the whole good.

I listed in this chapter six instances of pain. They are six different kinds of pain. In all six instances, the person *is* in their very pain *with* the other person. The pain is the same in that respect. Yet it is a different kind of being with in each case. My point is not that pain means different things at different times. I'm saying that pain can *be* different things at different times. Pain does not mean. It is.

The different kinds of pain we consider are different kinds of being with another. It is a different kind of being with someone precisely in being a different feeling of pain. This pain is nothing but a feeling. Before any subsequent interpretation by the individual, his or her pain is this or that kind of pain at someone, this or that kind of being with someone.

This pain is undoubtedly the result of prior interpretations. It is informed by previous experiences, interpretations by the individual, society and culture, etc. This fact is crucial for certain inquiries, but not for ours, at least not at this stage. Whatever be the causes and whatever be accumulated from the past, the pain as felt here and now by this individual is its conscious reality. That conscious feeling is a being with another person.

Much of my classifying of pains may be subsequent interpretation but the pain at losing my daughter's love and the pain at the pain of the man on Thayer St. are before any interpretation by me or you two different feelings, two different pains. They feel different. Even the pain of Ella and the pain of Bonhoeffer, similar as they are, feel different as we imagine ourselves feeling them. They differ precisely—if we use our concept pointer—in their way of being with the absent loved one. In that Ella's and Bonhoeffer's longing feels different, it is a different being with. Applying the concept of "being with" gives us no new knowledge but points to the similarity-in-difference of the two aches-for-loved-ones.

Pain is clay taking an unending variety of shapes. My pain can take a shape totally turned inward. In some pain we are not with anyone at all. Our pain closes us in on ourselves. In our examples, pain takes a shape turned outward. As I review memories of pain turned outward, I find no two that felt exactly the same.

Incredibly protean, pain is a million things. What am I saying? Pain does not take shapes. I in pain do. I in pain am. Pain is only me in pain. It is I who am protean and feel an infinite variety of pain, always ugly and bad, always desirable and good. Sometimes more bad than good. Sometimes more good than bad. It is I who turn inward or outward in pain in a million similar, different modes. It is I who am with myself or with another in a million modes.

Notes

1. Cf. Chapter 7 on our operative meaning of "good."

2. Cf. *U.S. News and World Report,* July 1, 1985, p. 12.

3. Cf. *S. Th.* II-II, 108, 1 and 2; 157, 1; 158, 1.

4. *S. Th.* I-II, 46, 2 and 6; II-II 158, 4; *Rhetoric*, II, 4.

5. Barbara Deming, "On Anger," *We Cannot Live Without Our Lives* (Grossman, 1974).

6. *S. Th.,* I-II. 23, 1; 24, 1, 2 and 4; 26, 4; 27, 4.

7. E.g. Dietrich Bonhoeffer, *Letters and Papers from Prison* (Macmillan, 1972), pp. 271-72, 310-12, 233-34; *Ethics* (Macmillan, 1972) pp. 146-159. Cf. J. Giles Milhaven and Terrence Reynolds, "Human Longing in the Later Theology of Dietrich Bonhoeffer," *Thought,* forthcoming.

10

To Cause Pain Can Be Good In Itself?

In the preceding chapter we reviewed experience where to feel pain is obviously a good thing, for all the bad in it. In those instances, it is manifestly good in itself. One can and should will it for itself, prize it, be glad that one feels it All our instances were of pain that one person feels because of another person. It is pain felt at something happening to or being done by the other person. My pain is a unique way of my being with the other. Clearly, at least in some of these instances, it is good for me to feel the pain. It is good that I want to feel such pain.

But what of times when I want someone else to feel pain at my pain? Suppose that I by sarcastic remark communicate to my colleague my pain at his success. I thrust us thus into sudden intimacy with each other. He may compound our intimacy further and feel what I want him to feel. He may feel pain at my pain. He may, by word or expression of face or tone of voice, show me the pain he feels. To use my pointer concept: we would *be with* each other to a degree unusual in academe. Since I imagine this as a first time occurrence, we would be with each other in a way we never have been before. This is probably why I only imagine it and don't do it.

I imagine the happening as not tragic, but comic. My guess is that we would be startled, embarrassed, exposed. We would probably both regret afterwards that we felt the way we did and revealed our feelings to the other. This moment of revelation might affect our dealing with each other in the future. My only point is that this showing each other the pain we felt at each other would be an abrupt intimacy, new to the two of us, raw and disturbing.

158

Suppose the contrary. Suppose my colleague feels no pain at my evident displeasure at his success. He understands my displeasure, thinks his own thoughts about it, and resolves to see less of me in the future. But he feels no pain. He doesn't care. He has no inclination to be with me in reciprocal pain at each other. I am disappointed at his indifference, his lack of pain at my pain. (I would rather even that he felt pleasure at my pain.)

In this and myriad other instances we want others to feel pain at our pain and to show that they do. Consider another obvious instance, which passes into mystery if we try to understand. Why am I glad that at my father's wake, towards the end of the evening, one visitor finally shows real pain at my loss? Why am I glad at the evident anguish of this old friend of the family? His choking up so he cannot speak? His reaching out with his hand but being too overcome to direct it? Why do I want and need someone to feel this way and show it to me?

The answer is obvious and, as I ponder it, a mystery. It is a mystery right off because I sense myself divided. Part of me wishes our family friend were not suffering like this. Part of me does not want our old friend to be in pain. Another part of me, embarrassed, wishes he would keep his pain to himself.

But why does yet a fourth part of me dumbly, gratefully, take in this pain he shows just as my hand takes his groping hand? I am glad and want that he feel and show his pain at and with my pain. I feel less alone. We two are for the moment closely with each other in mutual awareness. It is intimacy, confused, out of control, real. It is obviously good for me and him. Why?

Why is it so good that we be together in his pain? Possibly, it was above all to get this that I stood for hours in the funeral home, baring my suffering? Why am I not content with the calm understanding and willingness to comfort which is all that the other visitors show? Why, as I go home afterwards, do I keep remembering how one person showed he feels pain at my pain? My solitary pain multiplied like a cancer over into him. He took it in, let me see this and it was good.

It is banal but mysterious. What my friend showed that no other visitor showed was his pain. That was the only difference. Nothing but pain. Yet his pain disclosed was a being together different from what I had with the others. It was the best thing that happened to me that grim evening.

Why then did I have that strong wish for him to keep his pain to himself? Why did he struggle so hard with his face and head to keep from bawling? TV news catches people in sudden, unexpected grief. They must know that most observers will respect their grief. Yet the griefstricken struggle desperately not to let their face show their pain.

This comes, of course, from conditioning by our culture. It makes us afraid to show our pain. All the more are we afraid to show to others the pain we feel in regard to them. I still have not told my daughter the pain I felt which I described above. We do not want others to show their pain at what is happening to us. We also do want all these things. But our culture, while extolling them in name, pressures us to flee them in reality. For the inquiry of this book it is essential to see that this cultural deprecation of bared pain is forced and costly. For one thing, it can lead us not merely to show pain less but to feel it less.

Not all strata of our culture discourage all baring of pain. Maria and Cori and Christopher, second generation Americans, testify in our discussion to the openness of grief and frustration and anger in the ethnic milieus in which they grew up. Certain popular religious movements, scorned generally by the educated, give outlet to intense emotions. But the more one listens to testimony of this emotional freedom of expression, the more evident it is that the freedom even in these environments is limited. Evident, too, is that freedom of emotional expression has its problems and drawbacks. Our culture's determination to choke off personal and interpersonal passion is a bad choice, but not unintelligible.

For most of us discussants, "being together with another in freely expressed pain" is something we praise in principle and rarely do. Consequently we do not know what it really is. When we look closer at actual experience of unquestionably praiseworthy instances of sharing pain, it is different from what we praise. It calls for new ideas. We find none at hand.

*   *   *   *   *   *

But the inquiry of this book concerns a questionable sharing of pain. Perhaps, after the preceding discussion, we have a glimmer of how in my anger I want you to feel pain at my pain. But what of the fact that in my rage I lunge to *make* you feel the pain!? As we saw, it is essential to anger that I, by myself or through another, want to make you suffer for what you did. Identifying with the raped woman, I do not merely want the rapist to suffer for what he did. I want her and me, through our legal system, to make the rapist suffer.

To evaluate this, let us back away a bit from anger and ask generally: What about wanting to cause somebody pain? This is more than my wanting you to feel and show your pain at my suffering, as my friend did at the wake. I want to actively cause you pain. I want this for its own sake. I do not want it for any subsequent benefits that might ensue from it for you or me or anyone else. Can this passion be good?

As a matter of fact, yes. It can be. In certain instances, no one denies it. Let us follow Aristotle's advice and start with the more evident before moving to the less evident. In what situations have we experienced that it was unquestionably good for one individual to cause another individual pain just for the sake of doing so? Some of the most obvious instances resemble ones we just considered.

A lawyer friend, married for years without a child and yearning to have one, tells me that she had a miscarriage yesterday. She is not looking for advice or practical help from me. She knows I have none to give. She wants to, and I let her willingly, cause in me shock, sadness, disappointment with and at her loss.

The miscarriage is unmitigated disaster. But we are both fortunate in that she can cause me pain, pain at her pain. That is the mystery: in all this disaster, somehow it is very good, that she makes me suffer. My regret is that I cannot let her cause me all the pain she wants to. I empathize easily, but most of the time and this time shallowly.

Still it is a valuable being with her. Not just in my feeling pain at her pain. What is also precious is her deliberately telling me so that I feel the pain and my willingly letting her do so. It's an everyday occurrence. But if life in our vale of tears be worthwhile, this can be one of its worthwhile moments—especially if the receiver of the pain is willing and able to feel the pain deeply. It is not "meaningful," because it does not mean anything. It simply is what it is: an intimacy of giving and taking pain, an intimacy evanescent and precious.

Right, it is not clear *what* this intimacy is. Our crisp words and crystal abstractions point to cloudy experience. It gets cloudier and more intriguing if one reflect on other, very different instances of one person's causing another person pain and both persons' agreeing it's good. Lovebites, for instance. Here, too, giving and receiving pain can be a desirable being with, a prized intimacy. (Do you agree?)

Consider, too, mystics exulting in the wounds which their Divine Lover inflicts on their soul. John of the Cross writes:

> With his serenest hand
> My neck he wounded, and
> Suspended every sense with its caresses.

> Why then did you so pierce
> My heart, nor heal it with your touch sublime?
> . . . Reveal your presence clearly
> And kill me with the beauty you discover,
> For pains acquired so dearly
> From Love, cannot recover
> Save only through the presence of the lover.[1]

Divine Love speaks to the soul of Mechtilde of Magdeburg:

> I hunted thee for my pleasure,
> I caught thee for my desire,
> I bound thee for my joy,
> Thy wounds have made us one,
> My cunning blows, me thine.[2]

* * * * * *

We could learn a lot by poring over bits of everyday drama like telling our troubles to a friend or lovebites of a lover or over extraordinary phenomena like mystical rapture at being wounded by the Divine Lover. We might ponder the similarity of the three. We might meditate on the similarity not just in the concepts we apply, but, much more, in the actual experience itself, so far as we can remember or imagine it.

But our trail leads on. The examples of inflicting pain we have just reviewed are all with the consent of the "victim." In anger one lusts to cause the other pain against their will. One gets a special satisfaction if they resist and try vainly to escape the punishment.

I willingly let my friend make me suffer at her miscarriage. Lovers, sacred or profane, willingly let the other nip them if passion so move. But when I'm enraged, I want to say hurtful things you don't want to hear. I want to say them because you don't want to hear them. That is part of the pain I want to inflict on you. I force you to undergo something against your will.

I succeed and I know it. Perhaps I tell you something you might otherwise never have known. The fact agonizes you, as I expected. I am surely "with you" as my words sink into you and our eyes meet. Our intimacy is real, intense, personal, all the more because you tried to fend me off. I force on you a closeness of just you and me. But it's horrible! How could it ever be a good thing?

The objection we made in an earlier chapter applies here, too. "What you claim to be good in anger is what makes rape, battering, etc. the worst kind of evil. The fact that causing pain can constitute an intimacy, a being with, does not weaken the objection. It reinforces it. It constitutes its atrocious evil."

The objection now runs: "It is clearly evil, in the first place, to force someone against their will to feel pain when I do this not to gain anything further from it but simply to do it. To force pain on someone is evil. It is all the more evil because the pain you force on me is a being with, an intimacy with you. It is an intimacy I do not want! You force it on me over my refusal. If pain at times has intrinsic good that outweighs its evil, it cannot be when one violates another's freedom and puts them in agony against their will."

Well, I reply to the objection, real life is not that simple. There are different ways of causing another pain against their will. Some ways of so doing are obviously fine.

Scott, a student discussant, narrates in detail, to the delight of all us hearers, how he and his roommates plot and perpetrate the whole school year to give one another "the perfect putdown." Some of his examples are rough stuff. The roommates are great friends. They enjoy living together.

Teasing is making someone suffer against their will. Teasing can be cruel, but it can be a light, welcome connecting. I walk behind Clare leafing a book by the Library door. I touch her left shoulder as I go past so that she looks back over the shoulder and sees no one. I then send her a greeting from her right side as I stride off.

My brother writes me a letter containing a few impish, loving digs at me. My wife's and my friends, Bren and Mary, retired, love to have us for dinner in their cottage by the sea. They make us at home by gentle witticisms at our expense. Their witticisms are like hugs.

My tiny grandson and his mother indulge regularly in roughhouse mayhem. They love to play jokes on each other. She returning from shopping kneels and opens her arms for him to run into her embrace. He flees in the opposite direction as if she disgusts him. She chases him, gets him down, and beats him up, to his squeals of laughter.

What about sport? Women athletes take my seminar on anger. They need usually a little prodding to admit it even to themselves, but they do admit that the joy of victory would be greatly lessened without the sight of the defeated team walking dejectedly off the field. For those of us who like to play or watch sports, joy in causing the "opponents" pain is essential. Victory is victory over somebody. The other team certainly does not go down to defeat willingly. Athletes tell of good times with opposing players after the game. Of friendships and reunions over the years with their onetime opponents.

All these are banal facts of life. In ways that are unquestionably fine and good we cause each other pain against our will. We think about it little. We do it for its own sake. We like doing it. We like having it done to us. We prize the relationship that the inflicting of pain constitutes.

True, all the examples given above are playful. But the fact that it is play does not deny the fact that the making someone suffer against his will is here a welcome interpersonal union. It is not often we are in contact so warmly and pleasantly with the other. A card game or pickup game of basketball or a practical joke or some gentle teasing can make one of the best moments in our day.

We see something similar in dead serious interactions. Here, too, on occasion, it is blatantly fine and good that we want to cause each other pain against our will. Recall what we touched on earlier in the book: the fighting between those who love each other—spouses, lovers, siblings, parent-child, close friends, good friends, work partners, etc.—is in some relationships or on certain occasions something more good than evil. Perhaps the exception, not the rule, but still a common exception.

Here, as throughout the book, our method is to spiral. We keep coming back to the same experiences. Each time, in pondering the experience again, we move—we hope—more clearly and deeply into it. Like a corkscrew. Ponder once more, now in the light of our present perspective, your experience, personal or vicarious, of good fighting. Recall Paul and Luce's fight on the stairs, the father's snapping in "Blaming for Blaming's Sake," the climactic fight of Didi and Emma in the film, *The Turning Point,* the fight of the two men in *The Quiet Man,* or—?

The attorney who organized my discussion of anger with Brown alumni and parents in Norfolk, Virginia, told of a violent shouting match he had once with another attorney. He had not done anything like it before. Both, despite habitual self control and years of experience in the courtroom, lost their cool. "The judge had to threaten to have us arrested, before we would stop. . . . The two of us have been friends ever since." Do you have a personal memory of a fight of this sort?

Perhaps fights with loved ones are more often bad than good. I don't know. I have no advice to give as to when it will be wise to fight and when not. But we do at times have "good fights" with someone we love. Most of my discussants have no trouble recalling their own "good fights." They nod and smile. They seem a bit embarrassed, a bit proud, a bit amused, a bit grateful. All discussants easily recall or imagine others fighting in a way that ends up blatantly and mysteriously feeding their mutual love.

My continuing education class viewed the film *The Turning Point.* No one had trouble understanding its ending. No one objected to the general delight and appreciation by the seminar members of the ending of *The Turning Point.* What takes longer, even for my professional colleagues, is to get the fight itself into sharp focus, to focus on the vicious passion of Didi and Emma at each other, and to see how it, and not merely its good consequences, is already good and satisfying and precious as well as ugly and sad.

I submit that the very fighting of Paul and Luce was in itself good, satisfying and precious because their bared passion to hurt each other was a conscious being with, an intimacy, a live intertwining with the other. In this instance, unlike, for example, a rape, the intimacy was far more good than bad. It was, as the angel had to admit, a moment of love. Della, a psychiatric social worker, said of the fight on the stairs: "It's very erotic." Dana, a musician, said, "Only because they were so sure of each other, could they let themselves go that way. They wouldn't have done it with anyone else."

This book is a project in forming new ideas. I keep trotting forth anecdotes and images of common experience so that we can do what is uncommon: form clear ideas of what is common in the experience. In the next chapter, I will try, with new concepts, to get a little clearer idea of our experience of a person's passionately making another person suffer against their will, and not for any subsequent consequences of doing so. What does this interpersonal union consists of? What, if anything, is so good about it?

The instances just reviewed make already one thing clear. We cannot dismiss such causing of another's pain as always and completely evil. It is not, to use our working terminology, necessarily "more evil than good," or "on the whole evil." In the experiences we have recalled or imagined, it is mainly good. These experiences may be much less common than the contrary, but they happen often enough.[3]

Notes

1. *The Poems of John of the Cross,* transl. Roy Campbell (Grosset & Dunlap, 1967), pp. 13, 17.

2. St. Mechtilde of Magdeburg, quoted by Elmer O'Brien, S.J., *Varieties of Mystic Experience* (Mentor-Omega, 1964), p. 119, from *The Revelations of Mechtild of Magdeburg*, transl. Lucy Menzies (New York-London, 1953).

3. Such experience is neglected in Elaine Scarry's excellent *The body in pain: the making and unmaking of the world* (New York, Oxford University Press, 1985).

11

Feel My Power!
Feel My Pain!

My thesis is: to want to and to actually inflict pain on another against their will is in itself evil but can be also in itself good. I am not speaking of metaphysical good and evil. I claim only to describe good and evil as we find it in ordinary experience. Much of the good and evil in this passion to make someone suffer for what they've done becomes visible only if we violate the taboos of our culture and make ourselves look steadily at the experience. What do we experience, however dimly in consciousness, when we strain to give pain to another against his or her will?

We of our culture have so much trouble keeping our attention on this experience that I propose a *Denkexperiment*, an experiment of thought. Let us imagine a baby's first experience of making someone else feel pain. What I imagine is undoubtedly influenced by psychologies, notably the Aristotelian and the psychoanalytic. But, as usual, I appeal only to your experience.

I imagine, not an adult's, but a baby's experience in order to free the play of my and your imagination. Our imaginative construction of a baby's passion to hurt may help bring into relief, by comparison and contrast, vectors of what you and I, as adults, experience with other adults. I submit that what I will now fancifully describe takes place analogously in adult life. I appeal, therefore, only a little to your experience of babies and mainly to your experience of adults. If what I point is there in your experience, it will, of course, be only part of what you as baby or adult feel. The most I can hope for is to say something true, not anything comprehensive. In fact, women discussants taught me a second optic, disclosing a different truth. I will come to it after presenting this one.

Detour to babies. Imagine us babies first experiencing (1) *sensory pain*. We experience this pain at times as minor pain, discomfort, or irritation. We experience it at other times as intense pain: anguish greatly disturbing our infant consciousness. We may feel great hunger, thirst, cold or stomach ache. It may not be great hunger, thirst, etc. in terms of real harm or risk of harm. At least not when a parent is around to feed us or cover us or give us medicine. But we babies feel it as enormous pain, filling and absorbing our consciousness, disturbing our whole body, upsetting us totally.

As to sensory pain itself, of cold, hunger, etc., I find nothing enlightening to say. Thomas Aquinas explains pain as frustration of desire. His explanation, I will argue in the next paragraphs, fits some experience of pain. But sensory pain itself, I do not experience as frustration of desire. I experience it as simple agony and uproar. This seems to be true not only of the infant experience I imagine. It is evident in adult experience. I find no analogies, metaphors, words or concepts to make our knowledge of sensory pain any clearer than the original experience of it. I find nothing to distinguish or discern in sensory pain itself.

All the pain human beings feel is in part sensory. But other elements usually suffuse it. As the baby's experience of pain repeats over the days, it comes to experience pain as (2) *loss*. It remembers what pain has replaced, and what would replace pain, sucking milk, for example, or being warm. In its pain, it reaches eagerly for the breast or the warm enfolding arms. Its experience of pain is no longer just of sensory pain, but also of loss, deprivation, frustrated desire.

The loss it experiences in pain is not merely of what would replace the pain. It experiences the pain as disrupting its whole, generally satisfying, conscious life. When it feels strong pain, it feels nothing else. It can do nothing else but react helplessly to it. Pain crowds out of existence the infant's usual perceptions, activities, impressions, feelings, pleasures, desires, and fulfillment of desires. All this life was satisfying in varying degrees, and is now experienced as gone. (Whether or not the baby has any sense of possible death is not necessary for my point.)

The baby experiences pain, therefore, as almost total loss and deprivation. We are using concepts the infant does not have, but, I suggest, the infant experiences pain as devastating *loss of almost all power and life*. Just look and listen to a baby crying with all its might. What we imagine the baby to feel as we look at its red, howling face, can suggest what we feel under our layers of training, culture, denial, rationalization, etc. Note that the baby still experiences some power and life, as it reacts to the pain by yelling and twisting face, arms and body.

The baby's reflex to this agony and almost total deprivation of power and life is *to desire intensely to be rid of it and to get back the power and life*. It experiences pain as thoroughly undesirable and undesired, as "bad." We infants come to dread the onset of pain, knowing how it spreads into devastating loss of power and life. Power and life are what we most desire.

Here, as throughout the book, I have to use the word "desire," which our culture has so weakened that it no longer denotes a strong, elemental reality that permeates human lives, infants' or adults'. Our culture affords us no adequate word. We have no ordinary English word strong enough to designate generically that lunge of the bodied being in keen hunger, thirst, sex, fear, anger, loneliness, love. You come home from hours of unbroken work and a long trip home. You are hungry, thirsty, tired. What common verb can you use to express the strong, elemental feeling you have for food, drink and rest?

The least inadequate word is probably "want," which has managed to keep some of its Anglo-Saxon earthiness. But it is too general for what we want to designate. "Need," too, expresses some of the elemental drive of hunger, anger, etc. But "need" is not only too generic. It does not render the way our whole conscious being and person gathers itself into our pain-strain for food or vengeance. We meet again the thicket of nonlanguage that our culture erects around our passions.

The baby gradually experiences that this pain and loss is (3) *brought about by something or someone else*. At least, this other reality can at times stop the pain. It does so at times, but at other times it does not, though we imagine it could. We infants experience that we are in the power of others for our pain as for our power and life. These others are source of pain as of everything else for us.

In pain, we experience ourselves as helpless, powerless. We experience *the other as exercising power over us*. Pain is someone stripping us of power and life. Pain is invasion, domination, oppression, by that vague other. The other has knocked us down, levelled us, flattened us. The other is destroying our life.

One of our reactions, if we can do it, is to get away from the source of pain. We crawl from the cold room back to the heater. We throw away the rough material. Another reaction is to appeal to the source of the pain. We cry. But neither of these reactions is always successful. Far from it. In the course of time we hit upon a third.

One day we react in a new way to the source of pain. We must now be able to distinguish persons from objects for we do this only to persons. We perceive these beings to knowingly cause us pain. They refuse to give us something to suck or to pick us up and hold us. They take something from us which we want to have. We imitate this source of our pain. We bite it. We (4) *cause them pain.*

Since no one ever bit us, we are not imitating that physical act. The person whom we perceive as knowingly causing us pain is not doing so by biting. But we learned that biting causes pain by earlier reactions of others to our instinctive, innocent biting. An impulse wells up now in us to imitate the pain-causer in our own way. She makes us suffer. We'll make her suffer.

Our biting does not alleviate the particular pain we have. Biting our food-provider when we are hungry does not get us food. I do not believe that we infants, even at the beginning, think it would. In any case, we bite in order to do to the other what the other did to us: cause pain.

We bite back to equalize. To re-establish balance. I am fed up with depending on you and often not getting what I want. I bite you back to exercise power over you, as you are doing over me. I want to invade you, exercise power over you in depriving you of power and disrupting your life. All this I try to do by causing you pain, for I know what pain does to me. It gives me satisfaction to do so. I take pleasure in biting you.

Nature has given us the impulse to bite back apparently in order to help us fend off sources of pain. Only thus can we get what we need and want to live our natural life. But as with other instinctive impulses, we, infant or adult, when under the impulse, do not usually seek these vital goals consciously. We seek consciously something more immediate. It is usually pleasure, the pleasure of eating or drinking or walking or speaking or warmth or sleep or, later, sex.

We seek such pleasures for themselves, without reflecting how they may also enable and enrich our future life. Thus, in biting you, my parent or playmate, I seek the immediate pleasure of doing to your conscious life what you did to mine. For a moment, I have you in my power, putting you out of power and out of your usual, satisfactory life. Of course, I soon give up biting people because when I do, people more powerful than I, like my parents, give me pain far greater than my pleasure in biting.

In receiving and giving pain, the infant's experience evolves eventually to include, besides the dim feel of power, a dim feel of (5) *will*. When you cause me pain, I feel you not only exercise power over me, but you do what you will to me. You deprive me of power and life because you want to. By "will" and "want" I mean here an elemental, obscure, effective "willing" or "wanting." The self gathers itself together, takes over its impulse, and makes it now its own. Again, our language is lacking to designate this, whether in the infant's life or the adult's.

When I cause you pain back, I want to (6) *make you feel my engaged power and will* making you lose power and effective will. I sense hereby that (7) *I, individual, do something to you, individual,* as you did to me. I (8) *make me equal to you.* The biting back by the infant constitutes an intense interpersonal interaction. It is a painful, negative, destructive interaction. It is also a joyous, positive, constructive interaction for the infant. The infant's feelings and action are a pleasurable, positive, constructive movement of one individual onto another individual.

The interaction can be called a message from me to you, but the sole medium is pain and pleasure. The medium is the message, the whole message. My causing you pain says nothing, expresses nothing, means nothing. It is itself. It is what is happening between me and you. It is not that I want to exercise power over you and therefore I want to cause you pain. My response is from the beginning: I want in causing you pain *to* exercise power over you.

Words and concepts are not needed to communicate this message to you. In fact, they cannot. Words and concepts cannot extract or encapsulate this message. They do not even express it, really. Words and concepts only point, using metaphors from rational life, to what I do to you.

You showed me something in causing me pain. Now I show you something in causing you pain. As you jump back or cry or writhe in pain, you know me better. You know me in my live, willed power. You know me as your equal. This is why I enjoy your crying in pain. You see my grin and it increases your pain, as I want it to, and my pleasure. I love our conscious equality!

With these words and concepts we point to an interaction going on in a medium that is nonverbal, unintelligible, primitive, opaque, close. The interaction, the giving and undergoing of pain, absorbs the consciousness not only of the biting baby but also the bitten parent. The parent may stay totally in the same medium of feeling, as he or she forthwith, with no word or concept, slaps, spanks or bites back the baby.

I force the interaction, the message, on you. Here and now, in real life, by willing effectively to cause you pain against your will, I make you experience my live individuality in power and will. I force thus an intimate, individual union on you against your will. Is this evil or good or both?

The question makes sense though it is not yet a moral question. It is not a moral question whether we stay on the imagined infantile level or turn to real adult experience of similar "primitive," "instinctive" responses. Before asking moral questions one can usefully ask about premoral good and premoral evil. Something that is premorally evil can in situations be morally good. Killing another human being or letting oneself get killed, for instance. I'm thinking of someone who defends their family by such means. Something that is premorally good can in situations be morally evil. Getting sexual orgasm, for instance.

What I described fills the whole consciousness of the infant. It is hardly aware of anything else. This seems to happen to infants and children more than to adults. One advantage of our trying to fantasize being an infant is that it enlarges the experience to fill the whole screen. We can better trace its lines of force. They hold also in adult life, even when fenced off in a dark corner of consciousness. They may lose little, if any, of their primitive force affecting the individual even when they are much less conscious and all-absorbing. My attention may stay away from my wanting and relishing that I overpower the other in causing pain. But these barely conscious feelings may covertly skew the rest of my conscious activity.

My fellow discussants contributed true stories to illustrate this interpassion and interaction between child and parent, at the infant level and older. I list a few here without comment, leaving the reader to ponder. They may help us superimpose the picture I have drawn of infant anger upon our experience of adult anger. We may thus be better able to identify lineaments of the latter.

A father told of putting his two-year-old son, violently resisting, on the potty. He commanded him angrily to stay there till he had his poop. He came back to find that his son had had his poop and smeared it over everything he could reach in the bathroom.

A woman remembered herself at two running gleefully naked into the living room, having a BM on the carpet, and facing her mother, joyfully, tauntingly as she came into the room.

A basketball player recalled his tiny mother only two years ago, out of sorts with everything that day, picking up a dishrag and beating him with it frantically as he passed from shock to laughter and she finally hugged him and said, "I love you!"

Micah's early teens had been characterized by his declared pacifism and rigorous nonviolent behavior in daily life despite all provocation. This time was characterized also by the unrelenting persecution of him by his older sister. (We heard only one side of this story.) One day, she took over the small couch before the TV, spreading out her lunch so that the couch, could not, as usual, seat him as well as her. Seeing this, he stopped stock-still in shock. Then to the complete surprise of both of them and at close range, he flung his filet-of-fish sandwich at her. They stared at each other in silent horror, as the mayonnaise dripped. After a brief interval their relations became better and more equal.

*   *   *   *   *   *

The incidents were not as cute as they may seem. The first two were early instances of a tension that went on for years between parent and child. It was still going on as the story was told. The basketball player's tone of voice in recounting this typical rage of his mother was sad and puzzled. Micah, who told with humor and relish of his casting of the filet-of-fish, admitted that now, five years later, he still did not understand his deed. He felt unhappy when he had impulses to do anything like it, even with mere words. He accepted resignedly these impulses as normal and human. He had not done anything like it again.

To keep our question distinct may seem oversubtle and involuted, but I do not apologize. Life being what it is, it's the only way one can think hard about it. The persons of these four stories have still often the impulses they acted on in their stories. When, if ever, should they act on them in the future? That is one question. It is not ours. Should they, even when not acting on them, cherish and be proud of these impulses? That's a separate question. That's our question.

More precisely, our question is: *what* in these impulses can we cherish and be proud of, even when it be wrong or unwise to act on them? Our *Denkexperiment,* with the four stories as illustration, suggests what it is. In wanting to cause another pain, the person wants an interpersonal equality. She or he wants in making the other person suffer to have with that person equal power and will. To want equal power and freedom with another person is precious. One can cherish and be proud of it. Bigger Thomas, once more, articulates the point lucidly.

What drives Bigger to kill? It is the pain of his life as a black man. It is the shame and misery of the life he shares with his family and all black people in America. He knows that if he allows himself to feel this to its fullness, he will either kill himself or someone else.[1]

What is the shame and misery of his life? The whites "don't let us do nothing."[2] Bigger can't get used to the powerlessness and lack of freedom which whites force on him. "I swear to God I can't. I know I oughtn't think about it, but I can't help it. Everytime I think about it I feel like somebody's poking a red-hot iron down my throat."[3] The white folks, Bigger tells his friend Gus, live in his stomach. "Every time I think of 'em, I *feel* 'em." It's like fire. It makes Bigger feel something awful's going to happen to him. "It's like I was going to do something I can't help."[4]

What he does is murder a white girl, causing the white persons who love her and the whole white community horrible agony. Bigger does it unintentionally but subsequently endorses his deed. He has killed whites many times in fantasy. This is only the first time that he carried out the fantasy in reality. In willing to accept the deed he fulfils a deep debt to himself.[5]

Bigger does what whites most want to keep him from doing. He does what whites of his time did not believe a black man could do.[6] His anger leaves him. "Having done what they believed he never could do, he could look them in the eyes and not be angry."[7] "The knowledge he had killed a white girl they loved and regarded as their symbol of beauty made him feel the equal of them, like a man who had been somehow cheated, but had now evened the score."[8]

The whites of Chicago have taken black people as nobodies. Now in the suffering Bigger inflicts on them, they take this black man seriously. The shame of his and his family's lives, Bigger once opined, was that "none of them in all their lives had ever done, anything, right or wrong, that mattered much."[9] By murdering a white girl, Bigger does something that matters very much to himself and whites. This is the debt he pays to himself.[10] He becomes for the moment their equal in freedom and power.

Once he has murdered, Bigger's shame is gone.[11] He feels calm, relaxed, elated, proud.[12] Most of all he feels alive, free and powerful vis-a-vis the whites and also his own people. Lacking only in these first days after the murder is that whites know that he, Bigger Thomas, a black man, has struck them with this terrible blow.[13] He gained this freedom of will and power by striking back and it is what he prizes most. It is why he endorses his act after the fact.[14] By his act he created a new world and life for himself.[15]

The new life of freedom and power of will with others is what Bigger raged and killed for. This passion is what Bigger discovers and declares, the last time we see him, to be good. The desire and need to live free and strong of will vis-a-vis the whites was what he felt hard enough to kill for. To kill Mary was wrong. To want to live free and strong of will was good. His wanting to kill was his wanting to live this way. Bigger is ready to die because he is proud of having wanted this strongly enough to kill for it, though he is sorry he killed. As we last see him, he smiles. It is a faint, wry, bitter smile, as he hears the steel door clang shut on him. But he smiles. These are the final words of the novelist, Richard Wright.

What then is good about vindictive anger in itself? The first answer I came to was this answer of Bigger. Vindictive anger is good because it is an elemental lunge of our self to be with others as their equal in power and will. Our wanting to make others suffer for making us suffer is our wanting to make ourselves equal to them in personal power and freedom. However blind be our rage and however brutal and inhuman be the act we in our rage strain to do, we are straining to be by that act, with the other person as equal persons.

Our rage to cause others pain is a reflex to their putting us down. It is a violent move of our person to regain what has been taken from us: to be equal, recognized as such, among other persons. Inflicting pain can do it because our causing the other pain is interpersonal interaction and intimate being together. In our fury we strain to grab the other in mutually conscious equality. We love more than we think we do.

This answer explains further a fact we have discussed. We may or may not act on our rage. But this passion, if we feel it fully and will it firmly and if circumstances favor, moves often spontaneously into desire for an equality with others that is not vindictively wrought. We begin to desire an equality that does not involve inflicting pain. The once raging person wants now an equality richer and more satisfying than punishment or vengeance yield. Freed vindictive anger thus phases itself out often by its own momentum.

Thomas Aquinas, as we saw in chapter 8, explains this fact by showing vindictive anger to be a form of the passion to be taken seriously. Our present interpretation of vindictive anger develops this explanation further. We identify the passion to be taken seriously as a passion to exercise power and freedom equally with other human beings. Consequently, to feel fully and make my own my passion for revenge on someone is to loose into open consciousness this basic desire of mine to exercise power and freedom in equality with other human beings. The desire, now aroused and affirmed, moves spontaneously towards fuller satisfaction. It moves, therefore, to fuller exercise of fuller power and freedom in equality with other humans, if possibilities appear. Revenge, a minimal achievement of power and freedom, fades in attractiveness. Bigger, again, illustrates.

Bigger's initial exercise of power and freedom did not last long. The police captured him. The state brought him through questioning and trial to his execution. The whites dictated once more what he will do. Yet he did not return to his previous state of pent-up shame and rage and misery.

Even while he enjoyed the momentary life of freedom and power which his act of murder gained him in the face of the whites, he was not satisfied. He was not happy. He wanted something more. When in prison he struggles to become aware of what he wanted and still wants. He succeeds in feeling it consciously. He longs "to merge himself with others and be a part of this world, to lose himself in it so he could find himself, to be allowed a chance to live like others, even though he was black."[16] It was in order to be "at home" with other men and to be in recognized power and freedom like and among other men that Bigger Thomas murdered.

Only in the last page and a half of the novel does Bigger realize how passionately he wanted this. He realizes, too, that it is good. He is proud of it. As a result, Bigger feels and acts now in a new way. So sharp a change does he make in feelings and actions that most readers—in my teaching experience—cannot focus on what happens at the ending of the book. Bigger acts with far more strength and will than he ever has. He is able to share confidently his discovery, though it shocks and terrifies Max.

> Maybe it ain't fair to kill, and I reckon I really didn't want to kill. But when I think of why all the killing was, I begin to feel what I wanted, what I am . . .
>
> . . . I didn't want to kill! But what I killed for, I *am!* It must've been pretty deep in me to make me kill! I must have felt it awful hard to murder . . .
>
> . . . What I killed for must've been good!

He says this to express his peace and to reassure Max. He tells Max repeatedly, "I'm all right!" He means it. As he shakes hands in farewell to Max, his strength and will contrast with Max's state. Max's eyes are wet. He cannot face Bigger. He gropes blindly for the door. Bigger says to Max other things he has never said before. "Just go and tell Ma I was all right and not to worry none, see? Tell her I was all right and wasn't crying none." He sends a message to the young Communist who loved Mary, whom Bigger murdered, and who yet tried to help Bigger after his imprisonment. Bigger has treated him only with scorn. He address him now for the first time by his first name. "Tell Mister . . . Tell Jan hello." At the end, Max cannot look at Bigger. We do and see him faintly, wryly, bitterly smiling.[17]

We will return in the following chapter to consider more at length this tendency of vindictive anger, when fully felt, to phase into more constructive passion. Drawing on certain feminist writing on anger, I will try to show how the answers we come up with in the present chapter support and enrich active involvement against injustice. My present point is that vindictive anger is good because in striving to inflict pain, the angry person is striving to be with the other person in equal power and freedom.

* * * * * *

When first discussing the goodness of vindictive anger, I used to try to lead the discussants towards the answer I just sketched. I succeeded in leading many in that direction. But over and over a number of the discussants, principally women, lead me to a different answer to this question. They do not deny the first answer. They generally acknowledge its truth. But more immediate in their experience is a second answer, complementing the first. It is a new idea for me.

The two answers emerge in different responses that men and women tend to make to the same situation. Someone deliberately and flagrantly wrongs you. He or she treats you badly for no good reason. You are furious. You instinctively want to get back at them, get even, make them suffer for it. What do you in your blinding passion want to do? "Show him!" Show him what? Men often, women less often reply: "Show him he can't treat me this way!" Women often, men rarely, reply: "Show him what it's like!"

The first reply says something like this. Treating me this way, he took me as of no account, as someone he could step on with impunity. As a patsy, a weakling, a pushover. He could do with me what he willed. He was somebody with power and will. I was nobody, weak and irresolute.

In striking back I'll show him! He was wrong! I also am somebody with power and will. Let him feel me now in my cutting words or hammering blows. I'll show him. This first reply is a version of the answer which I have just offered with the help of my *Denkexperiment*, some anecdotes and Bigger Thomas' articulation.

The second reply says something like this. Treating me the way he did, he took me as of no account, like dirt. He was glad to make me go through hell. Let him feel what it's like to be treated that way. Let him know the hell he put me through. I'll show him!

Take a brutal incident of a recent TV drama. The man beats the woman into insensibility as he has many times before. He falls into a stuporous sleep on the bed. The woman eventually rises. She goes for a can of gasoline, douses the man's bed, sets it on fire and burns him to death. The woman's act is wrong, I believe. It is evil on the whole, though in her state she is probably not responsible for what she does. Her feelings of rage are evil in wanting the burning to death. Her feelings of rage are good in wanting what they want in that burning. As Bigger Thomas cried: "What I killed for was good! What I wanted was good!" What does she want? What does she kill for?

According to our first answer, the woman lights the gasoline to show her husband that she is not someone negligible. He can not treat her like dirt. He can not do to her whatever he wants. She is somebody! She is like him a person with will and power. He will learn this in his agony, terror and despair when he wakes up on fire. They will be equal then and he will know it.

According to the second response, the woman lights the gas to make the man feel what he made her feel. In his physical pain, terror, horror and despair at her hands when he wakes up on fire, he will learn what it's like. He will go through what he put her through. They will be equal then and he will know it.

My discussants and I identify with the woman. In reimagining the whole story, most of us feel something of what she feels. Part of us wants to do what she wants to do, though we believe we would not do it. But, as I say, what some of us in identifying want to do differs, in emphasis at least, from what others want. All of us want the man to start "taking seriously" the woman. For all of us, his very terror, horror and despair at his burning flesh will be his taking the woman seriously as he had not before. That is what in her savage passion she wants and we want. But some of us envision him taking her seriously primarily in that his agony is an experience of her power and will. Others envision him taking her seriously primarily in that he experiences the agony she went through at his hands.

Look at it from a slightly different angle. All of us want, with the woman, that the man be with her in pain, since he refuses to be with her in any other way. As we saw in preceding chapters, one of my deepest desires in real, painful life is to be with others in pain. There is unique intimacy when in mutual awareness one person feels pain at another's pain. Recall the experience of my old friend and me at the wake, or my lawyer friend and me at the news of her miscarriage. My vindictive anger is passion for such intimacy though of an uglier sort. For all its evil, it can be mainly good, to be striven for in itself.

Why? We said: because the pain that the victim inflicts is the offender's conscious pain at the pain he caused the victim. Some add now: because the pain is the offender's experience of unsuspected power and freedom of his victim. Others stress that the pain is desirable because the pain is the offender's experience of what he put his victim through.

Both perspectives show, differently, how in fury we want the other to take us seriously. From both perspectives, we, in vicious, vindictive striking back, want to bring the offender in his pain to be with us or with whoever the victim is. We love more than we think we do.

Both perspectives, I submit, ring true to experience. They complement each other. The answers need to be pressed and expanded. Both paths of inquiry, dim, tangled and little used, beckon. Perhaps in another book? By you, reader, if not by me?

* * * * * *

As our first perspective did, so, too, our second perspective casts light on the fact that those who feel fully and prize their vindictive anger begin often to feel it less. They begin to feel more constructive passions. If vindictive anger is my elemental thrust to have others feel the agony I feel, it makes sense that this thrust gets more satisfaction from a more positive sharing of my agony. As Thomas pointed out, our anger tends to die and no longer to insist on punishment if our offender feels and expresses pain at what he did to us. The vindictive thrust of anger weakens, too, if the angry person, without acting out the anger, expresses her fury to others who respond empathetically and assure her that this feeling is good. To want to make others feel with me is a kind of love, however odd it seem in my passion for revenge. It makes sense that such a strand of love, felt openly and encouraged, thrusts to unfold and expand and grow into more loving forms.

It makes sense, but does it not call in question the worth of having gotten these two answers to our question? Does it not call in question any point to pursuing further the question and answer? If vindictive anger, when felt openly and encouraged, tends to phase itself into something better, why spend time and effort to get reasons why this anger should be willed for itself, prized for itself, etc.?

This is the same objection we dealt with in Chapter 6. It arises now from those who sympathize with vindictive anger of the oppressed and whose main concern is to better their lot. The large majority of these objectors are feminists. Serving in battered women shelters, big sistering, campaigning for change of law, picketing, teaching in classroom, leading support group, writing, etc., they work to help oppressed women.

These discussants strongly encourage oppressed persons to feel and express their vindictive anger at their oppressors. But they so encourage only because such anger can liberate the person to rise to more positive passion and constructive action. Though these discussants take initially an active part in our discussion, they lose interest when, as in the present and preceding chapters, I start answering our question. Then these discussants realize that they are not interested in discerning whether vindictive anger is *in itself* a good thing, to be willed for itself, prized for itself, to be glad of for itself, etc. The question seems to them idle, if innocuous, speculation, for, if I hear them right, the only real-life value of vengeful anger is in freeing the oppressed person and moving her on to better feelings and attitudes and actions and living.

This is a serious objection since I am ending the book with what is at best an initial, incomplete, tentative answer. I want you, reader, and me to walk away from the book pressing further its question and its suggested answer. You are not likely to do so if the question is of little practical moment. Let us discuss then, a final time, the practicality of the answers we have started to our question. I will repeat points made in Chapter 6, but this objection, as articulated by feminists I know, compels me to think the matter further along.

I am in good company, at least in my intent. Socrates, in his untiring thrust to press his philosophical question on his exasperated fellow citizens, had to keep showing them how practical the question also was.

Notes

1. *Native Son,* pp. 13-14, 108-109, 323-324.

2. Pp. 22-24, 100, 325-329.

3. Pp. 22-23; cf. 108-109.

4. P. 24.

5. Pp. 101, 225, 255; cf. 214. He also murders his black girlfriend, but we cannot show here how this strand of the story intertwines with the one we trace.

6. Pp. 102, 108, 141, 179.

7. Pp. 141-142; cf. 179.

8. P. 155.

9. P. 100.

10. P. 101.

11. Pp. 108-109; 141-142.

12. Pp. 101, 102, 108.

13. Pp. 102, 108, 141, 179, 208.

14. Pp. 101, 102, 108, 111, 141, 155, 179, 224, 225, 255. 326, 328.

15. Pp. 101, 225, 226.

16. Pp. 225-26, 255-6.

17. The last two pages of the novel. The immediately preceding pages help understand this dramatic turn.

12

Vindictive Anger, Activists and Feminists

In inquiring into vindictive anger, I discuss our question often with people who are actively engaged in combating injustice and oppression. They are interested in such anger. It is familiar to them. It is a common feeling of the oppressed against their oppressors. They know it well, sympathize with it, and often feel it themselves.

Some of these activists—my term, not theirs—are scholars and professional people. Some are students, graduate and undergraduate. Some live lives in which there rarely happens the kind of intellectual discussion I promote. All are primarily concerned not to think and talk, but to do things and change things. When they think and talk, their aim is always to better the lives of the oppressed. These may be blacks in this country or South Africa, or abused children or the mentally ill or women seeking abortion or the elderly poor or illiterate immigrants or gay men and lesbian women or the homeless or war victims or Jews or women generally.

The activists and I have congenial discussions. We each are interested in what the other has to say. We learn from each other. Yet we end discussion with a distance remaining between their thinking and my thinking about vindictive anger.

In part, the distance between them and me is inescapable and good. It helps make the kind of diversity that constitutes good community. Their main bent is to action. Their thinking is geared to action. What I do mostly is philosophy: phenomenology and foundational ethics. It is a kind of contemplation. What I Invite my discussion partners to do is to contemplate with me. It is contemplation by imagination and feeling as well as of intellect. It is a contemplation of real life experience. But it is still only contemplation. It is not action. It is not aimed immediately to action.

Contemplation can ultimately help shape action. That is one of my goals. But the contemplation I work at, as in this book, is not of strategies or tactics or goals of action. In my discussions we do not work to understand what members of a base community in Latin America strive to do or how a spouse of an active alcoholic can get help or how one can rescue an abused child. I am not competent to lead so practical a discussion. I do little thinking of this sort, except in side work related to alcoholism, abortion and homosexuality.[1]

But the fact that my inquiry is philosophical and contemplative is not the reason why activists keep distance from my question. Most activists do philosophy, too. The activists to whom I am about to respond are feminists. All of them seem to me to work to contemplate and get clear ideas of "mutuality" or "nurturing" or "self-esteem" or "community" and why these are intrinsic values of human life. They just have little interest in doing this with vindictive anger and any intrinsic worth it may have.

They say, or seem to me to presume, that in real life it doesn't matter what intrinsic worth vindictive anger has. It does matter what intrinsic worth community or mutuality have. What matters in real life is to live maturely. Mature living lies essentially in communal, mutual relationships and therefore it matters to understand what this truly is. Vindictive anger plays at most a small part in the lives of mature persons.

Vindictive anger can be extraordinarily valuable at a given moment of a person's life. Activists applaud breakthrough experiences like Bigger's, Celie's and Melanie's, where individuals are for the first time able to feel vengeful, punitive rage against their oppressor. Many recall similar breakthroughs of their own. But whether or not one has a breakthrough experience, one grows hopefully into a rhythm of life which is much less vindictively angry, much more positive and satisfying. Of what use then to analyze what is good *in* such anger?

This disinterest in the intrinsic value of vindictive anger is common among feminists I know. By looking long I found feminist writing that is punitively or vengefully angry, such as the passionate lines of Griffin, Morgan, Grahn, Piercy, Shange and Rich, cited in chapter 6. But these lines are in this respect exceptional for feminist poetry. They are exceptions within the opus of these poets. Of the feminist essays on anger which I read, few imply and hardly any affirm explicitly that what I label "vindictive anger" is good in itself.[2]

This should not have surprised me. The seasoned feminists whom I know personally cannot be characterized as "mad at men." They are not usually avid to get back at men or punish them. They rage on occasion to punish this or that man. They can be swept by passion to put a particular rapist or child-abuser in prison for life. They want this whether or not the sentence has a deterrent or rehabilitative effect. He should get what he deserves! But such anger is only occasional. It is usually subordinate to their other feelings and commitments. Most feminists I know seem to live mature, admirably passionate lives without vengeful or punitive anger being a frequent, strong passion of theirs.

This is not peculiar to feminists. It is obvious, once one reflects on it, that most men and women whose attitudes and emotional style we respect and admire are not often passionately vindictively angry. These mature persons may want to strike out to cause pain to oppressors. But their overriding passion is not to cause pain as revenge or punishment. It is to get the oppressors to stop oppressing. If anger dominates their day-by-day lives, it is not vindictive, but the passion to get freedom and equality for the oppressed by whatever means are effective.

It comes as a shock to me to realize that hardly any of the examples I have given of good vindictive anger are of anger seen to continue in ongoing mature life. I depict onetime experiences in which individuals discover their anger, discover it is good and ride off happily into the sunset. Recall Martin, Paul, Bigger, Celie. None of these is yet, at the time we see them, an emotionally mature person, leading a good emotional life. Melanie, Jeff's father-in-law, the father and son towards the end of chapter 1, may be mature persons, but I describe a single dramatic event. One has no idea what kind of lives they lead or what place anger takes in their continuing lives as a whole. Ella is a mature adult. Her anger is a fairly important current of her life. But I used her story only "to make clear what I want to ask about the attitude one should have towards anger." In concluding, I claimed only to come up with "a primitive and promising conceptual tool" to start asking this question.

This, therefore, is a question that may draw closer activists and myself if we tackle it. What is the relation of vindictive anger to ongoing mature living in mutuality and community? First, what do activists know about this relation which I have not yet grasped and which belong in my contemplative view of vindictive anger? Secondly, how can the contemplation I have offered in the preceding chapter of the intrinsic worth of vindictive anger contribute valuably to the action of activists? I take up the first question in the present chapter. I take up the second question in the following two chapters.

*   *   *   *   *   *

Activists say certain things which without denying the intrinsic worth of vindictive anger relativize any intrinsic worth it has. These things are true and pertinent to my inquiry. They locate this anger in real life.

The first truth I have already stated, but not given enough emphasis. It belongs at the center of any view of vindictive anger. *Vindictive anger is most valuable for what it can lead to. By far its greatest value is that it can be energy for more constructive passion and action.* As we saw, vindictive anger, under the right circumstances, often rises, without achieving its negative goal, into a broader, positive passion. The individual now wants equality with others whether or not he or she gets it by striking back. The individual now has more inner strength for constructive action. For oppressed individuals anger may be the only energy they have to move into more constructive passion and action. The point that needs to be put front and center is that far more valuable than the vindictive anger for the individual is the more constructive passion.[3]

Only constructive passion and action can in the long run help the individual. It seldom helps matters for the put-upon individual to carry out the urge, however justified, to punish or get revenge on the other. The tragedy of Sophia in the early part of *Color Purple* is exemplary. Much more often than not, it does more harm than good if in normal social life one simply gets one's vindictive anger out against the offender. Anyone who gets it out automatically and on general principle suffers for it. This behavior, encouraged by some modern counselling, does, on the whole, little good and much harm.

We rejoice above all at the impulses for constructive action which Bigger feels at the end of his story and which have replaced his earlier rage. At the end of "One Moment of Love," when Paul has relived his fight with Luce and nears home with his house key out, we imagine him eager, but not for another fight. Look at what Martin is doing as his story fades from our view.

A person at Al-Anon confesses that last night, when her husband staggered in drunk last night as he does every night, she felt something different. She did not feel what she usually did: pity for him or pity for herself or, more recently, despair. She felt, unbidden and unexpected, a strong impulse to grab him by the neck and throw him back down the stairs. The Al-Anon group applauds.

There is no question of her doing it. But this spontaneous urge to punish her spouse is not only an appropriate, justified, laudable feeling in itself. Much more importantly, as the group knows from experience, it is the emergence of new strength in her for positive action she needs to take. It is now possible that she may genuinely desire to take care of herself. She may thus be able to ask the spouse to move out, or to move out herself, or to consult a lawyer about separation or divorce. Or it may merely be that her new passion gives her the spine the next morning for the first time to speak calmly to her spouse and tell him that if he does not go to AA that evening, she will ask him to move out.

This metamorphosis of vindictive anger into more constructive passion, enabling more positive and more helpful action, is often spontaneous. It is striking how a passion with so destructive a thrust displaces itself, as it were, with much more constructive passion. This is a commonplace experience. But it is far less common than one would wish.

More often the change does not happen spontaneously. It happens only through the determined effort of the angry person. In one of the finest essays I have read on anger, Barbara Deming insists on this. *It is an imperative task of good, human life to work to "transmute" or "translate" our raw anger into disciplined passion and action for change.* For many it is extremely hard and they must work on it continually. It is particularly hard, says Deming, when our anger is anger, not at the oppression which others suffer, but at our own oppression. Other feminists, too, urge this ongoing task of human life.[4]

The energy that is anger needs not only transmutation into more constructive passion and action. *It needs direction into that constructive action that will be effective.* For oppressed people to have the passion to act for their rights is hard enough. It is far harder to act effectively, to get some of these rights. As Miriam Greenspan insists, it does not help much if all one does is "get one's anger out" in safe privacy, e.g. by permissive therapy, beating pillows, etc.[5] "It is part of the deeper work of ethics to help us move through all our feelings to adequate strategies of moral action."[6]

Those who can, therefore, should help the justly angry individual to find and take constructive actions that work. Therapists do not help women who are angry at their oppression when they merely enable the women to deal with their emotions internally. They help the women only who help them also to understand the unjust social situation they live in and to learn tactics by which they can lessen their unjust treatment and build a life of dignity and respect.[7]

In the real world it is extremely difficult, when possible, for oppressed people to act effectively to gain rightful freedom. Consider a spouse financially dependent on an alcoholic or a black in America or a child growing up abused or women in banking or all sorts of people in all sorts of life situations. *For an angry individual to find and take constructive action against injustice often becomes possible only by her or his grouping with others who have been similarly oppressed.*[8] *For effective liberation, the cooperation of the oppressor may be vital.* It is "urgent that men join women in doing feminist moral theology—that is, acting to keep the power of relationship alive in our world—because men have more public power than women and because there is so much to be done."[9]

If the individual does enter into an effective pattern of action and gains substantial freedom and equality with others, the individual's rage is likely to subside. It is replaced progressively by constructive, satisfying, personal and interpersonal feelings. An individual who has long suffered from oppression is, of course, likely to still feel some vindictive anger. This is not necessarily bad. *A mature person can and should accept his or her vindictive anger. One wants and expects that it will be relatively rare. It should not characterize the liberated person's mature lifestyle. One's main interest in it is to transmute it, when possible, to more constructive passion and action.*

*　*　*　*　*　*

These truths are slowly settling into my mind. I believe they are more important than any conclusions I have come to earlier in the book. They help me understand why activists tend to have little interest in the intrinsic worth of vindictive anger. The primary need of people suffering injustice is to grow in constructive passion and action that gain them the equality and freedom they deserve. To those who try to help them, the question of the intrinsic worth of vindictive anger may seem pretty irrelevant.

To argue, as I have done, that punitive, vengeful anger is a good thing in itself seems to risk encouraging persons to stay under the domination of this passion which achieves little, whatever be its intrinsic value. It seems to risk encouraging persons who have attained some degree of mature, liberated life to indulge at times an anger that by itself is usually impotent, childish and self-destructive. Better, therefore, not to waste time analyzing this raw, negative impulse, poking it intellectually to find some good amid its evident evil.

But this conclusion is not generally true. Appreciation of vindictive anger need not be a waste of time. First of all, most of us, however mature, do feel vindictive anger on occasion. Not everybody does, but, if my discussions be typical, most people can recognize that some feelings they regularly have meet the definition of vindictive anger. It cannot be a large part of a mature life, but it seems to be usually a part. In a mature life it may not often be felt strongly, but it is not infrequently felt. My discussants seem to agree here.

Most of us have not succeeded in rooting vindictive anger out of us. We don't seem likely to do so. Is it not then worthwhile to attend to this part and get more in touch with myself? To live more at one with myself? To understand myself and my life better? Truth about myself is surely gain over ignorance.

Is it not good to "feel whole"—as Melanie put it—by feeling in full awareness a passion one has long had and still has, but keeps in the shadow? Is it not valuable to experience with some clarity how I am "larger than I thought"—to use Alison's phrase? All the more if this buried passion, this larger self, is in itself "appropriate," "justified," "good"? All the more if, as we concluded in the preceding chapter, this part of me in the shadow is a lunging for the genuinely interpersonal, though in a primitive way not translatable to reason?

If this part of me is itself good in some respect, so much the more is it worthwhile for me to know it. It will build further my justified self-esteem. Appreciating fully the intrinsic worthiness of my rage is worth the effort, independently of any impact that the appreciation gained might have on the rest of my life.

I have just repeated an argument of Chapter 6. But interest in discerning the intrinsic value of vindictive anger follows also from the activist position sketched above! From a purely practical point of view, it is worthwhile to appreciate the intrinsic worth of vindictive anger. It can compound the energy that the anger gives me for more constructive passion and action. This can be true not only in breakthrough experiences but in ongoing, mature liberated lives when the individual feels vindictive anger.

Feminist authors I have read seem to me to agree. They imply that appreciating one's vindictive rage for itself compounds its energy for phasing into more constructive passion and action. Yet, strangely, none of the authors clearly says so. There is an empty place in these essays where the question of the intrinsic worth of vindictive anger is called for, but not taken up. I will try now to trace this lacuna in the writing of certain feminists. I want to show how the conclusions of this book about vindictive anger fit here. Contemplation can serve action directly!

What follows is no critique of feminist thought in general, for I have read only a small part of the literature. It is no critique of the whole thought of the feminists I cite, for I have read only one or two essays of each. What follows is, like my listing above of truths I learned from them, a first response to essays of theirs that challenge my thought. I respond to move discussion forward. I would like to open conversation with these authors and others who think like them.

Notes

1. Cf. my "How the Church Can Learn from Lesbian and Gay Experience," in *The Vatican and Homosexuality*, edd. Jeannine Gramick and Pat Furey (Crossroads/Continuum, 1988), pp. 216-223; "Becoming Prolife While Staying Prochoice," *Conscience*, IX, 5 (Sept./Oct., 1988), pp. 15-18; "The Problems with an Anti-Choice Amendment," *Conscience*, VII, 4 (July/August, 1986), p. 18; "How Prolife Beliefs Strengthen a Prochoice Position," *Conscience*, VII, 3 (May/June, 1986), pp. 17-18; "Catholic Theologians and the Abortion Debate," *Conscience*, V, 4 (July/August, 1984), pp. 12-13; essay in Amy Stromsten, *Recovery. Stories of Alcoholism and Survival* (Rutgers Center of Alcohol Studies, 1982).

2. As I will discuss shortly, affirming or implying the intrinsic goodness of vindictive anger are, in my judgment: Karen McCarthy Brown, "Why Women Need the War God," *Women's Spirit Bonding*, edd. Janet Kalven and Mary I. Buckley (N.Y.: Pilgrim Press,1984), pp. 190-201; Miriam Greenspan, *A New Approach to Women and Therapy* (N.Y.: McGraw-Hill, 1983); Audre Lorde, "The Uses of Anger: Women Responding to Racism" and "Eye to Eye: Black Women, Hatred and Anger," *Sister Outsider. Essays and Speeches* (The Crossing Press, 1984), pp. 124-133 and 145-175. Other feminist essays on anger which I have read are cited in note 3. They focus on anger as energy by which one can move into more constructive passion and action.

3. Cf., besides the work of Brown, Greenspan and Lorde cited in note 1, Barbara Deming, "On Anger," *We Cannot Live Without Our Lives* (Grossman, 1974); Beverly Harrison, "The Power of Anger in the Work of Love. Christian Ethics for Women and Other Strangers," *Making the Connections* (Boston: Beacon, 1985), pp. 3-21 (a slightly amended version of an essay that appeared in the *Union Seminary Quarterly Review*, vol. 36 Supplementary, 1981); Naomi Scheman, "Anger and the Politics of Naming," *Women and Language in Literature and Society*, edd. S. McConnell-Ginet, R. Borker, N. Furman (N.Y.: Praeger, 1980), pp. 174-187. Susan Griffin recounts the energizing discovery of her own anger, *Made from This Earth* (Harper and Row, 1982), pp. 3-20, as do Adrienne Rich, *Of Woman Born* (Bantam, 1977), pp. 1-22, and Miriam Greenspan, pp. 302 ff. Deming and Greenspan state clearly and the other five authors seem to imply that the initial, energizing anger includes a passion to strike back,

get even, punish, etc., though this is not the passion for constructive justice the passion rises to. Cf. also the poems of Griffin quoted in chapter 6.

4. Cf. the essays cited above of Deming, Harrison, Lorde (pp. 127-133) and Griffin.

5. Greenspan, pp. 131-133, 301-15.

6. Harrison, p. 14.

7. Carol Tavris, *op. cit.*; Scheman, *op. cit.;* Greenspan, pp. 131-133, 150, 183-185, 190, 203, 302-4.

8. Cf. Scheman, pp. 185-186. A conclusion of the essay is the importance, even indispensableness, of consciousness-raising groups for women to help them deal with their anger and develop it constructively. Similarly, Greenspan, e.g. pp. 301-15, 318, 324, 335.

9. Harrison, p. 21.

13

Contemplation In Action

The primary interest which activists have in vindictive anger is to channel it into more constructive passion and action. We others can only applaud and imitate. We should also learn from them. As we saw in the preceding chapter, they say valuable things which belong in the contemplative view of this book.

Do the activists whom we read or listen to have any interest in vindictive anger in itself? They seem at times to have some. They seem to say some things which fit with what we have concluded in this book. On the other hand, as I will argue in this chapter, what they say is ambiguous and incomplete. They could profitably say more.

They do, however, say the following. *When I feel anger, even if only occasionally, it is wise to know that I feel it.* This is true of any kind of anger. It is true of any kind of feeling. It is wise to know whatever feelings may be motivating my words and actions. As Beverly Harrison says,

> If we are not perceptive in discerning our feelings, or if we do not
> know what we feel, we cannot be effective moral agents. That is
> why psychotherapy has to be understood as a very basic form of
> moral education.[1]

Christians, Harrison observes, often fear deep feeling and avoid facing it. They mask their anger, and denied anger wreaks havoc.[2]

Barbara Deming stresses how necessary and difficult it is to "look at . . . anger about our own particular personal oppression." The task is urgent because "[one] *cannot transmute anger that one represses, but only anger that one faces honestly in its raw state.*"[3]

Harrison and Deming make clear that *anger works as energy for more constructive passion to the extent that we recognize our anger and let ourselves feel it in full consciousness.* Greenspan puts it,

> Through the process of allowing my "man-hating," I found a new way to love men that did not entail my subordination. In the process of feeling and letting go of my anger, I learned to love myself and other women.

> . . . I do not see letting go of anger as a matter of getting it out so that we can forget it. It is a matter of unleashing it from the repressed, indirect, and self-destructive forms that strangle us so that we can use it in more conscious, active, collective ways.

It is, therefore, essential to help women to "find, name and express their anger."[4]

Anger effects even more good, says Audre Lorde, *when we recognize each other's anger at each other,* when we have strength enough to confront each other in anger.[5] The two cited essays of Lorde illustrate this. One is a lecture which she gave white women on her anger at whites. The other, an essay in *Essence,* bares and probes her anger at other black women, and their anger at her as a lesbian.

The words of Harrison, Deming and Lorde make clear that they are not speaking of a purely cognitive process. They urge that we turn our full consciousness onto ourselves raging. They urge that we let ourselves rage consciously with all the passion that floods up in us. They urge

> . . . the terrifying and exhilarating process of finally, with the help of many other women, letting myself get good and angry. . .

> . . . allowing myself to rage at a society (and at all the particular men in my life) that had perpetuated my own worst ideas of who I was.[6]

Recognizing our anger, letting ourselves rage in full awareness, is difficult for many of us, to the extent that it is at all possible. Our culture has conditioned us not to feel it. *It becomes more possible, less difficult, to feel my anger if I understand that it is a justifiable, worthy passion. So, too, if, as I now consciously rage, I verify the justification and worth of my wrath,*

*then its thrust can more readily move forward and upward into more con-
structive passion.*

The question of the intrinsic worth of anger is, therefore, of crucial
practical importance. Naomi Scheman distinguishes "among the reality,
the legitimacy, and the justifiability of feelings." Not all our real feelings
are legitimate. Not all our legitimate feelings are justifiable. To discern
which feelings are justifiable and which are not, is, for Scheman, an indis-
pensable step towards building a better life.

In Scheman's example, Alice's guilt and depression are feelings that are
not even legitimate. They are insincere, self-deceptive, covering her feelings of anger. Her anger, on the other hand, is not only legitimate, but
also justifiable. Realizing its justifiability helps her to face and acknowledge it and thereby begin to change it into more constructive passion.[7]

Therapist Miriam Greenspan, too, asserts that anger can become energy
for nonpunitive, nonvengeful, constructive action only when the angry person becomes not only aware of his or her anger and but also how precious
it is. Therapists do not free a woman if all they do is enable her to feel
how angry she is at men. They need to help her experience the "beauty" of
her rage. They need to help her experience how "justified" is her passion
to strike out at those who abuse her. Only then can she be led to see that
actually striking out at her abuser may not be good for her. Only then may
she come to see that other, more constructive action is good and can give
her real satisfaction.[8]

Scheman and Greenspan describe as factual experience of therapy and
consciousness-raising groups what we saw dramatized in the last pages of
Native Son. A particular experience frees the person's anger to become
energy for more constructive passion and action. But the anger is freed to
rise only inasmuch as the person experiences his or her anger as good in itself, appropriate, justified. It takes a while before the individual begins to
feel more constructive passion. When they do, they see it as being in con-
tinuity with their anger. Seeing their vindictive anger as good opens the
way to seeing other, more constructive passion as better and feeling this
constructive passion more.[9]

Bigger's final feelings exemplify the kind of experience that Greenspan
and Scheman describe. The discovery and prizing of one's anger in itself
turns one's feelings upward into a new liberated, constructive, interper-

sonal life. As we have seen, feminists, such as Rich, Griffin, Brown and Greenspan, tell of similar breakthrough experiences which changed their lives. They state or imply that this kind of experience can, subordinated now and of minor moment, repeat itself usefully in a liberated life.[10]

Breakthrough experiences, such as Bigger's and that of Greenspan's patient Polly, model what can usefully happen regularly, rhythmically, in good emotional lives. Individuals may have worked through their anger. They may have done so with or without a single dramatic breakthrough experience. It helps many of them to repeat the process regularly. *Part of many good emotional lives is recurrent surges of anger. The anger may be a small part of our life, but it can be powerfully destructive if we deny it and it works underground within us. It can be powerfully constructive, if we regularly repeat something like Bigger's and Polly's progress from feeling rage to prizing the rage itself to feeling more constructive passion along with the rage and finally to choosing to act according to the more constructive passion, still using the rage as part of one's energy.*

To prize our anger for itself is not to ignore the evil in it. It is not to claim that such anger is always the most appropriate reaction conceivable. In every situation one might be able to imagine how better it would be if we were filled only with purely constructive passion. But in some situations we're not and can't be. Most of us cannot help feeling strong anger at times. We may react with positively loving passions but with this anger, too. We cannot always rise immediately and completely above our anger. The point is: If anger be never the most appropriate reaction conceivable, it may still be often appropriate. It may be, in a given situation, the most appropriate response possible. People do things to us that call for this anger. Our anger can be the only appropriate response we can muster. It makes sense to marry the wargod as Karen McCarthy Brown did.

> It seems to me that the Gods of war are necessary as long as there is anger in our hearts and war in the world. I am drawn to religious systems that take up all the stuff of life, whole cloth, and bring it into a central, well-lighted place for mutual negotiation. This type of spirituality works for me because it is rooted in an essentially tragic vision of life, and I feel at home there. I do not think humanity is ever going to do away with war . . .

> . . . I doubt we will ever have a world not characterized by some form of us-against-them thinking, although I hope we can find ways to understand one another better and to have more humane exchanges across the boundaries. I am thankful we will most likely not have to live in a world without self-assertion, anger, and energy. For me, the tragic vision is energizing, but not everyone must experience it my way.

> . . . it would be a mistake to think that those who wage war do out of a humanity essentially different from ours. I have held that particular truth in my own world through my marriage to the male God of war, Ogou. It would be a mistake in a feminist critique of war to paint women as only nurturers, only creative . . .[11]

Brown contrasts her tragic vision with the "idealistic vision" of other women. She respects this idealistic vision. Its spirituality can be moving, compelling, of transformative power. The danger of the tragic vision is resignation, acceptance of life as it is, a substitute for responsibility in the world.

> For me, however, the greater danger lies in not acknowledging that part of the spirit, that part of the human community, and that part of my own psyche that is anger-filled and war-making. I prefer to name it, to own it, and, from that place, to work to transform it.[12]

All this is obvious, once these writers make us think of it. (It is a mark of important literature that it enables the reader to see the obvious.) Many mature persons with good emotional lives feel anger from time to time. It is impossible for them not to. It is often good and appropriate for them to feel the anger. They strive to rise to more constructive passion but they are content when they do not fully succeed. They know and prize their anger.

They know and prize their anger not only because it is useful energy but also because it is in itself appropriate and justified. They make special effort to recognize and appreciate their anger when they feel it because naming it, owning it and prizing it helps it rise to more constructive and more valuable passion.

All this is obvious, once pointed out. It follows just as obviously, I submit, that discernment of spirits is essential to mature, socially engaged living. An elementary, recurrent phase of such lives must be to turn and face and feel fully one's anger and prize it. But (1) what anger is to be prized? All and every kind? And (2) what in the flooding passion itself makes it prizeworthy? What's good in it? The authors I have cited do not say. They break off here. They leave ambiguity and vagueness in their assertions which I have just recorded.

Their lack of clarity not only frustrates the philosopher. It also limits the practical effectiveness of these writers. They write to encourage women to acknowledge their anger and its appropriateness. They recognize how difficult it is in our culture to do so. Surely their encouragement would carry more force if they made clearer what they mean by "anger" and what they see as its appropriateness.

* * * * * *

Let me illustrate this obscurity. For Barbara Deming, our raw anger, inasmuch as it is a passion to do real harm, has no intrinsic worth. It is evil. One must labor unwearyingly to root it out and transmute it. But Deming does not say whether anger to cause the other pain without doing him "harm" is evil. She seems to imply that it can be intrinsically good when she replies to the "sister" who wrote criticizing Deming's nonviolent stance. The woman wrote:

> It's a rotten shame that middle-class people get so uptight, uneasy about so-called violence. Y'all, in fact, seem not to understand that often the most healthy, beautiful thing to happen is for people to have a knockdown, dragout fight. It's just another form of communication for ghetto folk. . . . All I hear is peace, peace, love, love, Barbara, that is not what I want. I want friction, confusion, confrontation—violent or not, it doesn't matter. People grow when they are agitated, put up against the wall, at war.

Deming grants the sister that many such confrontations ("including, I for one would grant her, certain knockdown fights") are not real violence and are welcome as real communication. But what kind of fight does she welcome? What kind of fighting communicates? How does it communicate? Deming does not say.[13]

Beverly Harrison accords anger an intrinsic worth in terms similar to those of the sister writing Barbara Deming from the ghetto. Harrison does not want "to suggest that feelings are an end in themselves. We should never seek feelings, least of all loving feelings." We should seek only actions. But she goes on, "Feelings deserve our respect for what they are."

> Anger is a mode of connectedness to others and it is always a vivid form of caring. To put the point another way: anger is— and it always is—a sign of some resistance in ourselves to the moral quality of the social relationships in which we are immersed. Extreme and intense anger signals a deep reaction to the action upon us or toward other to whom we are related.[14]

I would say that anger not only is "sign" and "signal" of the "resistance" and "reaction" which Harrison describes. Anger *is* a resistance and reaction of ours. It is a profoundly personal and interpersonal resistance and reaction of mine. Harrison must mean this, too, since she describes anger itself as a mode of connectedness, a form of caring. But how is anger connectedness? What kind of connection? What does anger care for? Care about? Harrison does not say.

To know what Harrison may imply here, one needs to know what she means by "anger." What kind of anger is she talking about? Does she mean by anger only what we labelled "anger for change" and "anger for liberation"? Or does she include also the kind of anger we inquire into? Does she include in the "anger" she encourages the common passion to cause someone pain and so get back at him or punish her justly? She does not say.

If it be *vindictive* anger or something like it that she means to say is a mode of connectedness, a vivid mode of caring, is it not important to say it? Vindictive anger is something most people feel at times. Among different kinds of "anger," it is one many of us like least to admit we feel. It is a kind of anger we find particularly hard to face and acknowledge. Yet ". . . if we do not know what we feel, we cannot be effective moral agents."[15] If vindictive anger can be caring and connectedness, knowing this would help us be open to it and recognize that we feel it when we feel it.

Harrison writes perceptively, "The group or person who confronts us in anger is demanding acknowledgement from us, asking for the recognition of their presence, their value."[16] This is a conclusion which we drew earlier about anger. Anger is good inasmuch as it is passion to get oneself or those one identifies with taken seriously for the excellence they have. But we meant vindictive anger. Does Harrison?

If a person or group rain on us hurtful blows or words in order to get back at us, are they thereby asking us for recognition of their presence and value? In a preceding chapter we argued phenomenologically for "Yes." I suspect Harrison would agree. Perhaps not. My present point is that to take up this question is called for by demands of moral living and of the struggle for justice. Harrison and other feminists whom I have read articulate powerfully these demands. They do not take up the question.

Brown, similarly, fails to identify what kinds of anger the wargod has. She does not make clear whether what she means by "anger" includes the passion to avenge or punish, to cause pain for its own sake, as in a knockdown, dragout fight.

I am not faulting insightful essays from which I have learned much. I argue simply, for further discussion, that *the writers leave an empty place in their own expressed thought. The place is worth filling not only for the sake of philosophical completeness but also to clarify and thereby meet better the demands of mature, liberated, interpersonal life.* To live such a life, as these authors insist, requires that one know and appreciate the anger one feels.

This lacuna in the essays read can be located without using categories of "vindictive anger," "revenge" and "punishment." The sister from the ghetto has her hand on the issue. In the heat of a fight, we tend to lose sight of constructive goals like mutuality or positive loving. The madder we get, all we have in our blazing minds is to hurt the other with our words. We just want to sting her, lash her, knock him down, drag him out. This is not one of your nobler kinds of anger. It is vulgar and vicious. Can it be also in itself good and valuable? If so, why? Perhaps I misread these authors. Perhaps most of them, even Brown, fail to see an appropriateness or goodness *in vengeful or punitive anger itself.* Perhaps the only good or appropriateness they see in it is what may result from it. Its only goodness or appropriateness is its being energy for some better feeling and action. They may see vindictive anger as itself completely ugly and repellent. Or they may see vindictive anger as itself neutral, valuefree, neither good nor bad—like the rush of adrenalin. Well, if this is what they hold, it would help if they said so. It remains true that to prize one's vindictive anger, as they say one should, one needs to know why.

The logic and psychologic of the cited essays demands, therefore, that we recognize such anger and discern its specific goodness or evil, appropriateness or inappropriateness. To do so we must ask: what can make this kind of anger appropriate? What can make it inappropriate? The essays lead up to the question, but do not ask it. Consequently, they offer no answer. The preceding chapters of this book do. Their conclusions fill the empty place in the feminist essays. Whether they fill it with truth, is matter for discussion.

The empty place is smallest in Miriam Greenspan's book. She concludes her book by narrating a fictional therapy session where Polly Patient feels strong vindictive anger. Greenspan calls it a fictionalized account of a "typical" feminist therapy session with a "typical" woman patient. It may clarify my point if in concluding this chapter we observe Greenspan's session with Polly Patient.[17]

* * * * * *

Polly Patient's boss has harassed her sexually for weeks. He is trying to coerce her into having sex with him. He implies that she will be rewarded on the job for sexual compliance. She will be punished, perhaps fired, for sexual "disobedience." Last night he tried openly to seduce her. She refused. She is very upset about the harassment and especially about last night.

In previous sessions therapist Greenspan has worked to help Polly understand her compliance with her boss's sexual harassment and yet not conclude that her boss's behavior is her fault. Obstacles to these efforts of Greenspan have been Polly's inordinate sense of Victim shame and her chronic Patient Routine. Polly has been trying to convince her therapist that all her feelings and responses to this problem are evidence that she is "fucked up." It *is* all her fault. She is attracted to the boss, has soft feelings for him and plays along with him.

In the narrated session, the therapist struggles to enable Polly to feel in full consciousness a feeling towards her boss that she does not know she feels. It is her anger at her boss. Finally, towards the end of the session, Polly bursts out, ". . . he's such a prick. . . . Sometimes I'd like to strangle him, I hate him so much."

Polly realizes now that she's been acting out her anger against her boss. She's been doing to him what she used to do by temper tantrums to her cool, distant, domineering father. Provoking him. She recognizes that with her father, amid all her frustration and pain, she "almost *liked* his hitting me because at least that was a sign that I'd really gotten to him, you know? I remember that he was all red and furious." She got to the boss yesterday by exasperating him through deliberate, dumb mistakes in a letter she typed for him. She got to the boss last night by sexually teasing him and then refusing to go further.[18]

Polly realizes now that she got pleasure from being "able to make [the boss] squirm after all these weeks of him making me squirm." With the boss, as with her father, it was now she who was in control. It was he who was in her power, not vice versa. It was up to her to say yes or no. "'I guess after feeling so much like he could take my job away from me, it felt good. It was like getting even. Revenge is sweet.' Polly giggles again." Polly had giggled just before "because I was also enjoying being attractive to him—having him salivating over me." She was relieved that the therapist understood what she meant: "There's something in particular isn't there, about being able to *refuse* him sexually, knowing how much he wants it?"[19]

Greenspan's effort is to help Polly see that she "has a right" to this anger of hers. It is justified and beautiful. It is also a valuable strength. But there are better ways of using this strength. There are better ways of "getting angry." Revenge felt to Polly like the only option available to her. But there are other, better options.[20]

Polly's passion is surely "vindictive anger." Of the feminist writers I read, only Greenspan affirms clearly that such anger is in itself good. She says in so many words that this anger is her right, justified and beautiful. But she does not say why. She does not say what in this anger is right, justified and beautiful. At least she does not say so explicitly and unequivocally.

This is no criticism of Greenspan's therapy. Much gets learned in therapy without being formulated as clear and distinct idea. It may get better learned if not so formulated. But our inquiry is contemplative. We seek clearer, more distinct ideas for more of our experience. Polly's breakthrough experience as described by Greenspan verifies our ideas and in so doing clarifies them further.

First of all—to pull in the idea we heard from Bonhoeffer, Aristotle and Thomas and saw illustrated in Bigger—a "good" passion is never in isolation. It is part of a whole passionate life. It is one of many good passions which the individual feels, even if only implicitly or perhaps not at all at a given moment.

Wanting to make the boss squirm and enjoying seeing him squirm would not be justified or beautiful if that were all that Polly felt about him. In fact, Polly has from the start other feelings about him. For one thing, she feels pain at the way he treats her. Polly wants and enjoys her revenge only as response to the pain that the boss made her feel. "Being able to make him squirm after all these weeks of him making me squirm." It is a different passion, and not what we are asking about, if a person simply wants to make someone squirm, with no relation to what that person has done in the past.

More importantly, Polly has also more positive feelings about the boss. She feels for him, for example, some compassion and admiration. She will hopefully continue to feel at least some compassion after last night's incident. Anger at a given individual is "intrinsically good" only if it is not the individual's whole emotional stance and is in a cluster of good passions that the individual feels about the individual. Anger is love only as one of a cluster of loving feelings about the individual in question. Good anger is relative, part of a whole. To absolutize or feel anger and nothing else for an individual is inhuman and evil.

Secondly, Greenspan and we agree that Polly should prize for itself her desire to make the boss squirm. She should prize for itself her enjoyment in doing so. She should be proud and glad she feels this way. Why? Greenspan suggests an answer.

"Today I got to him." Her therapist calls it using her anger "as a way of connecting to her father or her boss through distance."[21] As Greenspan stresses, this is generally, for Polly and for most women, an impractical, counterproductive way of connecting. It will increase their powerlessness because of more powerful male reprisals. Polly's passion to provoke, to get revenge, is welcome principally because it is movement which can move into more effective ways of connecting with men and exercising power with men.

But still Polly's anger, as it is, *is* a longing to *connect*. The child's tantrum and the woman's teasing come from an obscure, unbidden surge of their being to *be with* this other person. It is a surge to be with this person in a way that the person has continually prevented. Polly's anger, says Greenspan, is at the moment a surge to connect "through distance." Certainly, the connection by red-faced fury of father and boss is more distant than other connections Polly will hopefully go on to make with other men and women. But as she causes the man's red-faced fury at her and she and he know what she is doing, they are much closer than they usually are. It is one of the least desirable and satisfying ways of persons' connecting, but it still is connecting.

Why is it desirable? What is satisfying in this sudden intimacy that erupts in their customary distance of compliant individual and dominating individual? For one thing, he feels now what she has felt at his hands. He knows this dimly. More dimly still, and more powerfully, she knows he knows and he knows she knows this. This intimacy in his compelled pain shocks, revolts and terrorizes him, in part because it is what he forces regularly on her. With the blood pounding in his veins, they are momentarily equals in pain.

He not only feels the pain that she has been feeling, but he experiences that she makes him feel it. She exercises her will over him. She exercises power over him. In his pain he knows all this, and so does she. They both know that they both know. He takes her seriously as never before. He takes her seriously for the excellence she has. He knows her as an individual whose willed power can equalize things between them.

Because this is what Polly desires and what gives her some satisfaction, she is loving the boss as she loved her father in her tantrums. It may be a minimal love. It is more love than if she had been content to be the resigned slave of boss or father, or to be completely indifferent to them. Polly's experience in therapy echoes, I think, Greenspan's own experience:

> Through the process of allowing my "man-hating," I found a new way to love men that did not entail my subordination.[22]

Polly's anger is, therefore, in itself justified and beautiful, to be prized and glad about. But at the point where Greenspan leaves Polly's story, it is still almost completely a sad story. It is a bad story. If Polly had died before the described therapy session, her life would be an atrocity, a commonplace one. Something good happens in the last therapy session, but its value is mainly as a possible new start, wavering and uncertain.

What if Polly was suddenly killed by some accident right after the session? The point of this book is that her stubborn anger, with father, with boss and perhaps with others, was gain. It was tragically limited gain, but precious. Polly did connect then with her oppressor. She did willfully exercise real power in relation to him, tragically puny though the power was in the totality of her life. She did make him take her more seriously than ever before, for excellence she truly had. Yes, she was strong enough to keep loving men in this minimal way.

By Greenspan's account, most interpersonal life had been crushed out of Polly. She lacked mutuality in any relationship. But in her dogged anger an element of dignity and worth stayed in her life. She did not give up. She did not collapse into isolation and powerlessness. She persisted in provoking her oppressors, getting to them, making them share her feelings, exercising her small momentary power over them. They had not yet been able to crush that out of her.

This dignity of her life makes the atrocity of it all the greater. It cries all the more for justice. There is nothing to romanticize. Polly's oppressors have made her life a bad human life. It makes it all the more necessary that Polly move out of such futile, admirable anger into stronger, better aimed passion, moving her to stronger, freer and more satisfying action. My point is that her admiring her dignity and power in her vindictive passion, while realizing its futility in action, can be a new self-esteem and therefore a new self-confidence and hope. However limited, the self-esteem, self-confidence and hope can empower her to stronger passion and action.

To the extent that Polly discerns what she wanted in her anger, she learns in what direction to move on. So revenge was sweet because in it Polly felt the boss take her seriously as he experienced her power over him and shared her pain! Will it not be even sweeter, more satisfying, to make him and other men experience her power and share her feelings in more positive, more enduring ways? And, whether or not that be possible, will it not be more satisfying to turn to other women and get this greater esteem and sharing?

This is commonplace with passions. I begin to feel passion for enjoying music or for solving puzzles. At first my appetite is only for elementary music and puzzles. But the appetite becomes impatient. I am restless for something further. If I can make out what it is in music or puzzles that I particularly like, I can find more and more satisfying music or puzzles. I may lose most of my interest in the kinds of music and puzzles I first loved.

The comparison with passion for music or puzzles should not lead us to trivialize anger. Anger is an elemental human passion. It can make or break a life. It is like minor passions, e.g., for music or puzzles, in that it, too, tends to grow into more advanced desires and pleasures. It, too, tends to lose, to good extent, its original form. Unlike these minor passions, however, a good part of vindictive anger often remains, with the more mature passions developing out of it. Many mature persons need to confront their anger regularly. They need to keep working to "transmute" it. They need, therefore, to repeat something like Polly's progress and to "find, name and express" this dark passion of theirs. They need to taste regularly what is good and bad about it. The story of the next, final chapter illustrates this.

Notes

1. Harrison, p. 13.

2. P.15. Brown, too, pp. 198-201.

3. Deming, pp. 45-6.

4. Greenspan, pp. 302, 305, 315; cf. Lorde, e.g. pp. 124, 130, 131; Brown, *loc. cit.*

5. Lorde, pp. 128-131, Harrison, p. 15, the sister from the ghetto quoted by Deming, p. 43 and below in main text by me.

6. Greenspan, p. 301. Greenspan, like Thomas, sees anger as response to slight.

7. Scheman, pp. 177, 181.

8. Greenspan, pp. 300-317, e.g. 314.

9. See Chapter 12 for this progression in Bigger Thomas.

10. This is a major point of the essays of Brown, Harrison and Lorde.

11. Brown, pp. 198-99.

12. P. 199.

13. Deming, p. 43.

14. Harrison, p. 14.

15. P. 13.

16. P. 15.

17. Greenspan, pp. 316-335 and p. xxiii.

18. P. 330. The emphasis on "liked" is Greenspan's.

19. P. 332. The emphasis on "refuse" is Greenspan's. Cf. pp. 314-15.

20. Pp. 314-15, 331-5.

21. P.330.

22. P. 301; cf. pp. 305-311.

14

Saint Angela

The answer which I have now completed to the question of this book is incomplete as well as tentative. It stirs, I hope, in the reader, as in me, further troubling, promising questions. But it rings true, I contend, to ordinary experience. Angela illustrates this best for me.

When I first met Angela, friend of my daughter, five years ago, she was an "angry person." She was also a growing person. Abandoned at the age of two, she bounced from fosterparents to fosterparents for the next fourteen years. She got in various trouble for a few years more. When I met her, at the age of twenty-one, she, with the help of friends, professional counseling and her own indomitable drive, had taken charge of her life. Single parent of a one-year-old, she worked during the day, went to secretarial school at night, played on a women's softball team, and had other good times, alone, "with my songs," with her son and with friends. She was making it.

Angie has the fastest temper east of the Hudson. She had it mostly under control by then, but she still fired off once or twice a week. Coming home at midnight with her child after a long, hard day and a trying evening, she discovered that the landlord had put new locks in her door and neglected to give her the new keys. She could not get in.

Choosing not to sleep in her car, she drove to where the landlord lived, in one of his own apartment houses. She rang his apartment bell. When he did not answer promptly, she rang all the other apartment bells. When he opened the door, she commented very loudly on his character. When he asked her to quiet down, she yelled louder. He quickly gave her the keys.

Trouble was that Angie lived in a slum apartment without lease. It was all she could afford. The landlord, if he wanted to get rid of her, could force her out by simply raising the rent. At that time in Providence it was a sellers' market in apartments. Angie would have been lucky to get another apartment as cheap and suitable.

Being told of this incident the day after, I wished heartily that this impressive young woman would channel her anger more prudently. Her rages, I was told, rarely hurt anyone else seriously. They often hurt herself badly. I feared she had done so that morning at the landlord's.

But I had at the same time other reactions. Her fury took my breath away by its beauty. It later became one of my main inspirations to start thinking about good anger. Her jabbing away, baby in arm, at the landlord's tenants' doorbells at one in the morning was ugly, worrisome, comic, pathetic, frightening, inspiring, awesome, splendid. It shamed me. It gave me hope for humanity.

At that time I had witnessed her two or three times in full tantrum. It was not pretty. A beautiful woman, she did not look beautiful then. Her face was twisted, ugly. Her voice was a raw bellow, like scraping metal. Her body was taut, strained. Her eyes wild. She had for the moment lost touch with any other person or any other reality except the one she ranted at and what he had done to her or failed to do and what she was trying to do to him.

And yet my image of Angie storming the landlord's door moved me in strange ways. I wished to God she'd stop doing things like that. I smiled indulgently at her furious poking the bells, as I imagined the embarrassed landlord explaining later to awakened, irate tenants. I envied Angie. I wished I could act that way. Not "acted." But "could act."

I didn't want to do the kind of thing Angie did that early morning. But I wished I were able to. I wished I had passion like that to struggle with to keep it from moving me to regrettable action. I think it was the power of Angie's anger that I most admired. The main passion that would have surged in me in that situation would have been fear. Fear of how the landlord would respond. Or despair might have flooded me. Nothing I could do about it. I wouldn't have slept in the car with my kid. I'd have gone and woken friends, crashed in and got the keys in the morning.

Not so Angie. When Angie discovered her landlord had locked her out and not thought of giving her a key for the night, she feared neither God nor man. Despair never entered her little head. He was not going to treat her and her baby that way. She was not someone you push around like this. Angie used other words, I'm sure, but I heard her saying: "Bobbie and I are not nobody! We are somebody! You're going to take us seriously!" I heard her saying: "We're not going to suffer this alone. Join us in missing a good night's sleep."

Last week I ran into Angie. We had a cup of coffee together. She's doing well. Bank manager, married, homeowner, parent of two. Looks great. Sounds great. As she knew I was writing a book on good anger, I told her my problem of the last chapters. What of persons who once flew off the handle a lot but now rarely do? They live less angrily now, more constructively, more positively, more happily than in the days of their anger. Do they still feel that their anger is a good thing? Does it help them to feel that way?

Angie sipped her coffee and stared across the floor of Peaberry's. "Yes, I guess I was proud of being mad enough to tell off the frigging landlord. I still am proud I got that mad." Angie laughed. "I am proud I still get mad. I like being the kind of person whose blood pounds to smash you to pieces when you take me as nobody.

"I don't smash people any more. Not much anyway. Even back then, it was getting through my thick skull that when you smash people, they tend to smash you back. Did you know the landlord's new locks turned out to be defective? After the first day, they wouldn't open even with the new key. I discovered that, too, late at night. But I didn't hit the landlord again. I called the police, who called the fire department, who got in through my third storey window and opened up. The landlord raised my rent anyway. I was the only one in the building he raised the rent on. I had to move to a worse apartment.

"Still I like being mad. I like it at the time in a ferocious sort of way. And I like it afterwards in a mellow, patting-myself-on-the-head sort of way. My anger reminds me of who I am. It keeps me in touch with a part of me I love and don't want to lose. I want to be the kind of person I am. Before I think, I move to take you on if you treat me lightly. I'm gonna punch your eyes out. I'm a fighter and I like it. That's me. Some things about me I don't like. I'd change them if I could. Not my temper. That's the Angie I love!

"I love feeling my temper boiling up in me. You've got power, Giles, to the extent that you want something. The more you want it, the stronger you are. When I get mad, I really want what I want.

"But I don't get mad anywhere near as often as I used to. I admit I'm glad about that. I like my temper, but it's hard to handle. And often dumb. I can get excited like a dog who bites a bystander instead of the attacker. I can get mad at somebody at the bank, hold it in, and take it out on my family. Most of the things I do when I'm mad get me nowhere. They make things worse.

"I don't know why I get mad less often now. I've never tried to repress or suppress or whatever it is you do to stop feeling angry. I just have developed the habit of, when I'm mad, letting myself be mad but not doing what I feel like doing: lashing out. I've developed the habit, when I get mad, of trying to do not what will hurt but what is most likely to gain me the respect, recognition, rights, or whatever it is I want to get by hurting the guy. Somehow getting mad gives me power to do this. So did the speech class I took because I was so mad.

"People I live and work with take me seriously, as I do them. They make a fuss about me as I do about them. Even the VP. Why should I chew them out or tell them off when it's likely to shake our nice, friendly connections?

"Maybe that's why my feelings don't come charging up much now demanding your head on my platter. They seem to have learned that I can get much better by other means what they, or I, really want. My feelings still charge up a lot, but they're demanding usually that I get your respect in constructive ways. Maybe they're not so dumb. Can emotions learn?"

"Aristotle," I said, "claimed that human passions are like citizens of a democracy. You can't change them by command. You can change them by persuasion and by changing your pattern of acting. People who are treated unjustly, said Aristotle, tend not to get very angry when they've got or know they can get the positive respect they want. We want punishment or revenge only when every other alternative looks worse."

Angie lifted her cup and stared at it long. "That fits. Since the VP promoted me twice in one year and follows my advice pretty often, it's hard to get mad at those little putdowns of his. I'm on a roll right now. I don't expect ever to go back to those days when I got mad every day at one thing or another My life's filled now with so many other good passions I guess I have little energy to work up a head of steam against someone."

"But you still get mad now and then," I said.

"Yeah, I'm always going to have anger coiled inside me. I don't get all the respect I want and deserve. Nobody else does either, but that doesn't help me. I'm always going to resent that, and I want to resent it. When you see me resigned to life, put me in the crematorium.

"I'll always be mad at those two jerks who abandoned me. And some of the jerks who took care of me. And people like the VP. And men who have screwed me as a woman, and men who will. You don't know what it's like, Giles. People treating you like nobody! I want to stay mad at them. When I stop being mad at them, it'll be because I don't care. I want to always care.

"You know, getting furious at somebody is a way of caring. Say, somebody treats me as unimportant. If I didn't get mad, I might withdraw as some people at the bank do. They give up in a flash on somebody who annoys them. They pull into their shell, accommodate the person, and move away as soon as they can. If I'm mad, I move right towards the person. I want to hook into the other person. To engage him or her with me.

"There's a teller at the bank who has as short a fuse as I do. We slug it out about once a week. Neither of us takes it that seriously except as a way of communicating. People tend to disappear when they hear one of us starting to warm up. But ten minutes later both of us have forgotten the heat and remember the light.

"I made a great discovery. A lot of times I get mad, it's because I feel isolated. I want to draw blood so people will hurt *with* me. Well, I have found I can usually get more satisfied by telling them I hurt. I feel like snapping at things when I get home. Instead I tell Frank how bad a day I had. It's painful but we both feel closer. And it doesn't start off a chain of stupid nagging at each other. Or I tell Bobbie how hassled I feel. Six-year-olds can take that.

"Frank and I need a fight at times. Not often. Psychologists can figure out why, Giles, but I know it as a fact. The other night we had one of our longest arguments, both of us swinging from the floor at each other. At the end we were sitting on the couch, yelling at each other, saying anything we

could think of to sting the other. Not anything, of course. Anyway it occurred about the same time to both of us that we could not remember,
though we tried desperately, what we were arguing about. We stopped,
snuggled wearily and stared peacefully at the fire. It was nice. I couldn't
have gone through an hour like that with anyone else.

"Frank's and my fights are not nice. Frank and I try to keep them to a
minimum. We try to fight not at all. But I'm glad we do fight. Not just
because it clears the air, and the making up is nice. But our fighting is one
of those moments when Frank and I as adult human beings get closer to
each other, know each other more, take each other more seriously, love
each other more, than we ever have and probably ever will anyone else.
Our fight is one of those moments, ugly and frightening and vicious as it is.
If I could get close to Frank in that way in some other, nicer, less
dangerous way, it'd be great. But I can't. It's unique. Maybe I will some
day but I can't. You know, if by superhuman act of will the two of us
never fought, we'd lose a certain being close, communicating, being involved in each other. Do I make any sense?"

"You make a lot of sense," I said.

"Sometimes," Angie went on, "things are such that I have to keep my
rage to myself. No one to spill it out to. I'm not near the pillow I smash.
Can't go running. Smiling at myself helps. I know my temper is as quick
as it is hot. I get a headache when I keep it all to myself, but headache and
mad disappear after a while."

"Sounds like you've integrated your anger beautifully," I said.

"The bad news," Angie replied, "is that I lie a lot. I do often the opposite of everything I said. I like being me, but it's strenuous. If I let it
stop being strenuous, I go downhill. I let my anger disguise itself from me
and then I hurt myself and other people I don't want to hurt. I'm glad I
said all these things to you because I have to keep reminding myself of
them. I have to keep working my anger through.

"Part of me is ashamed of my anger. Part of me keeps trying to hide it
from others and myself. Part of me, a new part of me I think, just loves
passive aggression. You should see me some days with the VP. Or my
tellers. Or my family. I hate passive aggression! I hate taking out my
anger without admitting I'm doing it! I hate being ashamed of what I am
really proud of! I have to keep fighting with myself to admit I'm a fighter.

Part of me wants to be this big, dignified, calm person above the fray. Why do I want to be what I'm not?"

Well, she's Saint Angie to me. Like certain saints she illustrates preeminently a particular virtue. Her virtue is the virtue of good anger. As Aristotle and Thomas Aquinas remark, Western civilization knows the virtue but gives it no name. It's the virtue of feeling and acting on one's anger appropriately, as a harmonious part of one's realistic, responsible life. What name, reader, would you give it? In any case: Saint Angela, patron of the furious, help us.